PRE-INFERNO PLAYS

Pre-Inferno Plays

THE FATHER

LADY JULIE

CREDITORS

THE STRONGER

THE BOND

By August Strindberg

TRANSLATIONS AND INTRODUCTIONS

BY WALTER JOHNSON

University of Washington Press

SEATTLE AND LONDON

28032

COPYRIGHT © 1970 BY THE
UNIVERSITY OF WASHINGTON PRESS
LIBRARY OF CONGRESS
CATALOG CARD NUMBER 79-117735
PRINTED IN THE UNITED STATES OF AMERICA

Preface

IN THIS VOLUME are translations of five pre-Inferno plays that gave Strindberg a substantial claim to mastery of the modern drama. He had, to be sure, written the prose *Master Olof* back in 1872, but no one is likely to insist that the other plays he wrote before *The Father* in 1887 should be included in any list of great plays. All of them from the later versions of *Master Olof* through *The Journey of Lucky Peter* (1882) to *Comrades* (1886) are interesting primarily because they demonstrate in various ways Strindberg's potential as a dramatist. But none of them even approaches the high quality of *The Father* (1887), *Lady Julie* (1888), *Creditors* (1888), *The Stronger* (1889), and *The Bond* (1892). Every one of these has proved itself worthy as literature in the study and superbly suitable for production in the theater.

Both their form and substance have engaged students and scholars, actors and directors, laymen and professionals. While *The Father* with its three acts may strike a person exposed to it for the first time as decidedly like the Ibsen plays of the 1870's and 1880's in structure, re-examination and study will reveal subtle differences. The other four—each in its own way—represents ad-

vii

vances toward a compactness and tightness of form rarely achieved by later playwrights and certainly not by earlier ones.

While many people have been aware of such matters, the content of the plays has received far greater attention than their form. Written at a time when many Occidental women were insisting on equality with men, the plays could hardly escape notice, both favorable and unfavorable, because of their amazing revelations of Strindberg's analysis and presentations of human relationships, particularly the most personal and intimate. Sex, marriage, and the family were hardly novel human interests in the 1880's and 1890's. One playwright not only knew about them through his own experience and observations but had analyzed them far beyond the superficial and apparently obvious. Strindberg, through such nondramatic works as *Married* (1884, 1886), had already demonstrated that he could reveal his conclusions in literary forms that engaged his readers personally. The five plays gave a new dimension to his knack for "getting under people's skins"; few theatergoers and readers are likely to escape personal involvement when they read, hear, or see these studies in most important aspects of the human experience. They may be fascinated or repelled by what Strindberg called psychic murders, psychic suicides, unconscious crimes, vampirism, the battle of the brains, and animality, but, if they are honest, they are more than likely to sense the validity of what he has to say. They may even sense that Strindberg is making a positive contribution to the understanding of the human condition.

In translating the plays, I have tried to be faithful to the Strindberg text in both idiom and spirit. I have not attempted to adapt these plays for the stage, partly because they are already right for the stage, partly because directors and actors can readily make minor changes in lines in keeping with Strindberg's own conviction that a few such changes are occasionally necessary. For people who do not know Swedish, it seems to me, it is essential that they have an idiomatic translation that without being literal comes as close to the original as possible.

WALTER JOHNSON

Contents

The Stronger (1889)

The Bond (1892)

Bibliographic and Other Notes

PRE-INFERNO PLAYS

Introduction to
'The Father'

I<small>T IS CONCEIVABLE</small> and even probable that authors do not know the full significance of what they write but no one who approaches the study of one of Strindberg's major works can afford to disregard what he had to say about that work. While his statements rating his own plays, for example, were not always the results of thoughtful consideration but inclined instead in favor of the particular play just then in question, Strindberg usually knew very well what he intended to create and after sober consideration understood remarkably well how successful he had been. (The evidence supporting such assertions are available in his autobiographical works, not least in his letters.) Both what he says about his intentions and what he more than hints at in the titles of works are pertinent and valuable.

Strindberg had a great deal to say about *The Father*. Well aware of the fact that at least his Swedish contemporaries would regard the play as a camouflaged account of his own marriage, he insisted in one letter after the other in the late 1880's that his works are as much the products of his imagination and the creative pro-

cess as the works of any other writer, that *The Father* is not a segment of his life in dramatic form, but that it is, as he told his
brother Axel on February 25, 1887, a blend of reality and imagination:

> You can appreciate that as a creative writer I mix what I imagine
> with reality and that my hatred of women is completely theoretical,
> for I wouldn't be able to live without the company of women.
> You may believe that we [Strindberg and his wife] are two
> amusing birds. We sometimes quarrel enough to raise the roof
> and then we have a drink and play backgammon in the evenings
> and to this day we can talk and cut up through a whole night as
> if nothing had happened! So don't be upset in the least when you
> read *The Father,* for it is fiction! [*Strindbergs Brev* (Stockholm:
> Bonnier, 1948—), VI, 174]

Whatever may, and justifiably can, be said about the role of his own
marriage in the evolution of the play, the fact remains that it is not
a faithful, realistic account of that marriage. What Strindberg has
created is neither a sociological case report nor a report to a psych-
iatrist. *The Father* is a work of such superb art that it does not
require the support of sickly curiosity about the difficulties of fellow
human beings.

Even one reading or one performance of the play will be adequate for giving any sensitive person an appreciation of the obvious merits of the structure of the three-act tragedy. The careful
preparation for and foreshadowing of what is to come, the highly
skillful exposition of what happened in a marriage that has lasted
for more than twenty years, the seemingly effortless presentation
and illustration of the basic conflicts and the relationships between
the characters, the noticeably individualized dialogue, the restric-
tion of the action to the catastrophe without neglecting what has
led up to it, and—as every performance I have seen has demonstrated—the quick emergence of Adolf and Laura as flesh-and-
blood people are all, I should think, obvious. Certainly the intensity
of the basic struggle—much of it unacknowledged, some of it
hidden from the antagonists themselves, but the nature of all of it

at least sensed by the perceptive and honest reader or spectator with the shock of embarrassed or depressing recognition—is clear from the moment Adolf and Laura face each other for the first time on stage.

Strindberg is primarily interested here in one father and his role in his family. Until fairly recently the traditional, conventional Western view was of the father as Hercules, the strong man who carries the burdens of the world of his family on his shoulders. As the physically and intellectually superior member of the family group, the husband and father had certain rights and duties: the right, for example, to be respected and looked up to and the duty to look after the welfare of the "weaker" wife and children. But much as such a notion may have appealed to Strindberg and other men of his and other days, Strindberg knew quite well that the truth about man and woman and their relationships is never as simple as society and tradition suggest. Strindberg knew what Darwinism, naturalism, and determinism imply; he had, moreover, keen senses for observing the human scene. Both his observations and his reading had long since told him that an Adolf who had accepted without question or qualification the traditional concept of man and his role may have a deucedly hard time of it in a struggle with an Omphale, who not only wants the symbols of power but has the potential for getting them without the handicap of genuine scruples of any kind. In its way, *The Father* is a remarkable study of age-old notions about the ever interesting matters of man, woman, and their relationship.

Strindberg was anxious that Adolf not be misinterpreted. When the Swedish author Axel Lundegård proposed translating *The Father* into Danish for production in Copenhagen, Strindberg wrote to him on October 17, 1887:

> Who is going to play the captain, and what woman would want to play Laura? The play can easily be destroyed, be made ridiculous! I suggest . . . the captain ['s role] be assigned to an actor with a generally healthy temperament, who with a superior, self-ironic, lightly skeptical tone of a man of the world, who conscious of his advantages, goes to meet his fate in a relatively carefree

mood, wrapping himself in death in the spider's web he cannot tear to shreds because of natural laws ... No screaming, no sermons.

Let's remember that a cavalry officer is always a rich man's son, has been well brought up, makes high demands on himself in his relations with others and is refined even in dealing with the soldier [Nöjd].

So no crude fool of the traditional variety ... Besides, he has risen above his work, has exposed it, and is a scientist. To me he represents especially here a manliness people have tried to disparage, taken away from us and awarded to the third sex! It is only in the presence of woman he is unmanly, and that is how she wants him, and the law of accommodation forces us to play the role our mistress requires. Yes, we sometimes have to play chaste, ingenuous, ignorant just to get the sexual intercourse we want! [*Strindbergs Brev*, VI, 282]

How well these comments fit the content of the play a close reading will reveal.

Captain Adolf is obviously a rich man's son; there is still an estate that must be managed; there has been wealth beyond what the present estate represents. (Strindberg does not make it clear that it was a landed estate.) Did Adolf become an officer because it was a socially correct thing to do? Strindberg does not answer that question directly.

But it is clear that the captain is an intellectual who has been trained and disciplined to think freely and independently about most matters concerning God, man, and the universe. But not about all! He has thought through the matter of his profession and rejected it as anything more than an acceptable source of livelihood for himself and his houseful of women. He has considered the official doctrines concerning the Christian deity and found them wanting; he labels himself a free-thinker and sounds like an agnostic. While he has no illusions about the church and what it represents, he is so realistically sensible he will take no active issue with such a socially correct thing as confirmation. But the universe challenges him as something the investigation of which would justify the expenditure of his time and his energy. He has, then,

both the natural endowment and the interest for a successful, rewarding, and meaningful career in science.

Unfortunately, he does not always think clearly and objectively
about human beings, for, in the process of having been well brought
up, he has accepted blindly the traditional concepts of man, woman, and their natures and roles. Theoretically, he knows that
human beings are animals engaged in the struggle for existence,
but he cannot take advantage of that theoretical knowledge for
he is handicapped by traditional notions: that man is superior to
woman in every basic sense but the moral, that man as head of a
family has rights and duties, that a man must preserve his "honor,"
that there is something more to love than sex, and that somehow
human beings can rise above the animal condition.

The brilliant scientist engaged in rewarding and productive research, the disciplined captain highly competent in his military
activities, is (in spite of all that those who believe in the values of
self-restraint, civilization, and the like may say to the contrary)
the inferior in a struggle for power. For although Adolf senses
that his home is a cage full of tigers that need to be kept in line
and believes that a home should not be like that, he cannot in good
time bring himself to see the situation for what it is and certainly
not to use weapons and means comparable to his opponent's. The
sensitive Adolf, practitioner of self-restraint, is disarmed in an
unequal combat by an enemy who is only superficially concerned
about God and values, really not at all about the universe, but
very much so about man. And that concern is neither idealistic
nor sentimental, but clear-eyed and egotistic.

Laura is fascinating. But Strindberg had good reason to wonder
what actress would be willing to play Laura. She is indeed an
Omphale instinctively weaving the spider's web to catch her Hercules, a Hercules who was a prisoner of conventional notions
and ideals when she met him more than twenty years ago and
still is. Unlike Adolf, Laura not only knows what handicaps she
has in the struggle for power but recognizes them as handicaps
and does some rather interesting and rewarding things about them:

she not only senses what her strengths are but uses them successfully. And she senses possibilities and does all these things so
cleverly that she will reap neither pangs of conscience nor social
condemnation.

Those who consider Laura stupid should carefully define stupidity. She is certainly stupid if her goal is happiness within a
conventional marriage, but close scrutiny of the play will reveal
that Laura never had such a goal. Strindberg makes it quite clear
that Laura's mind has not been trained and disciplined in any
profound sense, but he also makes it equally clear that her mind
is a good one, good enough at least to recognize the implications—
good and bad—of her lot as a human female in a Western society.
For example: the lack of discipline that an inferior education for
women implies has permitted her self-expression qualified only by
the slight limitations imposed by the standards of acceptable social
behavior, or, to put it in a somewhat different way, she has been
permitted to function as a thoroughly egotistic animal behind the
camouflage of superficially correct social behavior. The lack of
training has forced her to use one of her most effective weapons—
sex—to gain a kind of security and a base of operating toward
the achievement of what she really wants.

Curiously enough what she does is not different, except perhaps
in degree, from what many women both in and out of books have
been doing for quite some time. She did not marry for love (note
the revealing scene between brother and sister, both of them, inci-
dentally, members of what at least one American disciple of Strindberg would call the animal kingdom); she became pregnant in
order to protect her security; she knows how to deal with other
people, none of whom she particularly respects; she not only has
been able to bring everyone in the household but Adolf under her
thumb but apparently has made them like it; and, what is so very
pleasant for her, she is able to conceal from herself the real implications of her actions. Laura is fascinating and, from a determin-
istic point of view, admirable. The Lauras will survive.

Most people who have read the play or seen it performed apparently agree with the Pastor's verdict that what Laura has done is to commit "an unconscious crime, an innocent little murder." Perhaps not so many have noticed that the story Strindberg has to tell is the story of a special kind of suicide as well as an innocent murder.

For over twenty years, Laura has thought of Adolf not as a man she loves, a partner, someone to work with, but as someone to be used—physically for the satisfaction of her sexual desires; socially for the attainment of a position in the community; and otherwise for securing her food, shelter, clothing, and base of operations. But in all the years of her life, Laura has always been at least nominally a subordinate, she has never occupied any position of primary power. She senses that she should have such a position, and she feels she can achieve it.

Except for those times when illness has brought Adolf low and permitted her to take control, Laura has made their marriage a Strindbergian (and a very human) hell for Adolf by questioning every move he has wanted to make and every decision he has tried to arrive at, by nagging and frustrating him whenever possible, by stirring him up and keeping him off balance, by never giving him—within their "home"—the chance to act calmly and decisively. She has done all this while convincing herself she was doing it for the general good of the family, never apparently consciously examining either her motives or her actions, sensing opportunities, and making instinctive use of them according to hints supplied by Adolf, who is unfortunately addicted to uttering aloud his analyses.

What one witnesses on stage is nothing more than the catastrophe: Laura's "unconscious" decision to indulge in quick final action when she at last sees her ultimate goal attainable. She simply intensifies what she has been doing for over twenty years: she makes use of "the rails" he and others have "laid down," destroys his will, and drives him mad, not by clear-cut conscious planning or any honesty with herself but by a process so complex that it permits her to keep the knowledge of her guilt comfortably below the surface of her consciousness. The actions she finally forces him to take are those of a broken irrational being, no longer the superior human being he had been.

Adolf does permit himself to be destroyed; in fact, one may indeed justifiably say that *The Father* tells the story not only of a murder but of a suicide as well. The intellectually trained Adolf refrains from studying Laura and her behavior realistically and scientifically although these have been two of the most important factors in his life for over twenty years. He shies away from the implications of what his senses and his good common sense tell him about her; he does not dare to face what he knows but is not willing to admit he knows. For over twenty years he has apparently blurted out the leads she needs to keep him off balance, and now in the crucial test to render him not only helpless but unnecessary. His psychic suicide is understandable: Adolf has been trained to talk *with* others; that is, he is able to communicate in the sense of considering and exchanging ideas. Laura never does this, although she comes close to doing so with her brother when he labels what she has done: the ugly little laugh that is quickly suppressed should not be forgotten. Her "unconscious crime," her "innocent little murder" is as unmerciful as can be, but then mercy is a factor that Laura, product of her environment and heredity just as Adolf is of his, has never considered beyond playing at it when she has others in her power.

Strindberg considered Adolf a tragic figure, and he is. In terms of endowment, achievement, and potential, Adolf is unquestionably a superior human being. But he has his tragic flaw, and he is guilty of pride. His flaw is far more complex than the implications of his loss of faith in the conviction that he is Bertha's father and his consequent loss of assurance of a kind of immortality. His flaw, it seems to me, lies in his inability to examine objectively what he has been taught about human beings, to take in what his senses tell him, and to deal with Laura in accordance with any objective standard. (Note that he is able to do this about

Bertha's future. Is Strindberg implying—in keeping with what he said in the letter to Lundegård above—that Adolf deliberately blinds himself to facts about Laura and has refrained from self-protective action over the years because he has been at her mercy sexually?) In other words, Adolf has never examined and weighed objectively the notions "society" has instilled in him about man and woman, love and sex, home and family, "artificial" and "natural" conduct. His fate or nemesis is thus the artificially instilled code of conduct that will not without loss of "honor" permit him to struggle successfully for his survival. He does have pride in his manliness, an arrogant assumption, if you will, of his superiority (as a male and because he is a male) physically, intellectually, socially, and, in his case, morally. In a world where the lightly concealed laws of the jungle permit a Laura to use every weapon and means to attain her goal in a struggle with an adversary who functions with his eyes closed to some basic facts and according to other and gentler laws of behavior, the latter must go down to defeat.

The Father is not only a remarkable play, but a remarkably good one. Its many merits include an intensely interesting plot, close enough to universality to affect every reader and spectator, with either fascinated engagement or horrified withdrawal from such frank revelation of truth. Perhaps it is this universality together with the intensity of the play that make some people call Adolf and Laura larger than life, but it is certain that anyone who witnesses a performance of The Father presented in keeping with Strindberg's intention will never doubt that he has brought Adolf and Laura alive as dynamic and complex flesh-and-blood human beings, and that he has succeeded as far as necessary in making the nominally Christian Pastor, the notion-ridden Nurse, the sexually careless Nöjd, the compromising Doctor, and Bertha (childlike for self-protection) believable. Structurally, The Father is a model of its kind—an extremely realistic modern tragedy. Perhaps as good a test of its greatness as any is the fact that the play can be read again and again with new rewards in terms of greater insight into what Strindberg intended and what he achieved both in form and substance.

But in 1887 recognition of its greatness came slowly. Antagonism toward Strindberg on the part of influential critics and other Swedes accounts in part for lack of immediate recognition. Theater people's reluctance to gamble with what is obviously different from most of the theatrical fare that they were used to is another reason. But what was probably most disturbing about *The Father* in the late 1880's was that Strindberg made the reader or spectator highly uncomfortable by making him face facts and possibilities about human nature and human conduct that generally are evaded.

Since its first performance in Copenhagen in November, 1887, however, *The Father* has gone on to win a leading place for itself in the occidental theater world. Productions have been numerous both in Sweden and in other European countries and even in the United States; many of them have been superb and have made important contributions to theater history. As good a criterion as any of the play's sure place in world drama is the certainty that no student of drama or theater can afford to disregard it: professors and their anthologies have seen to that. But what is most important is that *The Father* is still living, challenging theater and literature.

The Father · A Tragedy in Three Acts

Josef Sommer and Pauline Flanagan in *The Father* (Seattle Repertory Theatre)

Characters

CAPTAIN ADOLF
LAURA, *his wife*
BERTHA, *their daughter*
DR. ÖSTERMARK
PASTOR (JONAS), *Laura's half-brother*
MARGRET, *the nurse*
NÖJD
SVÄRD, *the orderly*

ACT I

A living room at the CAPTAIN'S. *At the back a door to the right. In the center a large round table with newspapers and magazines on it. To the right a leather-covered couch and small tables. In the right corner a door covered with wallpaper. At the left a chiffonier with a clock; a door leading to the rest of the living quarters. Weapons on the walls; guns and hunting bags. A hall tree by the door with military coats hanging on it. A lamp is burning on the large table.*

The CAPTAIN *and the* PASTOR *are sitting on the leather couch. The* CAPTAIN *is wearing his service uniform and riding boots with spurs. The* PASTOR *is dressed in black, is wearing a white tie but not a clerical collar, and is smoking a pipe.*

(CAPTAIN *rings.*)

ORDERLY *(enters):* Yes, Captain?

CAPTAIN: Is Nöjd out there?

ORDERLY: He's in the kitchen waiting for orders.

15

CAPTAIN: So he's in the kitchen again! Bring him in right away!

ORDERLY: Yes, sir. *(Goes)*

PASTOR: What's all this?

CAPTAIN: That rascal has been at it with the maid again. He's absolutely mad, that fellow!

PASTOR: Is it Nöjd? Why, he was up last year, too!

CAPTAIN: Yes, you remember! Say a few kind words to him this time so it takes! I've sworn at him, and I've let him have it, too, but that has had no effect.

PASTOR: Well, so you want me to preach at him. What effect do you think the word of God will have on a cavalryman?

CAPTAIN: Well, it hasn't any effect on me as you know . . .

PASTOR: I certainly do!

CAPTAIN: But it might on him! Try it anyhow.

(NÖJD *enters.*)

CAPTAIN: What have you been up to, Nöjd?

NÖJD: Bless you, captain, I can't say that when the pastor's here.

PASTOR: Oh, don't you be embarrassed, my boy!

CAPTAIN: Confess right now—if you don't, you know what will happen.

NÖJD: Well, see, it was like this . . . we were at a dance at Gabriel's, and then, and then Ludvig said . . .

CAPTAIN: What does Ludvig have to do with this matter? Stick to the truth.

NÖJD: Yes, and then Emma said we should go to the barn.

CAPTAIN: Oh, so it was Emma who led you astray?

NÖJD: Well, not far from it! And I'll say this: if the girl doesn't want to, nothing happens.

CAPTAIN: Out with it: are you the child's father, or aren't you?

NÖJD: How can I know?

CAPTAIN: What? Can't you know that?

NÖJD: No, see, you can never know that.

CAPTAIN: Weren't you the only one?

NÖJD: Yes, that time, but I can't be sure just because of that.

CAPTAIN: Are you blaming Ludvig? Is that what you mean?

NÖJD: It's not so easy to know who to blame.

CAPTAIN: Well, but you told Emma you wanted to marry her.

NÖJD: Yes, but one always has to say that . . .

CAPTAIN: (to PASTOR): This is terrible!

PASTOR: It's the same old story! But listen, Nöjd! Surely you're man enough to know if you're the father?

NÖJD: Well, I had her all right, but you know, Pastor, that that didn't need to lead to anything!

PASTOR: Listen, my boy, this has to do with you now! Surely you don't want to leave the girl in the lurch with the child! I don't suppose you can be forced to marry her, but you are going to support the child! That you are!

NÖJD: Well, then Ludvig's going to, too!

CAPTAIN: Then the case will have to be decided in court! I can't straighten it out, and I don't enjoy trying to. So . . . march!

PASTOR: Nöjd! One word! Hm! Don't you think it's dishonorable to leave the girl without support with a child like that? Don't you think so? Eh? Don't you think behaving like that . . . hm, hm! . . .

NÖJD: Yes, see, if I only knew I were the child's father, but, see, you can never know that, Pastor. And slaving for somebody else's child all through life isn't any fun! Both of you can surely understand that!

CAPTAIN: March!

NÖJD: Bless you, Captain! (Going)

CAPTAIN: But don't go to the kitchen, you rascal!

CAPTAIN: Well, why didn't you let him have it?

PASTOR: What? Didn't I?

CAPTAIN: Huh! You just sat there muttering to yourself!

PASTOR: Frankly speaking, I didn't know what to say. The girl's to be pitied, yes; the boy's to be pitied, yes. What if he isn't the father? The girl can nurse the child for four months at the orphanage, then the child will be supported permanently, but the boy can't nurse the child. The girl will get a good place afterward in some better family, but the boy's future can be destroyed if he's discharged from the regiment.

CAPTAIN: I wouldn't want to be in the judge's shoes and have to judge the case. The boy most likely isn't innocent; we can't know that, but we know one thing: the girl is guilty if there is any guilt.

PASTOR: Yes, yes! I don't judge anyone! But what were we talking about when this blessed story interrupted us? Wasn't it Bertha and her confirmation? Yes, it was!

CAPTAIN: It wasn't really about her confirmation, but about her whole bringing up. This house is filled with women, all of whom want to bring up my child. My mother-in-law wants to make her a spiritualist; Laura wants her to be an artist; the governess wants to make her a Methodist; old Margret wants her to be a Baptist; and the maids want her to be a member of the Salvation Army. You can't patch a soul together in that way, particularly since I who have the first right to guide her am constantly opposed in all my efforts. So I have to get her away from this house.

PASTOR: You have too many women who run your house.

CAPTAIN: Yes, don't I? It's like going into a cage with tigers in it. If I didn't hold my irons red hot under their noses, they'd tear me to pieces any time! Yes, you laugh, you scoundrel. It wasn't enough for me to marry your sister, but you fooled me into taking in your old stepmother, too.

PASTOR: Well, good heavens, one can't have stepmothers living with him.

CAPTAIN: No, but you think it's better to have mothers-in-law living with others, that is.

PASTOR: Yes, yes, we all have our burdens to bear.

CAPTAIN: Yes, but I've got too much. Then there's my old nurse who treats me as if I should still wear a bib. She's very kind, God knows, but she doesn't belong here!

PASTOR: Keep your women in line! You let them have the say entirely too much.

CAPTAIN: Listen, Jonas, will you tell me how to keep women in line?

PASTOR: Strictly speaking, Laura was . . . she's my own sister, but she has always been a little difficult.

CAPTAIN: No doubt Laura has her faults, but she's not such a problem.

PASTOR: Speak out—I know her.

CAPTAIN: The way she was brought up gave her a lot of romantic notions, and she has a hard time accepting reality, but in any case she is my wife . . .

PASTOR: And because she's your wife, she's the best of women. No, Adolf, I suspect she's the one who's troubling you most.

CAPTAIN: Be that as it may, the whole house has been turned upside down. Laura doesn't want to let Bertha leave home, and I can't let her stay in this madhouse!

PASTOR: So, Laura doesn't want to! Then I'm afraid you're in for trouble. When she was a child, she used to play dead until she got her way, and, when she had got what she wanted, she'd hand it back, if it were a thing, with the explanation that it wasn't the thing she wanted, but getting her way.

CAPTAIN: Really! So she was like that even then. Hm! She gets so furious now and then I'm afraid of her and think she's sick.

PASTOR: But what is it now about Bertha that can't be agreed on? Can't you compromise?

CAPTAIN: Don't think I want to make her either a child wonder or an image of me. I don't want to be my daughter's pimp and bring her up for marriage alone. If she doesn't marry, she'll have a hard time. But, on the other hand, I don't want to direct her into a masculine career that requires a long education which will be completely wasted if she should want to get married.

PASTOR: What do you want?

CAPTAIN: I want her to become a teacher. If she doesn't marry, she'll be able to support herself and won't have a harder time of it than those poor men teachers who have to share their wages with their families. If she gets married, she can use her knowledge in bringing up her children. Am I right?

PASTOR: Yes, you are! But, on the other hand, has she shown such talent for painting that it would be a crime against nature to repress it?

CAPTAIN: No! I showed her paintings to a distinguished painter, and he says they're the sort of thing anybody can learn in school. But a young fellow was here last summer who understands the matter better, and he said Bertha has exceptional talents, and that settled the matter—to Laura's advantage.

PASTOR: Was he in love with the girl?

CAPTAIN: I take that for granted!

PASTOR: God save you then, my friend, for then I don't see any way out. But this is too bad, and Laura has her supporters naturally . . . in there.

CAPTAIN: Yes, you can be sure of that! The whole houseful of them are up in arms, and, just between you and me, it isn't an exactly noble fight they're waging.

PASTOR: *(gets up):* Don't you think I know how it is?

CAPTAIN: You, too?

PASTOR: Too?

CAPTAIN: The worst, it seems to me, is that Bertha's future is being decided in there from despicable motives. They spit out that men are going to find out that women can do both this and that. It's man against woman in there constantly, all day long.—Are you leaving? No, stay and have dinner with us. There's nothing special, I suppose, but all the same. You know we're expecting the new doctor. Have you seen him?

PASTOR: I caught a glimpse of him when I went by. He looks pleasant and sound.

CAPTAIN: Oh? That's good. Do you think he'll be an ally for me?

PASTOR: Who knows? That depends on how much he knows about women.

CAPTAIN: Yes, but won't you stay?

PASTOR: No, thank you. I promised to get home for dinner, and my wife gets uneasy when I'm late.

CAPTAIN: Uneasy? Angry, you mean. Well, as you will. May I help you with your coat?

n the door leading to the living quarters): I'll bring it very
(Goes to the outer door at the back, just as the ORDERLY
it and announces) Dr. Östermark!
Madame!

oes up to him and extends her hand): Welcome, Doctor!
very much welcome. The captain is out, but he'll be back

I apologize for coming so late, but I've already been mak-

on't you sit down?

Thank you.

s, there's a lot of illness in the neighborhood just now,
pe you'll like it here anyway. It's very important for us
isolated out in the country to find a doctor who's inter-
his patients, and I've heard so many nice things about
tor, I hope we'll get along famously.

ou're too kind, but I hope for your sake my calls
me from necessity too often. Your family is well, I un-
and . . .

tunately we haven't had any serious illnesses, but even
ing isn't as it should be.

ally?

it's not as good as we'd like to have it.

ally? You frighten me!

e are circumstances in a family that because of honor
ence a person has to conceal from the world . . .
ept from the doctor.

s my painful duty to tell you the whole truth right

't we postpone talking about it until I've had the
eeting the captain?

ou must hear me first before you meet him.

bout him then?

him, my poor dear husband.

PASTOR: It's apparently very cold tonight! Thank you. Take care
of your health, Adolf. You're looking very nervous.

CAPTAIN: Nervous?

PASTOR: Yes. Aren't you feeling well?

CAPTAIN: Has Laura made you think I'm sick? For twenty years
she has treated me as if I were about to die.

PASTOR: Laura? No, but, but you make me uneasy! Take care of
yourself! That's my advice! Good-bye, but didn't you want to
talk about Bertha's confirmation?

CAPTAIN: Not at all! I assure you she'll be confirmed, but it will be
on the public conscience.* For I'm neither a witness to the truth
nor a martyr. That sort of thing is behind us. Well, good-bye then.
Greet your wife!

PASTOR: Good-bye, Adolf. Greet Laura! [*Goes*]

CAPTAIN (*opens the desk and sits down to do accounts*): Thirty-
four—nine, forty-three—seven, eight, fifty-six.

LAURA (*enters from another room*): Would you be so good . . .

CAPTAIN: Just a minute!—Sixty-six, seventy-one, eighty-four,
eighty-nine, ninety-two, one hundred. What is it?

LAURA: Maybe I'm disturbing you.

CAPTAIN: Not at all! The household money, I suppose?

LAURA: Yes, the household money.

CAPTAIN: Put your accounts there. Then I'll go through them.

LAURA: My accounts?

CAPTAIN: Yes!

LAURA: Am I to account for what I've spent?

CAPTAIN: Of course you are. Our financial position's uncertain, and
if we had to report for a settlement, there'd have to be records.
Otherwise I could be legally punished as a careless debtor.

LAURA: If our financial position is bad, it's not my fault.

CAPTAIN: That's just what we'll find out through your accounts.

LAURA: If our tenant doesn't pay, it's not my fault.

CAPTAIN: Who recommended him most enthusiastically? You! Why
did you recommend a—let's say—such a careless fellow?

*The Church of Sweden is a state church.

LAURA: Why did you accept such a careless fellow?

CAPTAIN: Because you wouldn't let me eat in peace, sleep in peace, work in peace, before you women had got him in here. You wanted him because your brother wanted to get rid of him, your mother wanted him because I didn't want him, the governess wanted him because he was a pietist, and old Margret because she had known his grandmother from childhood. So I took him on, and, if I hadn't, I'd either be in an insane asylum or in the family grave. However, here's the household money and your pin money. You can give me your accounts later.

LAURA *(curtsies):* Thank you very much!—Do you keep accounts of what you spend outside the household?

CAPTAIN: That does not concern you!

LAURA: No, that's true, just as little as my child's bringing up is to be my concern. Have you men made your decision during your conference?

CAPTAIN: I had already made my decision so I had merely to tell the only friend I and the family have in common. Bertha's to stay in town—she'll leave in fourteen days.

LAURA: With whom is she to stay, if I may ask?

CAPTAIN: At Sävbergs'.

LAURA: That freethinker.

CAPTAIN: Children are to be brought up in their father's faith, according to the law.

LAURA: And their mother has nothing to say about it.

CAPTAIN: Nothing at all! She sold her birthright and gave up her rights in return for her husband's assuming responsibility for her and her children.

LAURA: So a mother has no rights over her child?

CAPTAIN: None at all! If you've sold something, you're not likely to get it back and keep the money, too.

LAURA: But if both father and mother would decide together . . .

CAPTAIN: How could we? I want her to live in town; you want her to live at home. The compromise would be that she'd stay at the

railroad station halfway between

lem that can't be solved. You see

LAURA: Then something has to be

CAPTAIN: That's my professional s

LAURA: That everyone in the kitch

CAPTAIN: Fine! Then you ought t

LAURA: I do know it, too.

CAPTAIN: And have sat in judgme

LAURA: The law has it in black a

CAPTAIN: The law doesn't say wh

LAURA: No, but people can gene

CAPTAIN: Wise people insist on

LAURA: That is strange! Can't o

CAPTAIN: That's what they say!

LAURA: That's strange! How
her child, then?

CAPTAIN: He has those rights
if he is forced to assume re
riage there can't be any dou

LAURA: There can't be any d

CAPTAIN: I hope not!

LAURA: Well, what if the wif

CAPTAIN: That doesn't app
about anything else?

LAURA: Nothing at all!

CAPTAIN: Then I'm going
when the doctor comes.

LAURA: I will!

CAPTAIN *(going out thro*
soon as he comes, bec
You understand! *(Goes*

LAURA: I do understand!

HER MOTHER'S VOICE *(fr*

LAURA: Yes!

VOICE: Is my tea ready?

LAURA *(i*
soon!
opens

DOCTOR:

LAURA *(*
You're
soon.

DOCTOR:
ing call

LAURA: W

DOCTOR:

LAURA: Ye
but I ho
who are
ested in
you, Doc

DOCTOR: Y
won't co
derstand,

LAURA: For
so everyth

DOCTOR: Re

LAURA: No,

DOCTOR: Re

LAURA: The
and consci

DOCTOR: Ex

LAURA: So it
away.

DOCTOR: Can
honor of m

LAURA: No! Y

DOCTOR: It's

LAURA: Abou

DOCTOR: You're making me uneasy, and you certainly have my sympathy in your misfortune!

LAURA *(takes up her handkerchief):* My husband is mentally sick. Now you know everything, and you can judge for yourself later.

DOCTOR: What are you saying? I've read the captain's excellent articles on mineralogy with great admiration—he has always demonstrated a clear and strong intellect.

LAURA: Really? I'd be happy if all of us close to him were mistaken.

DOCTOR: But it may be that he's disturbed in other areas. Tell me about it!

LAURA: That's what we're afraid of, too! You see, he sometimes has the strangest ideas which as a scholar he could have if they didn't affect the well-being of his whole family. For example: he has a mania for buying everything possible.

DOCTOR: That is serious. But what does he buy?

LAURA: Whole boxes of books he never reads.

DOCTOR: Well, a scholar's buying books isn't very dangerous.

LAURA: You don't believe what I'm saying?

DOCTOR: Yes, I'm convinced you believe what you're saying.

LAURA: Does it make sense that a human being can see through a microscope what's happening on another planet?

DOCTOR: Does he say he can do that?

LAURA: Yes, he does.

DOCTOR: Through a microscope?

LAURA: Through a microscope! Yes!

DOCTOR: This is serious if it's so!

LAURA: If it's so! So you don't have any confidence in me, Doctor, and I've told you our family secret . . .

DOCTOR: I'm honored by your confidence, but as a doctor I have to examine, investigate before I judge. Has the captain shown any symptoms of capriciousness of mind, uncertainty of will?

LAURA: Has he? We've been married for twenty years, and he has never made a decision without changing his mind about it.

DOCTOR: Is he stubborn?

LAURA: He always wants his way, but once he gets it, he gives it all up and asks me to decide.

DOCTOR: That is serious and will need close observation. It's the will, you see, that is the backbone of the mind; if the will is injured, the mind goes to pieces.

LAURA: God knows I've had to learn to do as he wishes during these long years of trial. Oh, if you only knew what a life I've struggled through by his side! If you only knew!

DOCTOR: Your misfortune moves me deeply, and I promise I'll find out what can be done. You have my deepest sympathy . . . do rely on me completely. But from what I've heard, I'll ask you one thing. Avoid arousing any thoughts with strong impressions in your sick husband, because they can develop hastily and easily become fixed ideas. Do you understand?

LAURA: I'm to avoid arousing his suspicions!

DOCTOR: Exactly! You can persuade a sick person to believe anything just because he's receptive to everything.

LAURA: So! Then I understand! Yes!—Yes! *(Her mother's bell rings.)* Excuse me—my mother has something to say to me. Just a minute . . . There, there's Adolf . . . [*Laura leaves as the captain enters through the wallpaper-covered door*]

CAPTAIN: Ah, you have already come, Doctor! You're very much welcome.

DOCTOR: Captain, it's a great pleasure for me to meet such a famous scientist!

CAPTAIN: Please! My official duties don't permit me to carry on research in depth, but all the same I think I'm on the trail of a discovery.

DOCTOR: So!

CAPTAIN: You see, I've exposed meteor stones to spectroanalysis and I've found carbon, traces of organic life! What do you think of that?

DOCTOR: Can you see that through a microscope?

CAPTAIN: No, good heavens—through a spectroscope!

DOCTOR: Spectroscope! Excuse me! Well, then you'll soon be able to tell us what's happening on Jupiter!

CAPTAIN: Not what is happening but what has happened. If that blessed bookdealer in Paris would only send me the books, but I think all the bookdealers in the world are conspiring against me. Can you imagine that not one of them has answered orders, letters, or nasty telegrams—in two months! This is driving me crazy, and I can't understand how this has happened!

DOCTOR: It's the usual carelessness, I expect. You mustn't take it so violently.

CAPTAIN: But, damn it, I can't get my paper ready in time, and I know they're working on the same thing in Berlin. But we weren't going to talk about that! But about you! If you want to live here, we have a little apartment in the wing. Or do you want to live in the old house?

DOCTOR: Whichever you wish.

CAPTAIN: No, as you wish! Decide!

DOCTOR: You'll have to decide that, Captain!

CAPTAIN: No, I don't decide anything. You're to say how you want it. I have no preference. Not in the least!

DOCTOR: No, but I can't decide . . .

CAPTAIN: For Christ's sake, sir, say which you want. I have no will about this, no opinion, no wish! Are you such a weakling you don't know what you want? Speak up, or I'll get angry!

DOCTOR: Since it's up to me, I'll live here!

CAPTAIN: Fine!—Thank you!—Forgive me, Doctor, but nothing pains me more than hearing people say something doesn't matter. *(Rings)*

(NURSE *enters.*)

CAPTAIN: Ah, it's you, Margret. Do you know if the apartment is ready for the doctor?

NURSE: Yes, it is, Captain!

CAPTAIN: So! Then I won't delay you, Doctor—you may be tired. Good-bye and again welcome. I'll see you tomorrow, I hope.

DOCTOR: Good night, Captain!

CAPTAIN: And I assume my wife has told you something about circumstances here so you know approximately how the land lies.

DOCTOR: Your excellent wife has given me hints about various things a stranger could need to know. Good night, Captain. [*Exits*]

CAPTAIN (*to the* NURSE): Was there something you wanted, my friend?

NURSE: Listen to me, Mr. Adolf!

CAPTAIN: Yes, old Margret. Speak out—you're the only one I can listen to without getting burned up!

NURSE: Listen, Mr. Adolf! Couldn't you go half ways to agree with the mistress about this matter of the child? Think of this—she is a mother . . .

CAPTAIN: Think of this—I am a father, Margret!

NURSE: There, there! A father has things beside his child, but a mother has only her child.

CAPTAIN: Precisely, old woman. She has only one burden, but I have three, and I bear hers. Don't you imagine I'd have had a position in life other than that of an old soldier if I hadn't had her and her child?

NURSE: Yes, but that's not what I wanted to say.

CAPTAIN: No, I suspect not—you wanted me to be in the wrong.

NURSE: Don't you think I wish you well, Mr. Adolf?

CAPTAIN: Yes, my friend, I do, but you don't know what's good for me. You see, it isn't enough for me to have given life to the child—I want to give her my soul, too.

NURSE: Yes, but I don't understand that. But I think you two could come to an agreement.

CAPTAIN: You aren't my friend, Margret!

NURSE: I'm not? Good heavens, what are you saying, Mr. Adolf? Do you think I can forget you were my child when you were small?

CAPTAIN: Well, have I forgotten? You have been like a mother to me, you have been on my side when all of them were against me, but now when it comes to a showdown, you fail me and go over to the enemy.

NURSE: The enemy!

CAPTAIN: Yes, the enemy! You certainly know what the situation is in this house—you've seen everything from beginning to end.

NURSE: I certainly have! But, good heavens, are you two going to torture the life out of each other—you two who otherwise are so good and want to do the right thing by all others? The mistress never behaves like that to me or to others . . .

CAPTAIN: Only to me, I know. But I tell you, Margret, if you desert me, you're committing a sin. They're spinning a web about me here, and that doctor isn't my friend!

NURSE: But, Mr. Adolf, you suspect everyone of evil, but that's because you don't have the right faith; yes, that's how it is.

CAPTAIN: But you and the Baptists have found the one true faith. You *are* fortunate!

NURSE: Yes, I'm surely not as unfortunate as you, Mr. Adolf! Bow down your heart, Mr. Adolf, and you'll see that God will make you fortunate in your love for your neighbor.

CAPTAIN: It's strange—as soon as you start talking about God and love your voice becomes hard and your eyes fill with hate. No, Margret, you definitely don't have the true faith.

NURSE: Yes, be proud of your learning—it won't be enough when you're up against it.

CAPTAIN: How arrogantly you speak, humble heart. Of course I do know learning doesn't help creatures like you!

NURSE: You ought to be ashamed! But all the same I like you, my big, big boy best, and you'll come to me like a good child when the storm strikes.

CAPTAIN: Margret! Forgive me, but believe me, you're the only one here who wishes me well. Help me—I have the feeling something is about to happen. I don't know what, but what is in the making isn't right. *(Someone screams in an inner room.)* What's that? Who's screaming? [BERTHA *runs in.*]

BERTHA: Dad, dad, help me! Save me!

CAPTAIN: What's wrong, dear child? Tell me!

BERTHA: Help me! I think she wants to hurt me!

CAPTAIN: Who wants to hurt you? Tell me!

BERTHA: Grandmother! But it's my fault—I fooled her!

CAPTAIN: Tell me!

BERTHA: Yes, but you mustn't say anything! Promise?

CAPTAIN: Yes, but tell me what's wrong then! (NURSE *exits.*)

BERTHA: Well! She usually screws down the lamp in the evening, and has me sit down at the table with a pen in my hand and with a piece of paper in front of me. And then she says the spirits will write.

CAPTAIN: What's that? And you haven't told me!

BERTHA: Forgive me, but I didn't dare—Grandmother says the spirits will avenge themselves if one tells. And then the pen writes, but I don't know if it's I. And sometimes it goes well, but sometimes not at all. And when I get tired, it won't come, but it has to all the same. And tonight I thought I was writing well, but then grandmother said it was right out of Stagnelius* and that I had fooled her. Then she got terribly angry.

CAPTAIN: Do you believe there are spirits?

BERTHA: I don't know!

CAPTAIN: But I know there aren't any!

BERTHA: But Grandmother says you don't understand and you have much worse things that can see all the way to other planets.

CAPTAIN: Does she say that? Does she indeed? What else does she say?

BERTHA: She says you can't perform magic!

CAPTAIN: I've never said I could. You know what meteors are! Rocks that fall down from other heavenly bodies. I can study those and tell if they contain the same elements as Earth. That's all I can see.

BERTHA: But Grandmother says there are things she can see that you can't!

CAPTAIN: Then she's lying!

BERTHA: Grandmother surely doesn't lie!

CAPTAIN: Why not?

*One of Sweden's greatest romantic poets (1793-1823).

BERTHA: Then Mother lies, too!

CAPTAIN: Hm!

BERTHA: And if you say Mother lies, I'll never believe you again!

CAPTAIN: I haven't said that, so believe me when I say that your well-being, your future, demands that you leave this home! Do you want to? Do you want to get to town to learn something useful?

BERTHA: Oh yes! How I'd like to get to town, away from here, anywhere at all! Just so I'll get to see you occasionally, often. It's always so heavy, so terrible in there as if it were a winter night, but when you come, Dad, it's as if we were taking out the double windows on a spring morning!

CAPTAIN: My dear child! My dear child!

BERTA: But, Dad, you have to be good to Mother. She cries so often!

CAPTAIN: Hm!—So you want to go to town?

BERTHA: Oh, yes!

CAPTAIN: But if Mother doesn't want you to?

BERTHA: She just has to!

CAPTAIN: But if she doesn't?

BERTHA: Then I don't know what will happen! But she has to! She has to!

CAPTAIN: Will you ask her?

BERTHA: You ask her nicely—she doesn't listen to me!

CAPTAIN: Hm!—Well, if you want to, and I want you to, and she doesn't, what shall we do?

BERTHA: Then there'll be trouble again! Why can't you both . . . (LAURA enters.)

LAURA: Ah, Bertha's here! Then maybe we can hear what she wants since it's her future that's to be decided.

CAPTAIN: The child can hardly have any sound idea of how a young girl's life is likely to take form, but we ought to be able to figure it out approximately since we've observed a great many young girls grow up.

LAURA: But since we can't agree, Bertha can decide.

CAPTAIN: No! I won't let anyone take over my rights, neither women nor children. Bertha, leave us! (BERTHA *goes out*.)

LAURA: You were afraid of what she'd say since you believed it would be to my advantage.

CAPTAIN: I know she wants to get away from home, but I know, too, that you have the power to change her mind as you wish.

LAURA: Oh, do I have that much power?

CAPTAIN: Yes, you have a satanic power to get your way, but the person who doesn't hesitate about means always does. For example: How did you get rid of Dr. Norling, and how did you get the new one to come?

LAURA: Yes, how did I?

CAPTAIN: You insulted Dr. Norling so he left, and had your brother dig up votes for this one.

LAURA: Well, that was easy and absolutely legal. Is Bertha going?

CAPTAIN: Yes, she's going in fourteen days.

LAURA: That's your decision?

CAPTAIN: Yes!

LAURA: Have you talked with Bertha about it?

CAPTAIN: Yes!

LAURA: Then I suppose I'll have to try to prevent it!

CAPTAIN: You can't!

LAURA: Can't I? Do you think a mother will let her child go out among bad people to learn that everything her mother has taught her is foolishness so she'll be despised by her daughter the rest of her life?

CAPTAIN: Do you think a father will permit ignorant women to teach his daughter her father is a fake?

LAURA: That would mean less to a father.

CAPTAIN: Why?

LAURA: Because a mother is closer to the child since they've discovered no one can really know who a child's father is.

CAPTAIN: What does that have to do with this case?

LAURA: Surely you don't know if you're Bertha's father!

CAPTAIN: Don't I know?

LAURA: No, what no one can know, I suppose you can't know!

CAPTAIN: Are you joking?

LAURA: No, I'm only using what you've taught me. Besides, how do you know I haven't been unfaithful?

CAPTAIN: I believe you're capable of a lot, but not that, and you wouldn't admit it if it were true.

LAURA: Assume I'd rather do anything, be driven out, be despised, do anything to keep and control my child, and that I'd tell the truth when I'd say: Bertha is *my* child but not yours! Assume . . .

CAPTAIN: Stop!

LAURA: Just assume this: then your power would be at an end!

CAPTAIN: After you had proved I wasn't her father!

LAURA: That wouldn't be hard! Do you want me to?

CAPTAIN: Stop!

LAURA: Naturally I'd just have to name the real father, fix the place and the time, for example—when was Bertha born?—The third year after we got married . . .

CAPTAIN: Stop! Otherwise . . .

LAURA: Otherwise what? Now we will stop! But consider carefully what you do and decide! And above all don't make yourself ridiculous!

CAPTAIN: I find all this extremely sad!

LAURA: The more ridiculous you'll be!

CAPTAIN: But not you!

LAURA: No! That's how wisely it has been arranged for us women!

CAPTAIN: That's why we can't fight you.

LAURA: Why do you let yourself in for a fight with a superior enemy?

CAPTAIN: Superior?

LAURA: Yes! It's strange, but I've never been able to look at a man without feeling superior.

CAPTAIN: Well, then you're going to see your superior for once so you'll never forget it.

LAURA: That would be interesting.

NURSE *(enters):* Dinner is served. Won't you come?

LAURA: Yes, thank you!

(CAPTAIN *sits down in an easy chair next to the divan table*.)

LAURA: Aren't you coming to dinner?

CAPTAIN: No, thanks! I don't want any!

LAURA: What! Are you upset?

CAPTAIN: No, but I'm not hungry.

LAURA: Come, or they'll ask questions—that are unnecessary! Please—You don't want to—well, sit there then! *(Exits)*

NURSE *(enters):* Mr. Adolf! What is this?

CAPTAIN: I don't know what it is. Can you tell me how you can treat a grown-up man as if he were a child?

NURSE: I don't understand, but I suppose it's because all men, big and small, are women's children . . .

CAPTAIN: But no woman is born of man. Yes, but I *am* Bertha's father. Tell me, Margret, don't you believe I am? Don't you?

NURSE: Good heavens, how childish you are. Of course you're your own child's father. Come and eat now, and don't sit there sulking! There, there, just come!

CAPTAIN *(gets up):* Get out, woman! Go to hell, you witches! *(To the hall door)* Svärd! Svärd!

ORDERLY *(enters):* Captain!

CAPTAIN: Hitch up to the racing sleigh! Right now!

NURSE: Captain! Listen to . . .

CAPTAIN: Get out, woman! Right now!

NURSE: Lord preserve us, what's going to happen now?

CAPTAIN *(puts on his cap and gets ready to go out):* Don't expect me! before midnight! *(Goes)*

NURSE: Jesus, help us! What's going to happen now?

CURTAIN

ACT II

The same setting as in Act I. The lamp on the table is burning; it is night.

DOCTOR: Judging by our conversation, I'd say the evidence isn't absolute. In the first place, you made a mistake when you said he made these amazing discoveries about other heavenly bodies through a microscope. Now that I've learned it was a spectroscope, he's not only freed from suspicion of having an unbalanced mind but has also served science to a remarkable degree.

LAURA: Yes, but I never said that!

DOCTOR: I made notes on our conversation, and I remember asking you about the main point particularly since I thought I hadn't heard right. A person has to be scrupulously accurate in making charges that may lead to a man's being certified.

LAURA: Certified?

DOCTOR: Yes, you must know an insane person loses all civil and family rights.

LAURA: No, I didn't know that!

DOCTOR: And I wonder about another matter! He told me his letters to bookdealers had not been answered. May I ask if you—from mistaken but good intentions—have interfered with his mail?

LAURA: Yes, I have. But it was my duty to protect the interests of our family, and I couldn't just stand by while he ruined us all.

DOCTOR: Excuse me, but I don't think you could have foreseen the consequences of such an act. If he finds out you've interfered secretly in his activities, his suspicion will have a foundation and will grow like a landslide. Besides, by doing that you've curbed his will and have stirred up his impatience still more. You know how one feels in one's innermost being when one's strongest wishes are frustrated, when one's will is thwarted.

LAURA: Do I!

DOCTOR: Well, then judge how he has felt!

LAURA *(gets up):* It's midnight, and he hasn't come home. Now we can expect the worst.

DOCTOR: But tell me what happened this evening after I left. I have to know it all.

LAURA: He was imagining—having the strangest ideas. Can you imagine his getting the notion he isn't the father of his own child?

DOCTOR: Strange! How did he hit upon that thought?

LAURA: I don't really know, unless . . . he had one of the men on the carpet in a paternity case, and when I took the girl's part, he got excited and said no one can say who is the father of a child. God knows I did everything I could to make him calm, but now I think there's no more help. *(Weeps)*

DOCTOR: But this mustn't go on; something has to be done without arousing his suspicion at the same time. Tell me, has the captain had notions like this before?

LAURA: Things were like this six years ago, and then he admitted himself, yes, in his own letter to the doctor at that, that he was afraid he was losing his mind.

DOCTOR: Yes, yes, this is a case with deep roots, and the sanctity of family life—and all that—I can't ask about everything but must keep to what can be observed. What's done can't be undone, unfortunately, and the cure should have been applied to what's done.—Where do you think he is?

LAURA: I haven't the slightest idea. But then he has such wild notions.

DOCTOR: Do you want me to wait until he gets back? To avoid making him suspicious, I could say I was calling on your mother, who isn't feeling well.

LAURA: Yes, that will do nicely! But don't leave us, Doctor. If you only knew how worried I am. But wouldn't it be better to tell him right out what you think of his condition?

DOCTOR: One never says that to mentally sick people until they bring up the subject themselves, and only rarely then. It depends on what turn things take. But let's not sit here. Maybe I can go into the next room so it will look more natural.

LAURA: Yes, that will be better, and Margret can sit here. She always stays up when he's out, and she's the only one who can do anything with him. *(Goes to the left door)* Margret! Margret!

NURSE [*enters*]: Yes, ma'am! Is the master home?

LAURA: No, but you're to sit here to wait for him; and when he comes, you're to say my mother's sick and that's why the doctor's here.

NURSE: Yes, yes! I'll see that everything will be fine.

LAURA *(opens the door leading to the inner room)*: Doctor, won't you please come in here?

DOCTOR: Thank you! [*they exit.*]

NURSE *(at the table; picks up a psalmbook and puts on her glasses:*

Yes, yes! Yes, yes! *(Reads softly)*

> A mournful and a wretched thing
> Is life, and yet too soon it ends.
> The angel of death soars o'er all
> And ever to the world calls out:
>
> Vanity, mortality!

Yes, yes! Yes, yes!

> All that breathes and lives on earth
> Must fall to earth before his sword,
> And only Sorrow then lives on
> To carve upon the spacious tomb:
>
> Vanity, mortality!

Yes, yes!

BERTHA *(enters with a coffeepot and a piece of embroidery work; speaks softly)*: Margret, may I sit up with you? It's so ghastly up there!

NURSE: Good Lord, are you still up, Bertha?

BERTHA: I have to sew away at Dad's Christmas gift, you see. And here I have something good for you.

NURSE: Yes, but good heavens, this won't do! You have to get up tomorrow, and it's after twelve.

BERTHA: What difference does that make? I don't dare sit up there alone, for I think there are ghosts up there.

NURSE: There! What did I say? Yes, you'll see there's no good elf in this house. What was it you heard?

BERTHA: Oh, you know—I heard someone singing in the attic.

NURSE: In the attic! At this time of night!

BERTHA: Yes, it was a sad, a very sad song I had never heard before. And it sounded as if it came from the attic room where the cradle is—you know, to the left . . .

NURSE: My, oh my! And what a terrible storm tonight! I think the chimneys will blow down. "What is this our earthly life?—A vale of tears and of strife.—When it was the very best.—It was only trial and test."—Yes, dear child, God give us a good Christmas!

BERTHA: Is it true Dad is sick?

NURSE: Yes, he certainly is!

BERTHA: Then we won't get to celebrate Christmas eve. But how can he be up and about when he's sick?

NURSE: Well, my child—he has the kind of sickness he still can be up. Sh-h! Someone's in the entry. Go to bed and take the coffee-pot. Otherwise he'll be angry.

BERTHA *(goes out with the tray):* Good night, Margret!

NURSE: Good night, my child! God bless you!

CAPTAIN *(enters; takes off his coat and cap):* Are you still up? Go to bed!

NURSE: I only wanted to wait . . .

(CAPTAIN *lights a candle; pulls out the chiffonier leaf; sits down; and takes letters and newspapers out of his pocket.)*

NURSE: Mr. Adolf!

CAPTAIN: What do you want?

NURSE: The old lady is sick. And the doctor's here!

CAPTAIN: Is it serious?

NURSE: No, I don't think so. It's only a cold.

CAPTAIN *(gets up):* Who was your child's father, Margret?

NURSE: But I've told you many times it was that no-good Johansson.

CAPTAIN: Are you sure it was he?

NURSE: That's childish! Of course I'm sure, when he was the only one.

CAPTAIN: Yes, but was he sure he was the only one? No, he couldn't be, but you could. You see, there's a difference.

NURSE: Well, I don't see any difference.

CAPTAIN: No, you can't, but there's a difference all the same! *(Leafs through a photograph album on the table)* Do you think Bertha looks like me? *(Looks at a photograph in the album)*

NURSE: Yes, she looks just like you.

CAPTAIN: Did Johansson admit he was the father?

NURSE: Oh, he had to.

CAPTAIN: That's terrible! There's the doctor! *(Doctor enters.)* Good evening, Doctor! How is my mother-in-law?

DOCTOR: Oh, it isn't anything serious! It's just a slight sprain in her left foot.

CAPTAIN: I thought you said it was a cold, Margret. There seem to be different opinions of the ailment. Go to bed, Margret! *(The nurse goes. Pause)* Please sit down, Doctor.

DOCTOR *(sits down):* Thank you.

CAPTAIN: Is it true one gets striped foals if one crosses a zebra and a mare?

DOCTOR *(amazed):* Absolutely right!

CAPTAIN: Is it true later offspring are striped if one continues breeding with a stallion?

DOCTOR: Yes, that's true, too.

CAPTAIN: So under certain conditions a stallion can be the father of striped foals and vice versa?

DOCTOR: Yes, that seems possible.

CAPTAIN: That's to say: the offspring's resemblance to the father proves nothing.

DOCTOR: Oh . . .

CAPTAIN: That's to say: paternity can't be proved.

DOCTOR: Oh . . . hm . . .

CAPTAIN: You are a widower and have children?

DOCTOR: Yes—s . . .

CAPTAIN: Didn't you occasionally feel ridiculous as a father? I
know of nothing so hilarious as seeing a father walking with his
child on the street or hearing a father talk about his children.
"My wife's children," he should say. Didn't you ever feel there
was something false about your position, didn't you ever have
twinges of doubt—I don't want to say suspicions—for I assume
that as a gentleman you considered your wife above reproach?

DOCTOR: No, I never really had, but, Captain, a man has to take
his children in good faith as Goethe, I think, says.

CAPTAIN: Good faith, when it has to do with a woman? That's risky.

DOCTOR: Oh, there are many kinds of women.

CAPTAIN: Recent research says there's really only one kind!—When
I was young, I was strong—and—I'll admit—handsome. I remember two momentary impressions that later roused my fears.
One time I took a trip on a steamer. A few friends and I were
sitting in the cabin. The young waitress, her eyes red from weeping, came in and sat down directly opposite me. She told us her
fiancé had been lost at sea. We sympathized with her, and I
brought in champagne. After the second glass I touched her foot;
after the fourth, her knee; and before morning I had comforted
her.

DOCTOR: That was only a winter fly!

CAPTAIN: The second one was a summer fly. I was in Lysekil.*
There was a young wife, who had her children along, but her
husband was in town. She was religious, had extremely strict
standards, preached morality to me, was absolutely honorable—
I think. I lent her a book, two books; when she was going home,
she returned them—strangely enough. Three months later I
found a calling card in the books with a fairly clear declaration.
It was innocent, as innocent as a declaration of love from a married woman to a comparatively strange man, who has never made

*A resort town on Sweden's west coast (pronounced Lü-se-cheel).

any advances, can be. Now comes the moral. Just don't believe
too much!

DOCTOR: Don't believe too little either!

CAPTAIN: No, just so much, no more! But you see, Doctor, that
woman was so unconsciously bad that she told her husband she
was mad about me. That's just the danger—they're unconscious
of their instinctive evil. That's the extenuating circumstance, but
that can't cancel the judgment, just reduce it.

DOCTOR: Captain, your thoughts are taking a sickly direction, and
you should control them.

CAPTAIN: Don't use the word sickly! You see, all boilers explode
when the gauge reaches the boiling point, but the boiling point
isn't always the same for all boilers. You understand? But you're
here to keep an eye on me. If I weren't a man, I'd have the
right to complain, or lament as it's so shrewdly called, and I
probably could give you the complete diagnosis and what's more
the complete case history, but, unfortunately, I am a man, and
the only thing I can do is to cross my arms on my chest like the
Roman and hold my breath until I die. Good night!

DOCTOR: Captain! If you are ill, it won't hurt your honor as a man
to tell me everything. I have to hear your side, too.

CAPTAIN: I suspect it's been enough to have heard her side.

DOCTOR: No, Captain! And you know, when I heard Mrs. Alving*
talk about her dead husband, I thought to myself: It's a damn
shame the man's dead!

CAPTAIN: Do you think he would have said anything if he had been
alive? And do you think if any of the dead men rose from the
dead, he'd be believed? Good night, Doctor! You can hear
I'm calm, and you can safely go to bed!

DOCTOR: Good night, Captain. I can't have anything more to do
with this matter.

CAPTAIN: Are we enemies?

DOCTOR: Far from it! It's a shame we can't be friends. Good night.

*See Ibsen's Ghosts.

(The CAPTAIN *follows the doctor to the door at the back. Then the* CAPTAIN *goes to the left door and opens it slightly.)*

CAPTAIN: Come in so we may talk. I heard you were eavesdropping.

(LAURA *enters, embarrassed. The* CAPTAIN *sits down at the chiffonier.)*

CAPTAIN: It's late, but we have to settle this. Sit down! *(Pause)* I've been at the post office this evening and picked up letters! I gather from these you've kept back both outgoing and incoming letters. The consequence is that the loss of time has practically destroyed the results of my research.

LAURA: I did it with good intentions, because you were neglecting your job for the other work.

CAPTAIN: It wasn't a matter of your good intentions, I suspect, because you knew for a certainty I'd win more honor through my research than through my position, and above all you didn't want me to gain any honor, because that pressed heavily on your insignificance. And I have picked up letters addressed to you.

LAURA: That was nobly done.

CAPTAIN: See, you do have higher thoughts of me, as they're called. From these letters I gather you've been lining up—for a long time—all my former friends against me by supporting the rumor about my mental condition. And you have succeeded in your efforts, because there's not more than one person, from my commanding officer to the kitchen maid, who thinks I'm sane. Now my sickness amounts to this: my reason is unharmed, as you know, so I can take care of both my work and my duties as a father; I still have my feelings under control as long as my will remains relatively unharmed; but you have gnawed and gnawed away at it so it soon will slip its cogs and then the whole works will whir backward. I don't want to appeal to your feelings, for you don't have any—that's your strength—but I do appeal to your interests.

LAURA: Go on!

CAPTAIN: Through your behavior you've succeeded in rousing my suspicions so that my power of judgment will soon be blurred, and my thoughts are beginning to wander. That's the approaching madness you've waited for, and that can come any time. This is the question you must answer: Would it be more worthwhile to you for me to remain well? Or not well? Think carefully! If I collapse I'll lose my position, and then you'll have nothing. If I die, you'll get my insurance. But if I take my life, you get nothing. So it's to your interest that I live out my life.

LAURA: Is this a trap?

CAPTAIN: Of course! It's up to you to walk around it or stick your head in it.

LAURA: You say you'll commit suicide. You won't!

CAPTAIN: Are you sure? Do you think a man can live when he has nothing and nobody to live for?

LAURA: So you surrender?

CAPTAIN: No, I propose peace.

LAURA: The conditions?

CAPTAIN: That I may keep my sanity. Free me from my suspicions, and I'll give up the struggle.

LAURA: What suspicions?

CAPTAIN: About Bertha's paternity!

LAURA: Have you any suspicions about that?

CAPTAIN: Yes, I have, and you've awakened them.

LAURA: I?

CAPTAIN: Yes, you've dripped them like drops of henbane in my ear, and circumstances have made them grow. Free me from uncertainty; tell me plainly: it's like this, and I'll forgive you in advance.

LAURA: I certainly can't take on a guilt I don't have.

CAPTAIN: What does it matter to you when you can know I won't reveal it? Do you think a man will trumpet out his shame?

LAURA: If I say it isn't so, you won't know for sure, but if I say it's so, then you'll know. So you're wishing it's so.

CAPTAIN: It's strange, but I suppose that's because the first can't be proved, and the second can.

LAURA: Have you any reasons for your suspicions?

CAPTAIN: Yes and no!

LAURA: I think you want me to be guilty so you can get rid of me and then be the only one to have power over the child. But you won't catch me with those traps.

CAPTAIN: Do you think I want to have responsibility for another man's child if I get proof of your guilt?

LAURA: No, I'm convinced of that, so I see you were lying just now when you forgave me in advance.

CAPTAIN *(gets up):* Laura, save me and my sanity. You don't understand what I say. If the child isn't mine, I have no rights over her and I don't want any, and that's all you want. Isn't it? Or do you want still more? You want to have the power over the child but want me as the means of support, too?

LAURA: The power, yes. What has this whole struggle for life or death been about but power?

CAPTAIN: For me, since I don't believe in a next life, the child was my life after this. That was my concept of eternal life, and it's probably the only one that has any basis in reality. If you take that from me, my life is cut off.

LAURA: Why didn't we separate in time?

CAPTAIN: Because the child bound us together, but the bond became a chain. How did that happen? How? I've never thought about it, but now memories rise, accusing, judging perhaps. We had been married two years and had no children. Why, you know best. I became ill and was on the point of death. During a moment when I was free of fever, I heard voices out in the living room. You and the lawyer were talking about the fortune which I still had. He explained you couldn't inherit anything since we didn't have any children, and he asked you if you were pregnant. I didn't hear what you answered. I became well, and we got a child. Who is the father?

LAURA: You!

CAPTAIN: No, it's not I! There's a buried crime here that's beginning to smell. What a hellish crime! You've been tender-minded enough to free black slaves, but you still have white ones. I have worked and slaved for you, your child, your mother, your servants; I have sacrificed my career and advancement; I have suffered torture, beating, sleeplessness, worry about your existence so my hair has turned gray—all this so you could have the pleasure of living without worries and when you got old you could enjoy life again through your child. I've taken everything without complaining because I thought I was the father of this child. That's the lowest form of theft, the most brutal slavery. I've had seventeen years of penal labor and been innocent. What can you give me in return?

LAURA: Now you're absolutely insane!

CAPTAIN *(sits down):* That is your hope! And I have seen how you've worked to conceal your crime. I have pitied you because I didn't understand your sorrow; I have often caressed your bad conscience to rest as I believed I was driving away a sickly thought; I have heard you scream in your sleep without wanting to listen. I remember the night before last—it was Bertha's birthday. It was between two and three o'clock in the morning, and I was sitting up reading. You screamed as if someone wanted to choke you: "Don't! Don't!" I pounded on the wall because— I didn't want to hear any more. I've had suspicions for a long time, but I didn't dare to have them verified. All this I have suffered for you. What do you want to do for me in return?

LAURA: What can I do? I'll swear in the name of God and everything that's sacred to me that you are Bertha's father.

CAPTAIN: What good would that do when you've said a mother can and ought to commit all crimes for her child? I beg you in the name of memories of the past, I beg you as someone wounded for the merciful blow: tell me everything. Don't you see I'm as helpless as a child? Don't you hear I'm asking for pity as from a mother? Won't you forget I'm a man, that I'm a soldier who with one word can tame people and animals? I ask only sympathy as a sick human being. I lay down the tokens of my power, and I cry out for mercy, for my life!

LAURA *(has come up to him and put her hand on his forehead):* What! You're weeping, man!

CAPTAIN: Yes, I'm weeping though I am a man. But doesn't a man have eyes? Doesn't a man have hands, limbs, senses, likes, passions? Doesn't he live on the same food, isn't he wounded by the same weapons, isn't he warmed and made cold by the same winter and summer as a woman? If you prick us, don't we bleed? If you tickle us, don't we laugh? If you poison us, don't we die? Why shouldn't a man complain, a soldier weep? Because it's unmanly! Why is it unmanly?

LAURA: Weep, my child; then you'll have your mother with you again. Do you remember it was as your second mother I first came into your life? Your big strong body lacked nerves, and you were a gigantic child, who had come too early into the world or probably hadn't been wanted.

CAPTAIN: Yes, that's how it was, I suspect. Mother and Father didn't *want* me, and that's why I was born without a strong will. I thought I was becoming whole when you and I became one, so you got to have the say. I, who in the barracks, before the troops, was the one to give orders, was the one to obey you. I became part of you, looked up to you as to a more highly gifted being, listened to you as if I were your foolish child.

LAURA: Yes, that's how it was then, so I loved you as my child. But, you know, every time your feelings changed nature and you came as my lover, I was ashamed, and your embrace was a joy, that was followed by pangs of conscience as if I had committed incest. The mother became the mistress! *(Makes an exclamation of disgust)*

CAPTAIN: I saw it, but didn't understand. And when I thought you were contemptuous of my lack of manliness, I wanted to win you as a woman by being a man.

LAURA: But the mistake lay in that! The mother was your friend, you see, but the woman was your enemy, and love between the sexes is struggle; and don't think I gave myself; I didn't give, but I took—what I wanted. But you had an advantage, which I felt and which I wanted you to feel.

CAPTAIN: You always had the advantage; you could hypnotize me while I was awake so that I neither saw nor heard but simply obeyed; you could give me a raw potato and make me think it was a peach; you could make me admire your naïve notions as words of wisdom; you could have made me commit crimes, yes even despicable acts. For you lacked sense, and instead of becoming the one to accomplish what I suggested, you acted according to your own head. But when I started thinking things over and felt my honor injured, I wanted to wipe that out through a great act, a deed, a discovery, or an honorable suicide. I wanted to get into the war, but wasn't allowed to. That's when I turned to science. Now, when I should stretch out my hand to receive the reward, you cut off my arm. Now I'm stripped of honor and can't live any longer, for a man can't live without honor.

LAURA: But a woman can?

CAPTAIN: Yes, because she has her children, but he doesn't—But we and other people have lived our lives, unconscious as children, full of notions, ideals, and illusions, and then we've awakened. That would do, but we awoke with our feet on the pillows, and the one who awakened us was a sleepwalker, too. When women get old and have ceased to be women, they get beards on their chins. I wonder what men get when they become old and have ceased being men? Those who had crowed were no longer males but capons, and the pullets answered the call so that when the sun was going to rise we found ourselves sitting in full moonlight with ruins, just as in the good old days. It had been only a little morning nap with wild dreams, and it wasn't any awakening.

LAURA: You should have become a writer, you know.

CAPTAIN: Who knows!

LAURA: Now I'm sleepy. If you have any more fancies, save them for tomorrow.

CAPTAIN: First, a word about reality. Do you hate me?

LAURA: Yes, sometimes. When you're a man.

CAPTAIN: This is like race hatred. If it's true we're descended from the ape, it must have been from two species. We aren't like each other, are we?

LAURA: What do you mean by all this?

CAPTAIN: I feel that in this struggle one of us must go under.

LAURA: Who?

CAPTAIN: The weaker, naturally.

LAURA: And the stronger is right?

CAPTAIN: Always right since he has the power.

LAURA: Then I'm right.

CAPTAIN: Do you already have the power?

LAURA: Yes, legally, when I put you under a guardian tomorrow.

CAPTAIN: Under a guardian?

LAURA: Yes! And then I'll bring up my child myself without listening to your notions.

CAPTAIN: And who'll provide for the upbringing when I'm no longer about?

LAURA: Your pension!

CAPTAIN *(walks toward her threateningly)*: How can you get me put under a guardian?

LAURA *(Takes up a letter):* Through this letter! The family court has a certified copy.

CAPTAIN: Which letter?

LAURA *(retreating backward toward the left door):* Yours! Your declaration to the doctor that you are insane!

(CAPTAIN *watches her; silent.*)

LAURA: Now you have fulfilled your function as an unfortunately necessary father and breadwinner. You're not needed any more, and you may go. You may go—you've understood my reasoning power was as strong as my will—and you don't want to stay and admit it!

(CAPTAIN *goes to the table; takes the lighted lamp and throws it toward* LAURA, *who has retreated backward through the door.*)

CURTAIN

ACT III

The same setting. The lamp has been replaced. The wall-paper-covered door has been barricaded with a chair.

LAURA: Did you get the keys?

NURSE: Get them? No, good heavens, but I took them out of the master's clothes Nöjd had put out for brushing.

LAURA: So it's Nöjd who's on duty today.

NURSE: Yes, it's Nöjd himself.

LAURA: Give me the keys!

NURSE: Yes, but this is just like stealing. Do you hear his steps up there, ma'am? Back and forth, back and forth.

LAURA: Is the door securely shut?

NURSE: Oh yes, it's certainly securely shut.

LAURA *(opens the chiffonier and sits down by the writing leaf):* Control your feelings, Margret. Only if we're calm can we save ourselves. *(Someone knocks.)* Who is it?

NURSE *(opens the door to the entry):* It's Nöjd!

LAURA: Let him come in.

NÖJD *(enters):* A dispatch from the colonel!

LAURA: Give it to me. *(Reads)* Ah!—Nöjd, have you taken all the bullets out of his guns and bags?

NÖJD: That's done as ordered.

LAURA: Wait outside until I've answered the colonel's letter (NÖJD *goes.* LAURA *writes.)*

NURSE: Listen, ma'am! What is he up to up there?

LAURA: Quiet, while I'm writing! *(The sound of a saw can be heard.)*

NURSE *(half-aloud to herself):* Oh, may God in His mercy help us all! Where will this end?

LAURA: There! Give this to Nöjd. And my mother mustn't know anything about all this. Do you hear that?

(The NURSE *goes.* LAURA *pulls out drawers in the chiffonier and takes out papers. After a moment the* PASTOR *enters and sits down beside* LAURA *by the chiffonier.)*

PASTOR: Good evening, sister. I've been gone all day, as you've heard, and couldn't get here before. Serious things have happened here.

LAURA: Yes, brother, I've never lived through such a night and such a day before.

PASTOR: Well, I see you weren't injured in any case.

LAURA: No, thank goodness, but imagine what could have happened.

PASTOR: But tell me one thing: how did it start? I've heard so many versions.

LAURA: It began with his wildly imagining he's not Bertha's father and ended with his throwing the lighted lamp at my face.

PASTOR: Why, that's terrible! That's absolute insanity. And what's going to be done now?

LAURA: We'll have to prevent more outbursts of violence; the doctor has sent for a straitjacket from the insane asylum. In the meanwhile I've sent a message to the colonel and am trying to get an idea of household affairs, which he has managed in a disgraceful way.

PASTOR: It's a sad story, but I've always expected something like this. Fire and water end up in an explosion! What do you have in the drawer?

LAURA *(has pulled out a drawer)*: Look, he has hidden everything here.

PASTOR *(rummaging through the drawer)*: Good God! There he has your doll—and your christening cap—and Bertha's rattle—and your letters—and the medallion . . . *(Wipes his eyes)* He must have loved you very much all the same, Laura. I've never saved anything like that.

LAURA: I think he loved me once, but time . . . time changes so much.

PASTOR: What's this large document? . . . The deed to the grave! . . . Yes, rather the grave than the asylum! Laura! Tell me: aren't you at all to blame in this?

LAURA: I? What blame could I have in a person's going insane?

PASTOR: Well, well. I won't say anything. Blood *is* thicker than water!

LAURA: What do you have the nerve to say?

PASTOR *(fixing his glance on her):* Listen!

LAURA: Yes!

PASTOR: Listen! You can't deny all this fits in nicely with your wish to bring up your child yourself.

LAURA: I don't understand!

PASTOR: How I admire you!

LAURA: Me! Hm!

PASTOR: And I'll be the guardian of that freethinker. You know, I've always considered him a weed in our garden.

LAURA *(laughs briefly, then chokes off her laugh; adds hastily serious):* And you dare to say that to me, his wife?

PASTOR: You *are* strong, Laura. Unbelievably strong! Like a fox in the trap: you'd rather bite off your own leg than be caught! . . . Like a master thief: no accomplice, not even your own conscience! . . . Look in the mirror. You don't dare!

LAURA: I never use a mirror.

PASTOR: No, you don't dare—May I look at your hand?—Not a spot of blood to give you away, not a trace of the treacherous poison! An innocent little murder that the law can't get at . . .an unconscious crime . . . unconscious? That's a wonderful discovery! Do you hear how he's working away up there?—Take care! If that man gets loose, he'll saw you in two!

LAURA: You keep talking as if you had a bad conscience—Accuse me—if you can.

PASTOR: I can't!

LAURA: You see? You can't, so I'm innocent!—You look after your ward, and I'll look after mine—There's the doctor. *(The* DOCTOR *enters.)*

LAURA: *(gets up):* Welcome, Doctor! You at least want to help me, don't you? And unfortunately there's not much to be done here. Do you hear how he's behaving up there? Are you convinced now?

DOCTOR: I'm convinced he committed a violent act, but the question is if that act of violence is to be considered an outbreak of anger or insanity.

PASTOR: But disregard the outbreak and admit his ideas were fixed.

DOCTOR: I think your ideas, Pastor, are still more fixed!

PASTOR: My confirmed views of the highest things . . .

DOCTOR: We'll let the views go—[*Turning to* LAURA] It depends on you if you want your husband sentenced to prison and fined or committed to the insane asylum. What is your opinion of the captain's behavior?

LAURA: I can't answer that now.

DOCTOR: So you don't have a firm opinion of what would be best for the interests of the family? What do you say, Pastor?

PASTOR: Well, there'll be scandal either way . . . it's hard to say.

LAURA: But if he's simply fined for his violence, he can repeat it.

DOCTOR: And if he goes to prison, he'll soon be released. So we'll consider it most advantageous for everyone concerned to have him treated as insane immediately.—Where's the nurse?

LAURA: Why?

DOCTOR: She's to put the straitjacket on the patient when I've had a talk with him and told her to. But not before. I have—the garment out there. *(Goes out into the entry and returns with a large bundle)* Please ask the nurse to come in.

(LAURA *rings.*)

PASTOR: Ghastly, ghastly!

(NURSE *enters.*)

DOCTOR *(takes the straitjacket out of the bundle):* Now watch this. You're to put this jacket on the Captain from in back when I consider it necessary—to prevent violent outbursts. As you see, it has extremely long arms to hinder his movements. And you tie them behind his back. These two straps go through clasps and you'll fasten them to the arms of the chair or the sofa—whichever is handiest. Will you?

NURSE: No, I can't, Doctor; I can't.

LAURA: Why don't you do it yourself, Doctor?

DOCTOR: Because the patient is suspicious of me. You, Madame,

would be the one to do it, but I'm afraid he doesn't trust you either.

(LAURA *grimaces*.)

DOCTOR: Perhaps you, Pastor . . .

PASTOR: No, I'll have to say no! (NÖJD *enters*.)

LAURA: Have you already delivered the letter?

NÖJD: As ordered.

DOCTOR: So! It's you, Nöjd! You know the circumstances here and know the captain's mentally ill. You have to help us take care of him.

NÖJD: If I can do something for the captain, you know I'll do it!

DOCTOR: You're to put this jacket on him . . .

NURSE: No, he mayn't touch him; Nöjd mustn't hurt him. Then I'd rather do it—gently, very gently! But Nöjd may be outside and help me if necessary . . . Yes, you do that. *(Someone pounds on the wallpaper-covered door.)*

DOCTOR: There he is! Put the jacket under your shawl on the chair, and if all of you go out for the time being, I and the pastor will receive him . . . That door won't hold much longer.—There, out!

NURSE *(goes out to the left)*: Lord Jesus, help us!

(LAURA *closes the chiffonier; then goes out to the left.* NÖJD *goes out at the back.)*

(*The wallpaper-covered door is knocked open so that the chair is thrown out onto the floor and the lock is loosened. The* CAPTAIN *comes out with a pile of books under his arm.)*

CAPTAIN *(puts the books on the table)*: Here you can read all about it and in every one of these books! So I wasn't crazy! It says in the first canto of the *Odyssey,* verse 215, page 6, in the Uppsala translation—it's Telemachus talking to Athene: "Of course, my mother insists he—that's to say Odysseus—is my father; but I do not know that myself, for no one as yet *knew* from what man he is descended." And Telemachus had a suspicion like that about Penelope, the most virtuous of women! That *is* nice! Eh? And the prophet Ezekiel says: "The fool says: See, here is my father, but who can know whose loins have en-

gendered him?" Why, the whole thing's clear! What's this I have?
The History of Russian Literature by Mersläkow. Alexander
Pushkin, Russia's greatest poet, died tortured to death by wide-
spread rumors about his wife's faithlessness more than from the
bullet he got in his chest in a duel. On his deathbed he swore she
was innocent. Ass! Ass! How could he swear to that? Now you
hear I do read my books, though!—Well, Jonas, are you here?
And the doctor, of course! Have you heard how I answered an
English lady who complained about Irishmen's throwing lighted
kerosene lamps in their wives' faces?—God, what women, I
said!—Women? she lisped!—Yes, of course! I answered. When
things have gone so far that a man, a man who has loved and
courted a woman, takes a lighted lamp and throws it in her face,
then one can understand!

PASTOR: What can one know?

CAPTAIN: Nothing! A man never knows anything; he only believes.
Isn't that right, Jonas? If you believe, you're saved! Yes, that
one would be! No, I know one can be damned because of his
faith. I know!

DOCTOR: Captain!

CAPTAIN: Silence! I don't want to talk with you; I don't want to
hear you pass on what they're saying in there. In there! You
know!—Listen, Jonas; do you believe you're the father of your
children? I remember you had a tutor in your house who was as
handsome as could be, and people gossiped about him.

PASTOR: Adolf! Watch it!

CAPTAIN: Feel your forehead to see if there aren't two bumps there.
My word, he's turning pale, I think! Yes, yes, they just talk, but
good God they talk such a lot! But aren't we all ridiculous dogs
all the same, we married men? Isn't that right, Doctor? How was
it with your marital bed? Didn't you have a lieutenant living in
your house, eh? Wait and I'll guess. His name was . . . *(whispers
in the* DOCTOR's *ear)* There, he's turning pale, too! Don't feel bad.
Why, she's dead and buried, and what's done can't be undone. I
knew him though, and he's now—look at me, Doctor—no, right

in my eyes—a major in the dragoons. By God, I think he has horns, too!

DOCTOR *(pained):* Captain, will you change the subject?

CAPTAIN: See! He wants to change the subject just when I want to talk about horns!

PASTOR: Adolf, do you know you're mentally ill?

CAPTAIN: Yes, I *know* I am! But if I could treat your crowned heads for a while, I'd soon get to lock you two up, too! Yes, I'm insane, but how did I get insane? It doesn't concern you, and it doesn't concern anybody. You want to talk about something else? *(Takes the photograph album from the table)* Good Lord, there's my child! Mine? But we can't know that, can we? Do you know what people should do to be sure of knowing that? First, they should get married to win the respect of the community; then they should get divorced immediately afterward, and become lovers; and then he should adopt the children. Then one can at least be sure they're one's adopted children. Isn't that right? But how does all this help me now? What can help me now when you've taken my hope for eternal life from me? What good are science and philosophy when I haven't anything to live for? What can I do with life when I haven't any honor? I grafted my right arm, half my brain, half the marrow in my backbone to another, because I believed they could grow into one and become a more perfect tree, and then someone came along with a knife and cut everything off just below the graft, and now I'm only half a tree, but the other keeps on growing with half my arm and half my brain, while I waste away and die, because it was the best in me I gave away. Now I want to die! Do with me what you wish. I no longer exist.

(The DOCTOR whispers with the PASTOR: they go out to the left; then BERTHA comes in.)

(CAPTAIN sits—collapsed—at the table.)

BERTHA *(goes up to him):* Are you ill, Dad?

CAPTAIN *(looks up dully):* I?

BERTHA: Do you know what you've done? Do you know you threw the lamp at Mother?

CAPTAIN: Did I?

BERTHA: Yes, you did! Just think, if she had got hurt!

CAPTAIN: Would that have mattered?

BERTHA: You're not my father if you can talk like that!

CAPTAIN: What's that? I'm not your father? How do you know? Who told you? And who is your father? Who?

BERTHA: At least it's not you!

CAPTAIN: Still not I! Who then? Who? You seem to be well informed. Who has told you? That I should live to hear my child tell me to my face I'm not her father! But don't you understand you're insulting your mother when you say that? Don't you understand it's her shame if that's how it is?

BERTHA: Don't say anything bad about Mother! You hear?

CAPTAIN: No, you stick together, all of you—against me! And that's what you've done all the way!

BERTHA: Dad!

CAPTAIN: Don't use that word again!

BERTHA: Dad, Dad!

CAPTAIN *(draws her to him):* Bertha, dear child, of course you're my child! Yes, yes! It can't be otherwise. It's so! The other was only sick thoughts which came with the wind like the plague and fevers. Look at me so I may see my soul in your eyes!—But I see her soul, too! You have two souls, and love me with the one and hate me with the other. But you're to love only me! You shall have only one soul; otherwise you'll never get any inner peace, and I won't either. You're to have only one thought, child of my thought; you're to have only one will, mine.

BERTHA: I don't want that! I want to be myself.

CAPTAIN: You mayn't! You see, I'm a cannibal, and I want to eat you up. Your mother wanted to eat me, but I didn't let her. I'm Saturn, who ate his children, because they had prophesied that otherwise they'd eat him. Eat or be eaten! That's the question! If I don't eat you, you'll eat me, and you've already bared your teeth at me. But don't be afraid, dear child; I won't hurt you. *(Goes up to the collection of weapons and takes a revolver.)*

BERTHA *(tries to escape):* Help, Mother, help! He wants to kill me!

NURSE *(enters):* Mr. Adolf, what's wrong?

CAPTAIN *(examines the revolver):* Have you taken the bullets?

NURSE: Yes, I put them away, but sit down here quietly, and I'll get them! *(Takes the* CAPTAIN *by the arm and seats him on the chair where he sits; dull. Then she picks up the straitjacket and stations herself behind the chair.* BERTHA *steals out to the left.)* Mr. Adolf, do you remember when you were my dear child and I tucked you in at night, and I said your evening prayer? And do you remember how I got up at night and gave you a glass of water? Do you remember how I lighted candles and told nice stories when you had bad dreams and couldn't sleep? Do you remember?

CAPTAIN: Go on talking, Margret; it helps make my head feel calm! Go on talking!

NURSE: Yes, indeed, but then you have to listen! Do you remember once when you had taken the big kitchen knife and wanted to carve boats and how I came in and had to trick the knife away from you? You were a foolish child so I had to trick you, for you didn't believe I meant well by you.—Give me that snake, I said; otherwise, he'll bite! And then you let go the knife. *(Takes the revolver out of the* CAPTAIN'S *hand)* And when you were going to get dressed and didn't want to, then I had to play with you and say you'd get a gold coat and be dressed like a prince. And I'd take your underwaist, which was only of green wool, and I'd hold it in front of you and say: Nicely in with both arms! And then I said: Sit nice and quiet while I button it up the back! *(She has put the straitjacket on him.)* And then I said: Get up, and walk nicely across the floor so I can see how it fits . . . *(She leads him to the sofa.)* And then I said: Now you're to go to bed.

CAPTAIN: What did you say? Was he to go to bed when he was dressed?—Damnation! What have you done to me? *(Tries to get loose)* Ah, you devilishly cunning woman! Who could have be-

lieved you had that much sense! *(Lies down on the sofa)* Caught,
clipped, outmaneuvered, and not able to die!

NURSE: Forgive me, Mr. Adolf! Forgive me, but I wanted to prevent you from killing the child!

CAPTAIN: Why didn't you let me kill the child? Life is hell, and
death is heaven, and children belong to heaven!

NURSE: What do you know about what comes after death?

CAPTAIN: That's the only thing one knows, but about life one
knows nothing! If one had only known that from the beginning.

NURSE: Mr. Adolf! Humble your stubborn heart and pray to God
for mercy, for it's still not too late. It wasn't too late for the
robber on the cross when the Savior said: Today you shall be
with me in Paradise!

CAPTAIN: Are you already cawing for corpses, you old crow?

(NURSE *takes her psalmbook out of her pocket.*)

CAPTAIN *(shouts):* Nöjd! Are you there, Nöjd?

(NÖJD *enters.*)

CAPTAIN: Throw out that woman! She wants to choke me to death
with that psalmbook. Throw her out through the window or the
chimney or anywhere.

NÖJD *(looks at the* NURSE): God bless you, Captain, but, but I
can't! I just can't! If it were only six men, but a woman!

CAPTAIN: Can't you manage a woman?

NÖJD: I can manage her all right, but there's something special so
a man doesn't want to lay a hand on a woman.

CAPTAIN: What's special? Haven't they laid a hand on me?

NÖJD: Yes, but I can't, Captain! It's just as if you were asking me
to beat up the pastor. It's like religion. I can't!

(LAURA *enters; Signals to* NÖJD *to go; he does.*)

CAPTAIN: Omphale! Omphale! Now you're playing with the club
while Hercules spins your wool!

LAURA *(Goes up to the sofa):* Adolf! Look at me! Do you think
I'm your enemy?

CAPTAIN: Yes, I do. I think all of you are my enemies! My mother,
who didn't want me to be born because my birth would give her

pain, was my enemy when she robbed me of nourishment in the womb and made me a half cripple. My sister was my enemy when she taught me to be obsequious to her. The first woman I slept with was my enemy when she gave me ten years of illness in return for the love I gave her. My daughter became my enemy when she was to choose between you and me. And you, my wife, were my enemy to the death, because you didn't leave me until I was lying lifeless!

LAURA: I don't know I ever thought of or intended what you think I've done. I've probably had a vague desire to get rid of you as a hindrance, but, if you see any plan in my way of acting, it's possible it was there, though I didn't see it. I've never reflected about my actions, but they have glided along on rails you yourself have laid down, and before God and my conscience I feel innocent even if I'm not. Your existence has been like a stone pressing on my heart, which has pressed and pressed until my heart has wanted to shake off the frustrating weight. That's how it is, I think, and if I've unintentionally hurt you, I ask you to forgive me.

CAPTAIN: That sounds reasonable. But what good does it do me? And whose is the fault? Perhaps spiritual marriage? In the old days a man married a wife; now he sets up business with a woman member of a profession, or moves in with a friend!—And then he takes his partner and rapes his friend! Where did love— good, healthy, sensual love—go? It died as a result. And what an offspring from this love in bonds and shares, placed with the bearer, without joint responsibility! Who is the bearer when the crash comes? Who is the physical father of the spiritual child?

LAURA: And as far as your suspicions about the child go, they were absolutely unfounded.

CAPTAIN: That's just what is terrible! If they had been well founded, I would have had something to take hold of. Now there are only shadows, which hide in bushes and stick their heads out to laugh. Now it's like fighting with air, to simulate shooting with loose powder. A fatal reality would have called for resistance, have strained life and spirit to action, but now . . . My thoughts dissolve in vapors, and my brain grinds empty until it'll catch fire! Put a pillow under my head. And throw something over me—I'm freezing! I'm so terribly cold!

(LAURA *takes her shawl and spreads it over him.*)

(NURSE *goes to fetch a pillow.*)

LAURA: Give me your hand, my friend!

CAPTAIN: My hand! That you've tied behind my back . . . Omphale! Omphale! But I feel your soft shawl against my mouth; it is as warm and soft as your arm, and it smells of vanilla as your hair did when you were young. Laura, when you were young, and we walked in the birch forest with its buttercups and thrushes— splendid, splendid! Just think how beautiful life was, and what it has become. You didn't want it to become like this; I didn't either, and still it did. Who rules over life, then?

LAURA: God alone does . . .

CAPTAIN: The god of strife then! Or the goddess nowadays! Take the cat away, the one that's lying on me! Take it away!

(NURSE *enters with the pillow; takes away the shawl.*)

CAPTAIN: Give me my tunic! Throw it over me!

(*The* NURSE *takes the tunic from the clothes tree and spreads it over him.*)

CAPTAIN: Ah, my tough lion's skin you wanted to take away from me, Omphale! Omphale! The cunning woman who was the friend of peace and hit upon disarmament. Wake up, Hercules, before they take the club away from you! You wanted to trick us out of our equipment, too, and pretended to believe it was only frills. No, it was iron before it became frills! It was the smith who used to make the coat of mail, but now it's the embroiderer! Omphale! Omphale! Brute strength has fallen before treacherous weakness. To hell with you, you devil of a woman, and damnation to your sex! (*He raises himself to spit but falls back on the sofa.*) What sort of pillow have you given me, Margret? It's hard and very cold, very cold! Come and sit next to me on the chair. There, like that! May I put my head in your lap? So!—It's warm! Bend over me so I may feel your breast.—Oh, it's a delight to fall asleep on a woman's breast—a mother's or a mistress', but most delightful one's mother's!

LAURA: Do you want to see your child, Adolf? Tell me!

CAPTAIN: My child? A man has no children, it's only women who get children, so the future is theirs when we men die childless!— Oh, God who loves children!*

NURSE: Listen, he's praying to God!

CAPTAIN: No, to you so you'll put me to sleep, for I'm tired, very tired! Good night, Margret, and blessed be you among women! *(He raises himself, but falls down with a cry of anguish in the* NURSE's *lap.)*

(LAURA *goes to the left and calls the* DOCTOR, *who enters with the* PASTOR.)

LAURA: Help us, Doctor, if it isn't too late! See, he isn't breathing any more!

DOCTOR *(takes the* CAPTAIN's *pulse):* It's a stroke!

PASTOR: Is he dead?

DOCTOR: No, he may yet awaken to life, but what sort of awakening it will be we don't know.

PASTOR: First, to die, and then the judgment . . .

DOCTOR: No judgment! And no accusations! You who believe a god controls the destinies of men may talk with him about this matter.

NURSE: Ah, Pastor, he prayed to God in his last moment!

PASTOR *(to* LAURA): Is that true?

LAURA: That's true!

DOCTOR: If that's so—and I can judge that as little as the causes of his illness—my skill is over. Now try yours, Pastor.

LAURA: Is that all you have to say by this deathbed, Doctor?

DOCTOR: That's all! I don't know any more. Let him who knows more speak!

---

*The beginning of the commonly used children's prayer that Margret referred to earlier in this act.

BERTHA *enters from the left, runs up to her mother):* Mother,
   Mother!
LAURA: My child! My own child!
PASTOR: Amen!

CURTAIN

Introduction to 'Lady Julie'

WHILE IT IS interesting that Strindberg wrote the Preface to *Lady Julie* after he completed the play, the fact is not particularly important in terms of the impact both the play and its Preface have had. The preface has been read, analyzed, and discussed by practically every Westerner who is interested in drama and theater. What Strindberg said in it has had a tremendous influence on later dramatists who have tried to write plays that are, for want of a better work, extremely realistic or, if you will, naturalistic. Strindberg emphasized the necessity of a theme of universal and timeless significance, a plot more or less taken from life itself, a dialogue that approaches actual conversation and gives the effect of human talk in its irregularity and drift, a one-act form that permits no interruption of the audience's attention, realistic staging, the elimination of what he then considered artificial and therefore undesirable lighting and make-up, and a happy formulation of a decidedly modern method of characterization. All of these matters have provoked both interest and imitation in later playwrights. Students of drama have on occasion pointed out that Strindberg in writing the Preface was not consistent at all points in his postanalysis of the play, but no one, as far as I have been able to determine, has ever denied that the Preface is one of the most important pieces of dramatic criticism produced by a playwright throughout the history of drama and theater, or that *Lady Julie* is a masterpiece of drama and of theater.

Since this is the first play he labeled a naturalistic tragedy, there is every reason for emphasizing the fact that it is thoroughly Strindbergian. While a naturalistic work of art theoretically should be the result of a scientific study of a segment of actual life itself—that is, a sort of sociological case report—Strindberg was too sound an artist to disregard the absolute necessities of selection and arrangement. In other words, he knew perfectly well that a drama presenting a segment of life without artistic editing would be not only unbearably dull but also unmanageable. His awareness that he had the gift for seeing the dramatic possibilities in any situation and changing it to bring out those possibilities saved him from attempting an uncritical representation of actual happenings. That is probably why some people have questioned whether Strindberg was indeed a literary naturalist. Be that as it may, Strindberg did select and arrange his materials for his own purposes.

During the time he was writing *Lady Julie* and the other plays in this volume, Strindberg tried to subscribe to essential elements of naturalism. While he could in general accept the concepts of determinism and a mechanistic universe, he could never really accept without question the consequent idea that there is no genuine freedom of the will. (Gustaf's remark to Tekla in *Creditors* that there is a margin of responsibility had personal application for Strindberg even in his "naturalistic" period.) He was convinced, however, that heredity and environment, time, and chance are determinative factors in any human being's development. He knew that life is a struggle for existence, that there is validity to the idea of natural selection, that all human beings are basically members of the animal kingdom, that the individual has a will to live, and that many if not all human problems arise from instincts and desires.

Such ideas, derived basically from his own acute observations of himself and others and reinforced by what contemporary scientists and psychologists had to say, helped him formulate most effectively in his Preface a concept of character. He had applied the concept appreciably in most of his earlier plays from *Master Olof* (1872) on, but he had never before formulated it as happily as he does in the Preface. He retained his concept of the human character as complex and dynamic; even in his so-called expressionistic plays in his later years one can find plenty of evidence for the validity of that statement although he did not attempt full characterizations of, say, a Hummel in *The Ghost Sonata* or the Lawyer in *A Dream Play*.

Strindberg did consider *Lady Julie* naturalistic, and, granting the qualifications of selection and arrangement, one will have to admit that Strindberg within those limits has given us an artist's presentation of an inner recreation of a segment of life. The one-act form; a theme that is universal and timeless; a plot that was partly taken right out of life and could have been almost completely; a dialogue that strikes one as natural conversation, in terms of the situation, the particular people, the time, and the place; the decidedly realistic setting and staging; and the characterization—all these are in keeping with what Strindberg believed was naturalistic, always, it must be remembered, as seen and heard through Strindberg's eyes and ears and transformed in the creative process.

The matter of social rising and falling will probably remain as much a fact of life in any society as it was in nineteenth-century Sweden. Social mobility, as Strindberg knew, may be delayed or even temporarily prevented by all that an aristocracy of birth implies, but in the struggle for existence—and advancement— crude native talents are likely to count far more than artificial safeguards designed to keep the members of a family protected generation after generation through position, power, and possessions. Strindberg had good reason to apply the theme to a daughter of the old aristocracy. He had lived through a period in his nation's history when the aristocracy had lost one form of power and prestige after another; the elimination of the system of four estates in the Riksdag in the 1860's, for example, had not only meant the disappearance of a House of Lords in the Swedish parliament but promised eventual control by slowly but surely rising lower classes. He had, moreover, dealt with the theme in various works, the best known of which are the novel *The Red Room* (1879), the short stories in *Married* (1884, 1886), his autobiographical *Son of a Servant* (1886 ff.), and the autobiographical *Defense of a Madman* (1887).

He had, furthermore, access to contemporary illustrations of social mobility and its attendant problems not only in his own personal experience but in more or less scandalous newspaper accounts and general gossip about an actual case involving an aristocratic lady and her father's servant as well. In a letter to Edvard Brandes in September, 1888 (*Strindberg's Brev,* VII, 126) he says: "That the daughter of a count commits suicide after sexual intercourse with a lower creature [*tidelag*] and theft is extremely likely! And if she doesn't do so right away, she becomes a waitress in a bar [*skänkmamsell*] at Hasselbacken [Restaurant] as the real Julie became!" But the plot he used to illustrate the theme is no attempt to imitate the outlines either of his personal situation or of that in which the lady and the servant were involved. It is instead a plot that, while it makes use of some of the actual material, is essentially a product of his creative imagination. Selection, arrangement, and transformation during the creative process produced a plot that stripped to barest outline can be summarized as the lady and the servant before the seduction, the mutual seduction, the problems having to be faced after the seduction, and the solution; or, if you will, an aristocratic woman allows herself to give way to her animal attraction for a healthy, well-endowed, and ambitious young male servant and to indulge in sexual intercourse with him, and then out of fear has to find a solution to her dilemma in keeping with the code of her class.

The dialogue approaches that of life itself in the sense that it is not the extremely polished give and take that even brilliant conversationalists can only with great effort achieve and sustain. It has such qualities of actual human talk as polite patter, shifting from topic to topic without making certain that no end is left loose, and variation of tempo and intensity according to the speaker's mood and intention at the moment. It ranges all the way from brutal coarseness to polite nothings, from the artificial exchanges of set remarks to totally unrestrained expressions of egotistic feelings and responses. But the impact of the dialogue is great not because Strindberg has reproduced conversation out of life but because he has weighed every word, every nuance of expression to give us a dialogue that has the effect of real conversation in a series of highly dramatic situations. Even the dialogue—to Strindberg's credit— has been selected, arranged, and transformed for his artistic purposes.

Strindberg's selection of a structure for his play is a happy one. If a "naturalistic" play is to present a segment of life or, in Strindbergian practice, to present what might very well be such a segment, the one-act form surely is highly appropriate. It does eliminate such extraneous interruptions as imbibing and talking about other matters during intermissions, it does make the audience focus its attention on what is happening on and off stage, and it does give the interested theatergoer a *whole* experience. Strindberg is right in his defense of his use of ballet, mime, and monologues: a midsummer group can dance in a manor house kitchen; a woman can curl her hair; and a woman may very well talk to herself on occasion.

Nor can there be any valid objection to Strindberg's insistence on a thoroughly naturalistic or realistic setting, scenery and stage properties, and staging—within the limitations of an actual theater. The kitchen of a Swedish manor house and the glimpse of the park beyond are highly appropriate in a play that involves a nineteenth-century lady who, in entering the domain for servants, forgets that she is there primarily to check on the preparation of a concoction for her dog and stoops to behavior smacking of that of the servant's quarters rather than restricting herself to the behavior expected of someone whose quarters are elsewhere in the house. There is not a single stage property either in the kitchen or in the park beyond that does not heighten the distinctions between the classes. Consider, for example, the chopping block and the figure of Amor. Each in its way limits and defines the socially acceptable roles of the two; the first is right there ready for a very real and practical use, the other is glimpsed at a distance and represents a way of life strikingly different from that of, say, Kristin the cook.

Fascinating as all these matters are, there is nothing in the play that surpasses Strindberg's "naturalistic" characterizations of Lady Julie, Jean, and even Kristin. What he says in the Preface about characterless characters—that is, highly complex and dynamic human beings—is an exposition of what he has done in characterizing the two principal characters; what he says about secondary characters is precisely what he does in characterizing Kristin. Only the midsummer dancers remain types—for reasons he explains in the Preface.

As every student of Strindberg knows, he prided himself on his skill in using parallel actions. Not only does he use them in *Lady Julie,* but, because he labeled the play a naturalistic tragedy, the parallels are exceptionally important. Diana, the blue-blooded bitch significantly given the same name as the chaste goddess of the hunt, is, without doubt, a product of her heredity as an animal and of her environment as her lady's pet. The implications of both are obvious enough—an animal taken out of her natural environment and protected artificially from contact with plebeians of her own species, cared for and restrained by more than the literal leash, escapes from the artificial bond only to give way to her instinctive need for mating. That the gatekeeper's cur is hardly a suitable mate—from Lady Julie's point of view—is significant enough. The whole situation is, of course, no more nor less than a parallel to Lady Julie's own. But in terms of her time and place the administering of an evil-smelling concoction will hardly solve Lady Julie's own dilemma and perhaps not the "unclean" Diana's—at least not if she succeeds in escaping from artificial restraint again on other occasions. The curs—human or not—and the bluebloods have, from a naturalistic point of view, the overwhelming tendency to find expression for their sexuality without too great regard for the niceties of the latter's artificial codes.

Isn't there justification, too, in taking a close look at Serena, Lady Julie's finch? Doesn't her very name imply the serenity of the artificially protected captive expected to sing appropriately for the pleasure of her human keepers? Theoretically, Lady Julie is a human Serena, a captive within a cage less material but just as confining. It is worth noting that the human captive of artificiality goes to die by means of a razor in her own hand, a highly refined artificial tool, while Serena perishes by means of an axe, a relatively crude instrument wielded by a brute. The latter happens without even a hint of "civilized" hesitation; the former results from what is at least in appearance the voluntary act of a person of honor and refinement.

Any detailed examination of the human Diana, the human Serena, will demonstrate that she is indeed a product of her heredity and her environment, of the time in which she lived and of chance. Lady Julie is an unforgettable illustration of the Strindbergian characterless character and a thoroughly believable characterization of a highly complex and dynamic woman.

The daughter of a count and a *fröken* (in her day the equivalent of the British "lady"), Julie is not entirely a product of an aristocratic environment. While her father was an aristocrat with a sense of honor who tried to rear his daughter to the point where she did not need visible restraints but could rely completely on inner ones, her mother had had no such standards. By means of little bits of servant gossip and a rather detailed account by Julie herself, Strindberg presents Lady Julie's mother—in what is close to a case report on a so-called emancipated woman who had no desire to rear her daughter as an aristocratic lady but rather as a human being, feminine to be sure because of accident of birth, who would show men that a woman is at least their equal if not their superior. Strindberg supplies the details that clarify the human result of the tug of war in Julie's conditioning—a half-woman, a man-hater, and, just as important, a twisted, confused human animal. For Julie is only to a degree a sheltered, artificial product of her father's and her mother's artificial worlds; she is basically a member of the animal kingdom at the mercy of her drives in spite of her conditioning.

Her "thinking" is in no sense her own; it is rather a conglomeration of notions ranging from the romantic and the sentimental to brutal notions about the nature of the male being. As Strindberg emphasizes in the Preface, she does not have an idea that is her own. The things she utters are only echoes of what she has heard or read: her almost literal repetition of Jean's plan for a future in Switzerland is a perfect illustration of the point. Her behavior, too, is in keeping with what she says; her coquetry, her use of French, her insistence on being toasted in a certain way, her erratic ambivalent conduct—from that of a lady to that of a slut—are merely a few aspects of a richly drawn characterless character. Yet Strindberg presents her in such a way that one cannot refrain from feeling both sympathy and pity for her: she is by no means far from the general human condition.

Strindberg has succeeded just as well in his characterization of Jean. From an aristocratic point of view just as much of a cur as the gatekeeper's cur, Jean is presented naturalistically as a healthy human animal on his way up. Potentially, Strindberg more than implies, Jean belongs to the aristocracy of brain and nerve; that, I take it, means that he has the endowment to be a superior being in an amoral world of rugged individualism. Unlike Lady Julie, Jean has no artificial or any other kind of scruples except insofar as an action may injure him. In his struggle for existence and advancement, Jean is handicapped not only by the facts of an unfavorable environment but by ingrained fear of those who have at least temporary power over him. But he does have the capacity to think, to play, and, when he sees no immediate or pressing danger to himself, to act. He has even a measure of sensitivity and a gift for learning what will pay off.

It is interesting that Strindberg emphasizes the ambivalence of Jean's thinking and behavior in ways parallel to those of Lady Julie. But the theme of social rising and falling would hardly have been adequately developed if Strindberg had not made it clear that Jean's ambivalence is a far more conscious and rational one than Julie's. When Jean needs to protect himself and his interests, he plays the role of a servant; when nothing seems to demand such self-protection, he thinks and acts as a person who, given a few breaks, may indeed become a Rumanian count and the progenitor of a family that in time will be considered blue-blooded.

Although Kristin as a secondary character is given a far less complete characterization than the two principals, she is brought thoroughly alive in her smugness, arrogance, curiously obtuse "religious" views, small thievery, and general egotism. Her frankly revealed plans for her future and Jean's, her condescending judgment of Julie as a fallen woman, and her ready seizure of power are merely a few of the many factors that reinforce the telling details of behavior and "thought" that stamp her a far from admirable member of the animal kingdom even though she has some superficial humanizing qualities. It is strange, however, that a Kristin can cancel her lady's orders. Is Strindberg implying that Lady Julie's position as mistress of her father's house is limited to relatively minor matters?

Strindberg believed he had written a naturalistic tragedy; within the limitations already suggested, he had. What there can be no question about, however, is that he had written a play that ranks among the best in world literature, one of the best modern tragedies, and one of the most widely acclaimed vehicles for theatrical production.

Lady Julie has had a brilliant record on the stage in many countries. Alf Sjöberg produced an outstanding film version; Elsa von Rosen created an internationally admired ballet based on the play; and it has even been transformed into opera. It is a play that has never ceased to interest students and scholars, actors and directors, artists and nonartists. It is excellent drama and theater.

Strindberg's Preface to 'Lady Julie'

For a long time theater like art in general has seemed to me a *Biblia pauperum,* a Bible in pictures for those who cannot read what is written or printed, and the dramatist a lay preacher, who peddles the ideas of his day in such a popular form that the middle class, which makes up most of the theater audiences, can without too much mental effort understand what it is all about. For that reason the theater has always been a public school for young people, the half-educated, and women, those who still have the inferior ability to deceive themselves and to let themselves be deceived, that is to say, get the illusion, receive the suggestion from the author. In our time when the rudimentary, incomplete thinking which takes the form of fantasy seems to be developing into reflection, analysis, and testing, it has occurred to me that the theater, like religion, is about to be discarded as a dying form, which we lack the necessary prerequisites to enjoy. The extremely serious theater crisis in effect throughout all of Europe now, and not least in England and Germany, the highly civilized nations which have given us the greatest thinkers of the age, supports the assumption that drama is dead along with most of the other fine arts.

In other countries people have believed they could create a new drama by filling the old forms with the content of a new age. But the new ideas have not yet had time to be popularized so that the public would be able to grasp what they are all about. Moreover, party strife has so stirred up people's minds that a pure disinterested pleasure has not been possible when people have had their innermost thoughts contradicted and when an applauding or whistling majority has brought pressure to bear as publicly as can be in a theater. The new form for the new content has not been found, so the new wine has burst the old bottles.

In this play I have not tried to do anything new—one cannot—but have only tried to modernize the form, according to the demands the people of our time would make on this art. To that end I have chosen or let myself be gripped by a theme that can be said to lie outside the party strife of our day, since the problem of social rising or falling, of higher and lower, better or worse, man or woman, is, has been, and will always remain interesting. When I took this theme out of real life—as I had heard it related some years ago when the incident made a strong impression on me—I found it suitable for tragedy, because it still seems tragic to see a fortunate individual go under and still more to see a family die out. But there probably will come a time when we shall have become so developed, so enlightened, that we will look with indifference at the crude, cynical, heartless dramas life offers; when we shall have closed up those lower, undependable instruments of thought which are called feelings, which become superfluous and injurious when our organs of rational judgment have fully developed. The fact that the heroine arouses our pity depends only on our weakness in not being able to resist the feeling of fear that the same fate can strike us. The very sensitive spectator will probably still not be satisfied with this pity, and the man with faith in the future will probably insist on some positive proposals for abolishing the evil, something of a program, in other words. But, in the first place, there is nothing absolutely evil, for the going under of one family is luck for another family which gets a chance to rise, and the alternation between rising and falling is one of the greatest sources of pleasure, since good fortune or luck exists only comparatively. And I want to ask the man with a program, the man who wants to remedy the unpleasant fact that the bird of prey eats the dove and lice eat the bird of prey: Why must it be remedied? Life is not so mathematically idiotic that only the big eat the small, but it happens just as often that the bee kills the lion or at least drives it mad.

That my tragedy makes a sad impression on many people is their fault. When we get as strong as the pioneers of the French Revolution, looking at the thinning out in royal parks of rotten, worn-out trees that have stood too long in the way of others who have just as much right to grow in their own set time will make an impression as unqualifiedly good and happy as when one sees an incurably sick person die.

People recently criticized my tragedy *The Father* because it was very sad—as if they demanded gay tragedies. People call pretentiously for the joy of life, and theater directors requisition farces as if the joy of life lay in being foolish and in depicting people as if they were all afflicted with St. Vitus dance or idiocy. I find the joy of life in the strong, cruel struggles of life, and my pleasure in getting to know something, in learning something. For that reason I have selected an unusual case, but an instructive one; an exception, but a great exception that proves the rule, a fact that undoubtedly will disturb those who love what is ordinary. What will also disturb a simple brain is the fact that my motivation of the action is not simple, and that the point of view is not merely one. An incident in life—and this is a rather new discovery!—is usually caused by a whole series of more or less deep-lying motives, but the spectator usually selects the one that he most easily understands or that he finds most favorable to his sense of honor. A suicide is committed. "Poor business!" says the businessman. —"Unfortunate in love!" say the women.—"Physical illness!" says the sick man.—"Crushed hopes!" the shipwrecked person. But it may be that the motive lay in all of these or in none of them, and that the dead man concealed his real motive by emphasizing a quite different one, one that threw the most favorable light on his memory!

I have motivated Lady Julie's tragic fate by means of a great many circumstances: her mother's basic instincts; her father's improper rearing of the girl; her own nature and the influence of her fiancé's suggestions on her weak degenerate brain; furthermore and even closer at hand: the festive mood during Midsummer Night; the absence of her father; her monthly period; her preoccupation with animals; the exciting influence of the dance; the night-long twilight; the strong aphrodisiac influence of the flowers; and finally chance, which brings the two together illicitly in a room, plus the excited man's agressiveness.

So my treatment is not one-sidedly physiological nor one-sidedly psychological. I have not merely blamed inheritance from the mother, not merely thrown the blame on her monthly condition or exclusively on "immorality," not merely preached morality! The last I have let a cook do—for want of a minister!

The great quantity of motives is—to my credit—in keeping with our times! And if others have done this before me, I flatter myself for not having been alone in using my paradoxes, as all discoveries are called.

As far as the characterization goes, I have made the characters rather "characterless" for the following reasons:

The word *character* has in the course of time taken on many meanings. I suppose it originally meant the dominant trait of the personality, and was confused with temperament. Then the word became the middle-class expression for the automaton, so that an individual whose nature had set once for all or who had adjusted himself to a certain role in life and had stopped growing has been called a character, and the one who is developing, the clever navigator on the river of life who does not sail with sheets set but who veers before the wind and luffs again is called characterless. In a derogatory sense, of course, since he is so hard to catch, classify, and keep under control. This bourgeois concept of the fixed state of the soul was transferred to the stage, where bourgeois people have always dominated. There a character became a man, fixed and set, who invariably appeared intoxicated, comical, or sad, and to characterize him all that was needed was to give him a bodily defect—a clubfoot, a wooden leg, a red nose, or have him repeat an expression such as "That's fine" or "Barkis is willin'." This simple way of seeing human beings still survives in the great Molière. Harpagon is merely a miser, although Harpagon could have been both a miser and an excellent financier, a superb father, and a good member of his community, and, what is worse, his "defect" is extremely advantageous for his daughter and son-in-law, who will inherit from him and therefore should not criticize him even if they have to wait a little to get into bed. So I do not believe in simple theater characters. And the author's summary judgments on human beings: that one is stupid, that one is brutal, that one is jealous, that one is stingy, and so forth ought to be rejected by naturalists, who know how rich the soul-complex is, and who feel that "vice" has a reverse side which pretty much resembles virtue.

I have depicted my characters as modern characters, living in a time of transition, more hysterically in a hurry than during the preceding period at least. I have presented them as vacillating, tattered mixtures of old and new. It seems to me not unlikely that modern ideas have through newspapers and talk penetrated down to levels where servants live.

My souls (characters) are conglomerations of past and present cultures, bits out of books and newspapers, pieces of human beings, torn-off shreds of holiday clothes that have become rags, exactly as the human soul is put together. And I have beside all this added a bit of evolutionary history, in which I let the weaker steal words from the stronger and repeat them, let the souls get "ideas," suggestions as they are called, from each other.

Lady Julie is a modern character—not that the half-woman,

the man hater, has not existed during all ages but because she
has now been discovered, has stepped forward, and has made herself heard. The half-woman is a type who thrusts herself forward,
who sells herself nowadays for power, decorations, honors, or di-
plomas as she used to for money. She signifies degeneration. She
is not a good type, for it is not sound, but unfortunately it can
reproduce itself and extend its misery into another generation;
and degenerate men seem instinctively to choose mates among half-
women, so that they increase in number, bring into being creatures
of uncertain sex who are tortured by life but fortunately go under,
either because of disharmony with reality or because of explosions
of their repressed passions or because of their crushed hopes of
being able to equal man. The type is tragic, offering the spectacle
of a desperate struggle against nature, tragic as a romantic inheritance, which is now being dispersed by naturalism, the only aim of
which is happiness; and happiness belongs to good and strong
types.

But Lady Julie is also a survival of the old war aristocracy,
which is now giving way to the new aristocracy of nerve or brain;
she is a victim of the discord a mother's "crime" has caused within
a family; a victim of the errors of an age, circumstances, and her
own deficient body, all of which together equal the old-fashioned
fate or universal law. The naturalist has erased guilt along with
God, but the consequences of the action—punishment, prison or
fear of prison—he cannot erase for the simple reason that they
remain whether he acquits the individual or not. Injured fellow
human beings are not so kind as those who have not been injured
and are not involved can easily be. Even if her father for com-
pelling reasons would not seek vengeance, the daughter would
revenge herself as she does here because of her inborn or acquired
sense of honor, which the higher classes inherit—from where?
From barbarism, from the original Aryan home, from the chivalry
of the Middle Ages? It is very beautiful though nowadays a disadvantage for the preservation of the human race. It is the nobleman's *harakiri,* the Japanese man's law of conscience, which makes

him cut his own stomach open when someone else insults him, which survives in modified form in the duel, the privilege of nobility. Therefore the servant Jean lives on, but Lady Julie cannot live without honor. It is the slave's advantage over the earl that he lacks this fatal prejudice about honor, and there is in every Aryan a little of the nobleman or Don Quixote, which makes us sympathize with the suicide who has committed a dishonorable act and thereby lost his honor, and we are noblemen enough to be tortured by seeing fallen greatness lying as a corpse, yes, even if the fallen person should redeem himself through compensating honorable acts. The servant Jean is the founder of a race, one in whom the promising differences are noted. He was a sharecropper's son and has trained himself as a nobleman-to-be. He has had an easy time learning, has highly developed senses (smell, taste, sight), and has a sense of beauty. He is already on the way up and is certainly strong enough not to be disturbed at using other people's services. He is already out of place in his native environment, which he despises as stages in his past, and which he fears and flees, because people know his secrets, spy out his intentions, see his rising enviously and look toward his defeat with pleasure. Out of all this comes his double, undecided character, wavering between sympathy for the exalted and hatred for those who have been exalted. He is an aristocrat, he himself says, has learned the secrets of good society, is polished, but crude below the surface, wears a formal coat with good taste, but does not give any guarantee that his body is clean.

He respects the young lady, but he is afraid of Kristin because she knows his dangerous secrets; he is sufficiently callous not to let the events of the night have any disturbing effect on his plans for the future. With the slave's crudity and the master's lack of squeamishness he can look at blood without fainting, take a piece of bad luck and throw it off; that is why he leaves the struggle unhurt and most likely will end his days as a hotel proprietor, and if *he* does not become a Rumanian count, his son will probably become a university student and possibly a government official.

The information he gives about the lower classes' concept of life as seen from below is rather important—that is, when he speaks the truth, which he frequently does not, for he says what is advantageous to him more than he says what is true. When Lady Julie suggests that all people in the lower classes feel the pressure from above very much, Jean agrees, naturally, since his intention is to win her sympathy, but he immediately corrects his own statement when he sees the advantage of separating himself from the crowd.

Aside from the fact that Jean is on the way up, he is also superior to Lady Julie because he is a man. Sexually he is the aristocrat because of his masculine strength, his more sensitively developed senses, and his ability to take the initiative. His inferiority consists mainly of the social environment in which he is temporarily living and which he most likely can put off along with his valet's jacket.

His slave temperament expresses itself in his respect for the count (the boots) and his religious superstition; but he respects the count particularly as the man who occupies the higher position for which he is aiming, and this respect remains when he has conquered the daughter of the house and seen the emptiness within the beautiful shell.

I do not believe that there can be any love in a "higher" sense between two such different people, so I let Lady Julie imagine she loves him as a means of protecting and excusing herself; and I let Jean assume that he could love her if his social circumstances were different. Love, I suspect, is like the hyacinth, which puts its roots down into the darkness before it can produce a strong flower. In the play love shoots up, blossoms, and goes to seed simultaneously; that is why the plant dies so swiftly.

Kristin, finally, is a female slave, filled with subservience and dullness, acquired before the kitchen fire, filled to overflowing with morality and religion which she uses as a cover for her own immorality and as a scapegoat. She goes to church to unload her household thefts on Christ easily and comfortably and to take on a new charge of innocence. She is, moreover, a minor character and is therefore intentionally merely sketched as I sketched the pastor and the doctor in *The Father,* for I wanted everyday people as country pastors and doctors usually are. My minor characters seem abstract to some people because everyday people are to a certain extent abstract in performing their work; that is to say not individualized, showing only one side while they are doing their work, and as long as the spectator does not feel any need of seeing them from several points of view my abstract depiction is fairly correct.

As far as the dialogue goes, I have broken with tradition somewhat in not making my characters catechists who ask stupid questions in order to elicit clever replies. I have avoided the symmetrical, mathematical artificiality of French dialogue and have let my characters' brains work irregularly as they do in real life, in which a conversational topic is never exhausted but in which one brain gets from another a cog to slip into at random. For that reason my dialogue rambles, too, presents material in the first scenes that is later reworked, taken up, repeated, expanded, and developed like the theme in a musical composition.

The action is tolerable enough, and since it really concerns two people I have limited myself to these, including only one minor character, the cook, and letting the father's unhappy spirit hover above and behind it all. This because I believe I have noticed that the psychological development is what interests people of our time most, and our desire for knowledge is such we are not satisfied with knowing what happened but we must also learn how it happened! We want to see the threads, see the machinery, examine the double-bottomed box, touch the magic ring to find the seam, and examine the cards to discover how they are marked.

I have had in mind the de Goncourt brothers' monographic novels, which of all contemporary literature have appealed to me most.

As far as the technique of composition goes, I have by way of experiment eliminated the division into acts, because it has seemed to me that our increasingly weak capacity for illusion possibly would be disturbed by intermissions, during which the spectator has time to think and thereby escapes the dramatist-hypnotist's suggestive influence. My play will probably take an hour and a half, and when people can listen to a lecture, a sermon, or a convention session for that long a time or longer, I imagine a play lasting ninety minutes would not exhaust them. In *The Outlaw* (1872), one of my first plays, I tried using this concentrated form, but with slight success. The play had been written in five acts. When I had completed it, I noticed the split, uneasy effect it had. I burned it, and out of its ashes arose one single, long, carefully developed act of fifty pages in print, which could be performed in an hour's time. The form [of *Lady Julie*] is not quite new, but seems to be mine and may because of changes in the laws of taste become timely. I would like to have an audience trained so that it could sit through a full-evening performance of a one-act play. But preliminary tests will have to be made. To give the audience and the actors opportunities to relax without their letting go of the illusion, I have used three art forms, all of them subordinate to drama: the monologue, the pantomime, and the ballet, originally part of the tragedy of antiquity—the monody becomes monologue and the chorus, ballet.

Our realists have banished the soliloquy or monologue as unbelievable, but if I motivate it, it becomes believable and can be used advantageously. It is natural that a speaker walks his floor alone rehearsing his speech aloud, that an actor runs through his role aloud, that a maid talks to her cat, that a mother prattles to her child, an old maid chatters to her parrot, and a sleeper talks in his sleep. To give an actor the opportunity to do independent work, for once, free of the dramatist's pointer, it is best that the monologue should be not written out but just indicated. Since it is rather unimportant what is said in sleep, to the parrot, or to the cat, providing it has no effect on the action, a gifted actor in the very midst of a mood and a situation can probably improvise better than the dramatist, who cannot know ahead of time how much may be said or at what length before the audience is awakened from the illusion.

As we know, some of the Italian theaters have returned to improvisation and thereby made actors creative—in keeping with the author's plans, however. This can be a step ahead or a new form of art, where one can talk about a really *creative* art.

Where the monologue would not seem true to life, I have used pantomime, and in that I give the actor still more freedom to create—and win independent honor for himself. In order not to try the audience beyond its limits, I have let the music, well motivated because of the midsummer dance, exercise its suggestive power during the silent action, and I ask the music director to choose the music carefully so that foreign moods are not aroused through recollections from current operettas, dances, or entirely too ethnographic folk tunes.

My ballet could not be replaced by a so-called folk scene, since folk scenes are badly performed and a lot of showoffs want to use the opportunity to be witty. They thereby disturb the illusion. Since the common people do not improvise their malicious remarks but use available material which can have a double meaning, I have not composed a malicious song but have taken a fairly unknown song-and-dance game, which I recorded in the neighborhood of Stockholm. The words hit only approximately, not directly and to the point, but that is the intention for the cunning (weak) nature of the slave does not permit a direct attack. So: no speaking buffoons in a serious play, no crude grins over a situation that puts the lid on a family's coffin.

As far as the scenery goes I have borrowed the asymmetry and economy of impressionistic painting and believe I have succeeded better in creating illusion; through not seeing the whole room and all the furniture, the audience has the opportunity to sense, that is, to imagine and complement. I have also got rid of the wearisome exits through doors, particularly theater doors made of canvas which sway at the slightest touch and cannot even express a furious husband's anger after a bad dinner when he goes out slamming the door "so the whole house shakes." (In the theater it sways.) I have limited myself to one setting to let the characters fit into their milieu and to break with the custom of having expensive settings. But when one has only one setting, one has to make it true to life. There is nothing harder than getting a room on stage that looks approximately like the real room, no matter how gifted the painter is at creating an erupting volcano and waterfalls. The walls will have to remain canvas, but it is about time to quit painting shelves and kitchen equipment on the canvas. We have so many other conventional things on the stage that we are expected to accept that we should not have to strain ourselves by believing in dishes painted on cloth.

I have placed the rear wall and the table diagonally to get the actors to play full face and in half profile when they sit by the table opposite each other. In the opera *Aida* I have seen a slanting backdrop that opened up unknown perspectives, and it looked as if it had been devised in the spirit of reacting against the wearisome straight line.

Another perhaps not unnecessary novelty would be the removal of the footlights. This lighting from below is probably designed to make the actor's faces fatter, but I ask: Why should all actors have fat faces? Doesn't this lighting from below eliminate a great many fine features in the lower parts of the face, especially the cheeks? Doesn't it falsify the shape of the nose? Doesn't it throw shadows over the eyes? If not, one thing is certain: the lights hurt the actors' eyes so that the effective play of their eyes is lost because lighting from below hits the eye in places which are generally protected (except in sailors, who see the sun in the water), and therefore we seldom see play of the eyes except for crude glances either to the side or along the balconies, when the white of the eye can be seen. Probably the actresses' tiresome fluttering of their eyelashes can be attributed particularly to the same cause. And when anyone on stage wants to speak with his eyes, he has only the unhappy solution of looking right out at the audience, with which he enters into direct communication outside the frame of the set—a bad practice rightly or wrongly called "greeting one's acquaintances"!

Wouldn't sufficiently strong sidelights (with parabolas or the like) give the actor this new resource: strengthening his acting by means of the face's greatest resource, the play of the eyes?

I have scarcely any illusions about getting the actor to play for the audience and not with it, although the former would be desirable. I am not dreaming of seeing the full back of any actor through the whole of an important scene, but I wish very, very much that decisive scenes would not be played as duets (next to the prompter's box) designed to be applauded, but at the place the situation dictates. So: no revolutions but simply little modifications, for getting the stage to be a room with the fourth wall removed and some pieces of furniture with their backs to the audience is still disturbing in effect, I suppose.

When I want to talk about make-up, I do not dare to hope to be heard by the ladies, who would rather be beautiful than true to life. But the actor might think about this: is it advantageous for him to be made up so that he has an abstract character on his face, which looks like a mask? Let's think of a gentleman who fixes a decidedly choleric feature between his eyes with soot, and let's assume that in spite of being so firmly grim he needs to smile when he delivers one line. What a ghastly grimace it will be! And how can the false forehead of his wig, shining like a billiard ball, be wrinkled when the old fellow gets angry?

In a modern psychological drama, in which the finest movements of the soul are to be mirrored more in the face than through gestures and sounds, it probably would be best to try a powerful sidelight on a little stage and actors without make-up, or at least a minimum of it.

Then if we could get rid of the visible orchestra with its irritating lights and with the faces turned toward the audience; if we could get the main floor raised so that the audience's eyes would reach a point higher than the actor's knees; if we could get rid of the boxes with their grinning diners and drinkers, and in addition have complete darkness in the auditorium during the performance, and first and last have a *little* stage and a *little* auditorium, then maybe we would get a new drama, and the theater could again be an institution for the pleasure of the refined. While waiting for such a theater, we shall have to write plays to have them ready for the repertory which will come.

I have made an attempt! If it has failed, there will be time to try again!

Lady Julie　　　·　　　A Naturalistic Tragedy

Ulf Palme and Inga Tidblad in *Lady Julie* (The Royal Dramatic Theater, Stockholm)

Characters

LADY JULIE, *twenty-five years old*
JEAN, *valet, thirty years old*
KRISTIN, *cook, thirty-five years old*

The action takes place in the count's kitchen on Midsummer Night.

SETTING

A large kitchen, whose ceiling and side walls are concealed by drapes and soffits. The rear wall goes diagonally across and up the stage from the left; on that wall to the left are two shelves on which are copper, bronze, iron, and pewter utensils; the shelves are edged with scalloped paper; somewhat to the right three fourths of the large arched exit with two large glass doors, through which can be seen a fountain with a cupid in it, lilac bushes in bloom, and projecting Lombardy poplars.

To the left on the stage, the corner of a large tiled stove with part of its hood showing.

To the right, one end of the servants' dining table of white pine with some chairs.

The stove is decorated with bunches of birch leaves; the floor is strewn with juniper twigs.

On the end of the table a large Japanese spice jar with lilac blossoms.

An icebox, a sink, a washstand.

89

A large old-fashioned handbell above the door and a speaking tube the mouthpiece of which is to the left of the bell.

KRISTIN *is at the stove frying something in a frying pan; she is dressed in a light cotton dress and a kitchen apron.* JEAN *enters, dressed in livery, carrying a pair of large riding boots with spurs, which he puts down where they can be seen—on the floor.*

JEAN: Tonight Lady Julie's crazy again—absolutely crazy!

KRISTIN: Oh, you're here?

JEAN: I took the count to the station, and when I came back I passed the barn and went in and was dancing when I saw the young lady leading the dance with the forester. But when she caught sight of me, she rushed right up and invited me to dance the ladies' waltz with her. And since then she's been waltzing so—I've never been in on anything like it. She *is* crazy!

KRISTIN: She always has been, but not quite as bad as the last fourteen days since her engagement was broken.

JEAN: Well, what's the truth about that? Why, he's a fine man, even if he isn't rich. Ah!! They have so many notions! *(Sits down at the end of the table)* It's strange, though, about a young lady . . . hm . . . to prefer staying home with the people, eh? Instead of going with her father to visit relatives?

KRISTIN: I suppose she's sort of embarrassed after that to-do with her fiancé.

JEAN: Most likely! But he was a man all the same! Do you know how it happened, Kristin? *I* saw it though I didn't want to let on.

KRISTIN: Really! Did you see it?

JEAN: Yes, I did!—They were down in the stable yard one evening, and the young lady was training him, as she put it—do you know how? Well, she had him jump over her riding whip like a dog you're training to jump. He jumped twice and got a blow each time; the third time he took the whip out of her hand and broke it into a thousand pieces; and then he took off.

KRISTIN: So that's how it happened! Well, what do you know!

JEAN: Yes, that's how it was!—But what do you have for me that's good, Kristin?

KRISTIN *(puts what she has been frying on a plate and places it in front of* JEAN*):* Oh, it's only a bit of kidney I cut out of the veal roast.

JEAN *(inhales the fragrance of the food):* Wonderful! That's my big *délice! (Feels the plate)* But you could have warmed the plate!

KRISTIN: You're harder to please than the count when you're in the mood! *(Pulls his hair affectionately).*

JEAN *(angry):* No, don't pull my hair! You know how sensitive I am.

KRISTIN: There, there! I was only being affectionate, you know! *(*JEAN *eats.* KRISTIN *opens a bottle of beer.)*

JEAN: Beer on Midsummer Eve! No, thank you! I have something better. *(Opens a table drawer and takes out a bottle of red wine with yellow sealing wax)* The yellow seal, see!—Give me a glass! A goblet, of course, when one's drinking the *real* thing!

KRISTIN *(goes back to the stove and puts on a small pan):* God save the one who'll get you for a husband! You are fussy.

JEAN: Nonsense! You'd be happy if you got a fine man like me; and I don't think it has hurt you to have them call me your boyfriend! *(Tastes the wine)* Good! Very good! Only a little too chilled! *(Warms the glass with his hand)* We bought this in Dijon. And it was four francs the liter in bulk, and then there was the duty, too!—What are you cooking? It has an infernal smell!

KRISTIN: Oh, it's a hellish concoction Lady Julie wants for Diana.

JEAN: You should express yourself properly, Kristin! But why should you stand there cooking for that bitch of a dog on a holiday evening? Is she sick, huh?

KRISTIN: Yes, she's sick! She stole out with the gatekeeper's mutt—and now she's in trouble—and, see, the young lady doesn't want to admit that.

JEAN: The young lady's too proud in some ways and not proud enough in others, exactly like the countess in her day. She felt

most at home in the kitchen and the barn, but she never wanted
to ride behind *one* horse: she wore dirty cuffs, but she had to
have the coat of arms on her cuff links.—Lady Julie, to talk
about her, doesn't take care of herself and her position. I'd say
she's not nice. Just now when she was dancing in the barn she
grabbed the forester from Anna and asked him to dance with
her. Surely we wouldn't behave like that, but that's how it is
when the gentry wants to be democratic—they get common!—
But she has a fine figure! Splendid! Ah! What shoulders! and—
etc.!

KRISTIN: Oh yes, don't overdo it! I've heard what Clara says, and
she dresses her.

JEAN: Puh, Clara! You're always envious of each other! I've been
out riding with her . . . And the way she dances!

KRISTIN: Listen, Jean! Won't you dance with me when I'm done?

JEAN: Yes, of course, I will!

KRISTIN: Do you promise?

JEAN: Promise? When I say I will, I will! Thank you for the food!
It was wonderful! *(Puts the cork in the bottle)*

LADY JULIE *(appears in the doorway; speaks to someone outside);*
I'll be back right away! You go on!

    *(*JEAN *hastily puts the bottle back in the drawer; gets up
respectfully.)*

JULIE *(in; up to* KRISTIN *by the stove):* Well, is it ready?
*(*KRISTIN *signals* JEAN *is present.)*

JEAN *(gallantly):* Are you ladies up to something secret?

JULIE *(strikes him in the face with her handkerchief):* Curious!

JEAN: Ah, but that was fragrant with violets!

JULIE *(coquettishly):* Shameless! Do you know about perfumes,
too? You certainly can dance . . . there, don't look! Go away.

JEAN *(impertinently but politely):* Are you ladies cooking a
witches' brew on Midsummer Night? Something to foretell by
your lucky star the husband you'll get?

JULIE *(sharply):* If you see him, you'll have to have strong eyes!

(*To* KRISTIN) Pour it in a small bottle and cork it carefully.—
Come and dance a schottische with me, Jean . . .

JEAN (*hesitantly*): I don't want to be impolite to anybody, but I
had promised this dance to Kristin . . .

JULIE: Well, she can get somebody else. Isn't that right, Kristin?
Won't you lend Jean to me?

KRISTIN: That's not up to me! If my lady is so condescending, it
won't do for him to say no. Go on, Jean, and thank my lady for
the honor.

JEAN: Frankly speaking but without wanting to hurt you, Lady
Julie, I wonder if it's wise for you to dance twice in succession
with the same partner, especially since the people aren't slow
about putting their interpretation . . .

JULIE (*flaring up*): What's that? What sort of interpretation? What
do you mean?

JEAN (*meekly*): Since my lady doesn't want to understand, I'll
have to speak more plainly. It looks bad to prefer one of her
servants to others who expect the same unusual honor . . .

JULIE: Prefer! What thoughts! I'm amazed! I, the mistress of the
house, honor the people's dance with my presence, and when I
really want to dance, I want to dance with someone who can
lead so I don't need to be the object of ridicule.

JEAN: As my lady commands! I am at your service!

JULIE (*blithely*): Don't take it as an order! Tonight we're all taking
part in a celebration as happy people and putting aside all rank!
So give me your arm!—Don't worry, Kristin! I won't take your
fiancé away from you!

(JEAN *offers his arm and conducts* LADY JULIE *out*.)

PANTOMIME

*To be played as if the actress really were alone; she turns her
back to the audience when she needs to; does not look out into
the theater; does not hurry as if she were afraid the audience
would become impatient.*

KRISTIN *is alone. One can hear distant violin music in schottische tempo.*

KRISTIN *hums in accompaniment to the music; clears up the table after* JEAN, *washes the plate at the sink, dries it, and puts it away in a cupboard.*

Then she takes off her kitchen apron, takes a little mirror out of the table drawer, puts it up against the vase containing the lilacs on the table; lights a candle and heats a hairpin with which she curls the hair on her forehead.

Then she goes to the door and listens. Returns to the table. Finds LADY JULIE'*s forgotten handkerchief, puts it to her nose, smells it; then she spreads it out automatically, stretches it, smooths it out, folds it twice, etc.*

JEAN (*enters alone*): Well, but she *is* crazy! The way she's dancing! And the people are standing grinning at her behind the doors. What do you say about that, Kristin?

KRISTIN: Ah, it's her time, and she's always queer then. But won't you dance with me now?

JEAN: I hope you're not angry because I danced the last one with her.

KRISTIN: Of course not!—Not for that little, you should know; and I know my place, too . . .

JEAN (*puts his arm about her waist*): You're a sensible girl, Kristin, and you'd make a good wife . . .

JULIE (*enters; unpleasantly surprised; with forced facetiousness*): You're a fine partner—running away from your lady.

JEAN: On the contrary, Lady Julie; as you see I've hurried to find the girl I left!

JULIE (*changes her tone*): You know, no one else can dance like you!—But why are you wearing livery on a holiday evening? Take it off at once!

JEAN: Then I'll have to ask my lady to step out for a minute, for my black coat's hanging here . . . (*Gestures as he goes to the right*)

JULIE: Are you embarrassed because of me? Changing a coat! Go into your room then and come back! Or you can stay—I'll turn my back.

JEAN: With your permission, my lady! (*Goes to the right; the audience can see his arm when he changes coats.*)

JULIE (*to* KRISTIN): Listen, Kristin! Is Jean your fiancé since he's so intimate?

KRISTIN: Fiancé? Yes, if you wish! We call it that.

JULIE: Call?

KRISTIN: Well, my lady has had a fiancé herself, and . . .

JULIE: Yes, we were properly engaged . . .

KRISTIN: But it didn't come to anything all the same . . .

(JEAN *enters wearing a black frock coat and a black top hat.*)

JULIE: *Trés gentil, monsieur Jean! Trés gentil!*

JEAN: *Vous voulez plaisanter, madame!*

JULIE: *Et vous voulez parler français!* Where did you learn that?

JEAN: In Switzerland while I was *sommelier* in one of the biggest hotels in Lucerne!

JULIE: Why, you look like a gentleman in that frock coat! *Charmant!* (*Sits down at the table*)

JEAN: Oh, you're flattering me!

JULIE (*annoyed*): Flatter you?

JEAN: My natural modesty forbids me to believe you're uttering bits of genuine politeness to someone like me, so I let myself assume you were exaggerating or, as it's called, flattering!

JULIE: Where did you learn to express yourself like that? You must have gone to the theater often?

JEAN: That, too! I've been many places!

JULIE: But you were born here in the neighborhood, weren't you?

JEAN: Yes, my father was a tenant farmer on the prosecuting attorney's estate nearby, and I certainly saw my lady as a child although you didn't notice me!

JULIE: Really!

JEAN: Yes, and I remember one time particularly . . . well, I can't tell about that!

JULIE: Oh yes! Do! Eh? By way of exception!

JEAN: No, I really can't! Some other time perhaps.

JULIE: Another time! Is now so dangerous?

JEAN: It isn't dangerous, but I don't feel like it!—Look at her! (*Points at Kristin, who has fallen asleep on a chair by the stove*)

JULIE: She'll make a delightful wife, that one! Perhaps she snores, too?

JEAN: No, she doesn't, but she talks in her sleep.

JULIE (*cynically*): How do you know she talks in her sleep?

JEAN (*coolly*): I've heard her! (*A pause, during which they observe each other*)

JULIE: Why don't you sit down?

JEAN: I can't allow myself to do that in your presence!

JULIE: But if I command you to?

JEAN: Then I'll obey!

JULIE: Sit down then!—But wait! Can't you give me something to drink first?

JEAN: I don't know what we have in the icebox. I think it's only beer.

JULIE: It's not *only* beer! I have such simple taste I prefer it to wine.

JEAN (*takes a bottle of beer from the icebox; opens the bottle; looks for a glass and a plate in the cupboard; serves the beer*): Here it is!

JULIE: Thank you! Won't you have some?

JEAN: I don't really care for beer, but if my lady orders me to!

JULIE: Order?—I think as a polite cavalier you ought to keep your lady company.

JEAN: That's very properly put! (*Opens a bottle, gets a glass*)

JULIE: Drink a toast to me!

(JEAN hesitates.)

JULIE: I think the man is shy!

JEAN (*on his knees, facetiously parodying "the manner"; lifting his glass*): A toast to my lady!

JULIE: Bravo!—Kiss my shoe, too, and you'll have done it just
right!
> (JEAN *hesitant; then he daringly takes her foot which he
> kisses lightly*.)

JULIE: Splendid! You should have been an actor!

JEAN (*gets up*): This won't do any longer! My lady, someone
might come and see us.

JULIE: Would that matter?

JEAN: People would talk, to put it simply! And if my lady knew
how their tongues were wagging up there just now . . .

JULIE: What were they saying? Tell me!—Sit down!

JEAN (*sits down*): I don't want to hurt you, but they used expressions—that cast suspicions of the kind that . . . well, you can
imagine what they were! Why, you're no child, and when they
see a lady drinking with a man while they're alone—and a servant
at that—at night—then . . .

JULIE: So what? Besides, we're not alone. Kristin is here.

JEAN: But asleep!

JULIE: Then I'll awaken her. (*Gets up*) Kristin! Are you asleep?
> (KRISTIN *mutters in her sleep*.)

JULIE: Kristin!—She certainly can sleep!

KRISTIN (*in her sleep*): The count's boots have been brushed—put
on the coffee—right away, right away—ho ho—puh!

JULIE (*takes Kristin by the nose*): Will you wake up?

JEAN (*sternly*): Don't disturb the one who's sleeping!

JULIE (*sharply*): What!

JEAN: The one who's stood by the stove all day can be tired when
night comes. And sleep should be respected . . .

JULIE (*changing her tone*): That's a lovely thought, and it does
credit to you—thank you! (*Puts out her hand to Jean*) Come
out and pick some lilacs for me!
> (*During the following speeches Kristin awakens, goes—stu-
> pefied with sleep—to the right to lie down*.)

JEAN: With my lady?

JULIE: With me!

JEAN: That will never do! Absolutely not!

JULIE: I can't understand what you mean! Are you possibly imagining something?

JEAN: No, not I, but the people.

JULIE: What? That I'm in love with a servant?

JEAN: I'm not conceited, but they've seen examples—and for the people nothing is sacred!

JULIE: You're an aristocrat, I think!

JEAN: Yes, I am.

JULIE: Then I'll come down . . .

JEAN: Don't come down, my lady; take my advice. There'll be no one who'll believe you came down voluntarily—the people will always say you fell!

JULIE: I have higher thoughts of the people than you! Come—and find out!—Come! (*She "examines" him searchingly with her eyes.*)

JEAN: You know you are strange!

JULIE: Perhaps. But so are you!—Besides, everything is strange! Life, people, everything, is dirt that's driven, driven on, on the water until it sinks, sinks! I have a dream that keeps coming back again and again, and I recall it now. I'm sitting on a pillar and can't see how I can get down; I get dizzy when I look down, yet I must get down; but I don't have the courage to jump; I can't hold on firmly, and I long to fall; but I don't fall. And still I get no peace until I get down, no rest before I get down, down on earth. And if I did get down on earth, I'd want to get down into the ground . . . Have you ever felt anything like that?

JEAN: No. I usually dream about lying under a high tree in a dark forest. I want to get up, up to the top and look about on the fair world where the sun shines, rob the bird's nest up there, where the golden eggs lie. And I climb and climb, but the trunk is so thick, so smooth, and it's so far to the first branch. But I know if I just reached the first branch, I could climb to the top as on a ladder. I haven't reached it yet, but I will reach it, even if it's only in my dreams!

JULIE: Here I'm talking with you about dreams! Come! Just out in the park! (*She gives him her arm, and they go out*).

JEAN: We'll sleep on nine midsummer flowers tonight; then our dreams will come true, my lady!

   (*They turn in the doorway. Jean is holding his hand to one of his eyes.*)

JULIE: Let me see what you have in your eye.

JEAN: Oh, it's nothing—just a speck—I'll be all right.

JULIE: It was my sleeve that brushed against you. Sit down, and I'll help you. (*Takes him by the arm, makes him sit down, takes hold of his head and bends it back; with the corner of her handkerchief she tries to remove the speck.*)

   Sit still, absolutely still! (*Strikes his hand*) There! Will you obey!—Why, I think you're trembling, you big strong man! (*Feels his upper arm*) With arms like that!

JEAN (*warningly*): Lady Julie!

JULIE: Yes, monsieur Jean?

JEAN: *Attention! Je ne suis qu'un homme!*

JULIE: Will you sit still!—There! Now it's gone! Kiss my hand, and thank me.

JEAN (*gets up*): Lady Julie! Listen to me!—Kristin has gone to bed!—Will you listen to me?

JULIE: Kiss my hand first!

JEAN: Listen to me!

JULIE: Kiss my hand first!

JEAN: Yes, but blame yourself!

JULIE: For what?

JEAN: For what? Are you a child at twenty-five? Don't you know its dangerous to play with fire?

JULIE: Not for me! I'm insured!

JEAN (*insolently*): No, you're not! And, if you were, there's inflammable substance near you!

JULIE: And that would be you?

JEAN: Yes, not because it's I, but because I'm a young man—

JULIE: With attractive looks—what unbelievable conceit! A Don
Juan, perhaps! Or a Joseph! My word, I think you're a Joseph!

JEAN: Do you?

JULIE: I'm afraid, almost!

   (JEAN *insolently up to her; wants to put his arm about her
   waist in order to kiss her.*)

JULIE (*slaps him*): Behave yourself!

JEAN: Was that serious or playful?

JULIE: Serious!

JEAN: Then it was serious just a minute ago! You play absolutely
too seriously, and that's what's dangerous! Now I'm tired of
playing and excuse myself to go back to my work. The count
wants his boots ready, and it's long past midnight.

JULIE: Put away the boots!

JEAN: No! It's a job I have to do, but I've never agreed to be your
playmate, and I never can be, for I consider myself too good
for that.

JULIE: You are proud!

JEAN: In some cases, yes; in others, no!

JULIE: Have you ever been in love?

JEAN: We don't use that word, but I've been fond of many girls.
Once I was sick because I couldn't get the one I wanted—sick,
you see, like the princes in the Arabian Nights! Who couldn't
eat or drink because of love!

JULIE: Who was she?

   (JEAN *silent.*)

JULIE: Who was she?

JEAN: You can't make me tell.

JULIE: If I ask you as an equal, ask a—friend! Who was she?

JEAN: You!

JULIE (*sits down*): How funny . . . !

JEAN: Yes, if you wish! It was ridiculous! You see, that was the
story I didn't want to tell, but now I will!

   Do you know what your world looks like from below—no,
you don't! Like hawks and falcons whose backs one seldom gets

to see because they're floating way up above! I lived in the tenant farmer's cottage with seven brothers and sisters, and one pig out on the gray field where not one tree grew. But from the windows I saw the wall of the count's park with the apple trees above. That was the Garden of Eden, and many evil angels with burning swords kept watch over it. Nonetheless I and other boys found the way to the tree of life—do you despise me?

JULIE: Ah! Why, all boys steal apples.

JEAN: That's what you say, but you despise me all the same! All right! Once I got into the garden with my mother to weed the flower beds. Next to the orchard was a Turkish pavilion in the shade of jasmine and overgrown with honeysuckle. I didn't know what it could be used for, but I had never seen such a beautiful building. People went in and came out again, and one day the door had been left open. I stole in and saw the walls covered with portraits of kings and emperors, and there were red curtains at the windows with fringes on them—now you understand what I mean. I—(*breaks off a lilac branch and holds it under Lady Julie's nose*)—I had never been in the castle, had never seen anything but the church—but this was more beautiful; and no matter how my thoughts flowed they always came back—to that place. So gradually I got a longing to experience the full pleasure of —*enfin,* I stole in, looked, and admired. But then somebody came! There was an exit for the gentry, but there was still another for me, and I had no choice but to take it!

(JULIE, *who has taken the lilac branch, lets it drop to the table.*)

JEAN: Then I really ran, plunged through a raspberry hedge, rushed across a strawberry field, and came up on the rose terrace. There I caught sight of a pink dress and a pair of white stockings—that was you. I lay down under a pile of weeds—*under* it, can you imagine, under thistles that pricked me and wet earth that smelled bad. And I looked at you while you walked among the roses, and I thought: If it's true a robber can get into heaven and be with the angels, then it's strange a tenant farmer's child here on God's earth can't get into the castle park to play with the count's daughter!

JULIE (*elegiacally*): Do you think all poor children have had the same thought?

JEAN (*first hesitatingly, then persuasively*): If all poor children— yes—of course! Of course!

JULIE: It must be extremely unfortunate to be poor!

JEAN (*with deep pain, strongly affected*): Oh Lady Julie!—A dog may lie on the countess' sofa, a horse may be caressed by a lady's hand, but a servant—(*changing his tone*)—well, there are the makings in an occasional one of them so he climbs up in the world, but that doesn't happen very often!—Do you know what I did, though?—I jumped into the mill stream with my clothes on, was pulled out, and got a beating. But the next Sunday when Dad and all the others at home were going to Grandmother's, I arranged to stay home. I washed myself with soap and warm water, put on my best clothes, and went to church, where I'd get to see you! I saw you and went home, determined to die, but I wanted to die beautifully and pleasantly, without pain. And then I remembered it was dangerous to sleep under an elderberry bush. We had a big one in full bloom. I stripped it of all its blossoms, and then bedded myself down in the oats bin. Have you ever noticed how smooth oats are? Soft to the touch as human skin . . . ! I pulled the lid down and closed my eyes; I fell asleep and woke up really very sick. But I didn't die as you can see.

What I was after—I don't know. There wasn't any hope of winning you—but you were a symbol of how hopeless it was to hope to rise from the class into which I had been born.

JULIE: You tell things in a charming way, you know. Have you gone to school?

JEAN: A little, but I've read a lot of novels and gone to the theater. Besides I've heard "better" people talk, and I've learned most from them.

JULIE: Do you stand there listening to what we say?

JEAN: Of course! And I've heard a lot . . . When I've sat on the driver's seat or rowed the boat. Once I heard you, Lady Julie, and one of your girl friends . . .

JULIE: Ah!—What did you hear?

JEAN: Well, I'd better not say, but I certainly was a little amazed and didn't understand where you had learned all those words. Maybe there isn't such a big difference as one thinks between people and people—basically!

JULIE: For shame! We certainly don't live as you do when we're engaged.

JEAN (*fixes her glance*): Is that so certain?—Well, there's no point in my lady's pretending innocence to me . . .

JULIE: It was a scoundrel to whom I had given my love.

JEAN: That's what women always say—afterward.

JULIE: Always?

JEAN: I think so—I've heard the expression several times before on occasion.

JULIE: What occasion?

JEAN: Like the one we're talking about! The last time . . .

JULIE (*gets up*): Sh-h! I don't want to hear any more!

JEAN: She didn't either—it is strange. Well, then, may I go to bed?

JULIE (*blithely*): Go to bed on midsummer night?

JEAN: Yes! I don't really enjoy dancing with that mob up there.

JULIE: Take the key to the boat and row me out on the lake. I want to see the sunrise!

JEAN: Is that wise?

JULIE: It sounds as if you were afraid for your reputation!

JEAN: Why not? I'm not anxious to be ridiculous, to be fired without a recommendation when I want to get ahead. And I think I have a certain obligation to Kristin.

JULIE: So . . . it's Kristin now . . .

JEAN: Yes, but it's you, too.—Take my advice and go to bed!

JULIE: Am I to obey you?

JEAN: Just this once—for your own sake! I beg you! It's very late, we're intoxicated for want of sleep, and one's head gets hot! Go

to bed! Besides, if I'm not hearing wrong—the people are coming over here to look for me. And if they find us here together,
you're lost!

CHORUS (*approaches singing*):

> There came two women out of the woods
> Tridiridi-ralla tridiridi-ra
> The one was wet about her feet
> Tridiridi-ralla tridiridi-ra.
>
> They talked about a hundred dollars
> Tridiridi-ralla tridiridi-ra
> But they had hardly a dollar
> Tridiridi-ralla-la.
>
> And I give you the wreath so fine
> Tridiridi-ralla tridiridi-ra
> But it's someone else I'm thinking of
> Tridiridi-ralla-la!

JULIE: I know my people, and I love them, just as they love me.
Let them come—you'll see!

JEAN: No, Lady Julie, they don't love you. They take your food,
but they spit after it! Believe me! Listen to them; just listen to
what they're singing!—No, don't listen to them!

JULIE (*listens*): What are they singing?

JEAN: It's a lampoon! About you and me!

JULIE: *Infamt!* How nasty! And so treacherously!—

JEAN: The mob is always cowardly! All you can do is to run away
from a set-to with them!

JULIE: Run away? Where? We can't get out! And we can't go into
Kristin's room!

JEAN: So! Into my room, then? Necessity has no law, and you can
rely on me, for I am your real, honest, and respectful friend!

JULIE: But . . . what if they should look for you there?

JEAN: I'll bolt the door, and, if they try to break in, I'll shoot!—
Come! (*On his knees*) Come.

JULIE (*pointedly*): Do you promise me . . . ?

JEAN: I promise!

(JULIE *out, quickly, to the right.* JEAN *follows her hastily.*)

BALLET

Dressed in their holiday finery and with flowers in their hats, the people on the estate enter; a fiddler at the head of the procession; a small barrel of near beer and a small keg of brännvin *(distilled liquor), both entwined with green leaves, are placed on the table; they take out glasses. Then they drink. After that they form a ring and sing and dance to the dance game, "Two women came from the forest." When they have done all this, they go out again singing.*

JULIE *enters, alone; sees the mess in the kitchen; strikes her hands together; then she takes out her powder puff and powders her face.*

JEAN (*enters; excited*): There you see, my lady! And you heard them! Do you think we can possibly stay here?

JULIE: No! I don't think so! But what are we going to do?

JEAN: Flee, travel, far from here!

JULIE: Travel? Yes, but where?

JEAN: To Switzerland, to the Italian lakes. You've never been there?

JULIE: No! Is it beautiful there?

JEAN: An eternal summer—oranges, laurels—marvelous!

JULIE: But what shall we do there afterward?

JEAN: I'll set up a hotel with first-class wares and first-class guests.

JULIE: A hotel?

JEAN: That's really living, believe me: always new faces, new languages; not a moment free for brooding or nerves; no looking for something to do—the work's there: night and day bells ringing, trains whistling, buses coming and going—gold coins rolling in all the time. That's living!

JULIE: Yes, that's living! But what about me?

JEAN: You'll be the mistress of the house; the ornament of the firm!

With your looks . . . and your ways—Oh—it'll be a success—we
can take that for granted! Colossal! You'll sit like a queen in the
office and set your slaves going by pressing a button; the guests
will march by your throne and shyly place their offerings on your
table—you'd never believe how people tremble when they get
their bills—I'll salt the bills, and you'll sweeten them with your
most beautiful smile—let's get away from here—(*Takes a train
timetable from his pocket.*)—Right away, on the next train!—
We'll be in Malmö at half past six; at Hamburg at 8:40 tomorrow
morning; Frankfurt-Basel, in a day, and in Como by way of the
Gotthard tunnel in—let's see, three days. Three days!

JULIE: All that's fine! But, Jean—you must give me courage—Say
that you love me! Come and embrace me!

JEAN (*hesitant*): I want to—but I don't dare! Not in this house
any more. I love you—no doubt of that—can you doubt that,
my lady?

JULIE (*shyly, in a genuinely feminine way*): My lady!—Say Julie!
There aren't any barriers between us any more!—Say Julie!

JEAN (*tortured*): I can't!—There are still barriers between us as
long as we stay in this house—there's the past, there's the count
—I've never met anyone for whom I have any more respect—all
I have to do to feel small is to see his gloves lying on a chair—I
only need to hear his bell up there to shy like a frightened horse
—and now when I see his boots standing there, erect and self-
confident, shivers run up and down my back! (*Kicks the boots*)
Superstition, prejudices, they taught us in childhood—but that
one can forget just as easily. If I just get to another country, to a
republic, they'll bow low before my porter's livery—they're to
bow low, see!—but I'm not going to! I wasn't born to bow low,
for I have what it takes, I have character, and if I can only reach
the first branch, you'll see me climb! I'm a servant today, but
next year I'll be a proprietor, in ten years I'll be a man of means,
and then I'll take a trip to Rumania, get myself decorated, and
can—note carefully, I say *can*—end up as a count!

JULIE: Wonderful, wonderful!

JEAN: In Rumania a person buys the title of count, and you'll be a countess just the same! My countess!

JULIE: What do I care about all that, that I'm now leaving behind me!—Say that you love me; otherwise—well, what am I otherwise?

JEAN: I'll tell you a thousand times—afterward! but not here! And, above all, no emotional outbursts, if everything's not to be lost. We have to look at this coolly, like sensible people. (*Takes up a cigar, snips off its end, and lights it*) Sit down there, and I'll sit here, and we'll talk things over as if nothing had happened.

JULIE (*in despair*): My God, my God! Don't you have any feelings?

JEAN: I! There isn't a human being who's so full of feeling as I, but I can control myself.

JULIE: A little while ago you could kiss my shoe—and now!

JEAN (*harshly*): Well, that was then! Now we have other things to think about.

JULIE: Don't speak harshly to me!

JEAN: No, but sensibly! A foolish thing has been committed. Don't commit more! The count can be here any time, and we have to decide our future before he gets here. What do you think of my plans for the future? Do you approve of them?

JULIE: They seem quite acceptable, but there's one question. There'll have to be capital for such a big undertaking. Do you have it?

JEAN (*chewing his cigar*): I? Absolutely! I have my skills, my excellent experience, my knowledge of languages! That's capital that will do, I should think!

JULIE: But you can't buy even a railroad ticket with it!

JEAN: That's true, of course; that's why I'm looking for a partner who can supply the funds!

JULIE: Where can you find one right now?

JEAN: You're to find him if you want to be my partner.

JULIE: I can't, and I don't own anything myself. (*Pause*)

JEAN: Then the whole project's off . . .

JULIE: And . . .

JEAN: Things will be as they are!

JULIE: Do you think I'll stay under this roof as your mistress? Do you think I'll let the people point their fingers at me? Do you think I can look my father in the eye after this? No! Take me away from here, from shame and dishonor!—My God, what have I done? (*Weeps*)

JEAN: There, there, so that's the tune now!—What you have done? The same as many before you!

JULIE (*screams convulsively*): And now you despise me!—I'm falling, I'm falling!

JEAN: Fall down to me; then I'll raise you up!

JULIE: What terrible power drew me to you? The weak to the strong? The falling to the rising! Or was it love? This . . . love? Do you know what love is?

JEAN: I? Yes, I certainly do! Do you think I've never been in on this before?

JULIE: What a language you speak, and what thoughts you think!

JEAN: That's what I've learned, and that's how I am! Don't get nervous now, and don't act refined, for now you're no better than I!—There, there, my girl, come here and I'll offer you a glass of fine wine! (*Opens the drawer in the table and takes out the bottle of wine; fills two used glasses*)

JULIE: Where did you get that wine?

JEAN: From the cellar.

JULIE: My father's burgundy!

JEAN: Won't that do for his son-in-law?

JULIE: And I drink beer! I!

JEAN: That only proves your taste is worse than mine.

JULIE: Thief!

JEAN: Are you going to tattle?

JULIE: My God! The accomplice of a house thief! Have I been intoxicated, have I been sleepwalking tonight? Midsummer night! The festival of innocent games . . .

JEAN: Innocent, hm!

JULIE (*walks back and forth*): Is there anyone on earth as unfortunate as I at this moment?

JEAN: Why are you? After such a conquest? Think of Kristin in there! Don't you think she has feelings, too?

JULIE: I did, but I don't any more! No, a servant is a servant . . .

JEAN: And a whore is a whore!

JULIE (*on her knees with clasped hands*): Oh, God in heaven, end my miserable life! Take me away from this filth, into which I am sinking! Save me! Save me!

JEAN: I can't deny I pity you! When I lay among the bulbs and saw you in the rose garden . . . I'll tell you now . . . I had the same nasty thoughts all boys have.

JULIE: And you wanted to die for me!

JEAN: In the oats bin? That was just talk.

JULIE: A lie, you mean!

JEAN (*beginning to get sleepy*): Just about! I think I read in a newspaper the story of a chimney sweep who lay down in a woodbox with heaps of lilacs because he had been sued in a paternity case . . .

JULIE: So, that's what you're like . . .

JEAN: What was I going to say? Why, you always have to use a line to catch women!

JULIE: Scoundrel!

JEAN: *Merde!*

JULIE: And now you've seen the hawk's back . . .

JEAN: Well, not exactly the *back* . . .

JULIE: And I was to be the first branch . . .

JEAN: But the branch was rotten . . .

JULIE: I was to be the sign on the hotel . . .

JEAN: And I the hotel . . .

JULIE: Sit behind your counter, attract your guests, falsify your bills . . .

JEAN: I was going to do that myself . . .

JULIE: That a human soul can be so thoroughly filthy!

JEAN: Wash it, then!

JULIE: Lackey, servant, stand up when I'm speaking!

JEAN: Servant's mistress, lackey's slut, shut your mouth and get out of here. Are you accusing me of being coarse? As coarsely as you've behaved tonight, none of the likes of me would have behaved. Do you think any maid accosts a man as you did? Have you ever seen a girl of my class offer herself in that way? I've seen the like only among animals and fallen women!

JULIE (*crushed*): That's right! Strike me, trample on me—I don't deserve anything better. I am a wretch, but help me! Help me get out of this if there's any possibility!

JEAN (*more gently*): I don't want to shame myself by denying my share in the seduction, but do you imagine anyone in my position would have dared to have looked at you that way if you hadn't issued the invitation yourself? I'm still amazed . . .

JULIE: And proud . . .

JEAN: Why not? Though I must admit that the victory was too easy to really go to my head.

JULIE: Go on—strike me!

JEAN (*gets up*): No! Forgive me for what I've said. I don't strike anyone who's defenseless, least of all a woman. I can't deny that, on one hand, it delights me to have found out it's only false gold that has blinded us down below, to have seen that the hawk was only gray on his back, that it was powder on the smooth cheek, and that there was dirt under the manicured nails, that the handkerchief was filthy though it smelled of perfume . . . ! But it hurts me, on the other hand, to have seen that what I have been struggling for wasn't anything higher, more solid; it hurts me to see you fallen so low you're far below your own cook; it hurts me in the same way as when I see autumn flowers torn to shreds by the rain and changed into filth.

JULIE: You talk as if you were already above me.

JEAN: I am: you see, I can make you a countess, but you can never make me a count.

JULIE: But I was born of a count, and that you never can be!

JEAN: That's true, but I can become the father of counts—if . . .

JULIE: But you're a thief; I'm not.

JEAN: A thief isn't the worst! There are worse people! And besides:
when I serve in a house, I consider myself a member of the family in a way, as a child of the house, and people don't consider it
stealing if a child takes a berry from a loaded bush! (*His passion
is again aroused.*) Lady Julie, you're a splendid woman, alto-
gether too good for someone like me! You're the victim of intoxi-
cation, and you want to conceal the error by pretending you love
me! You don't, unless my looks attract you—then your love
isn't any better than mine—but I can never be satisfied by being
simply an animal to you, and I can never awaken your love.

JULIE: Are you sure of that?

JEAN: You're trying to say it's possible!—I'd be able to love you
—without a doubt! You're beautiful, you're refined—(*comes up
to her and takes her hand*)—educated, charming when you want
to be, and the flame you've aroused in a man will surely never
be put out. (*Puts his arm about her waist*) You're like warmed
wine with strong spices, and a kiss from you . . . (*He tries to
lead her out, but she slowly tears herself loose.*)

JULIE: Leave me!—you won't win me in that way!

JEAN: *How* then?—Not in that way! No caresses and sweet words;
not through thought for the future, not through saving you from
shame! *How* then?

JULIE: How? How? I don't know—in no way!—I despise you as
I despise rats, but I can't escape you!

JEAN: Escape with me!

JULIE (*straightens up*): Escape? Yes, we must—But I'm so tired!
Give me a glass of wine!

  (JEAN *pours.*)

JULIE (*looks at her watch*): But we're going to talk first! We still
have a little time (*Empties her glass; holds it out for more*)

JEAN: Don't drink so much—you'll get drunk!

JULIE: Would that matter?

JEAN: Would that matter! It's vulgar to get drunk!—What did you
want to say to me?

JULIE: We must escape! But we must talk first; that is, I'm going to talk, for you're the only one who's done the talking so far. You've told me about your life; now I'll tell you about mine so we'll know each other thoroughly before we begin our wandering together.

JEAN: One minute! Excuse me! Be sure you won't regret it afterward when you've revealed secrets that can be held over you!

JULIE: Aren't you my friend?

JEAN: Yes, sometimes! But don't rely on me.

JULIE: You're just saying that—besides, everybody knows my secrets anyway.—You see, Mother was not a noblewoman by birth but came from a very humble family. She was brought up to believe the ideas of her time about equality, the emancipation of women, and all that; and she was decidedly opposed to marriage. When Father proposed to her, she said she'd never want to be his wife, but . . . he could be her lover. He told her he didn't want the woman he loved to be less respected than he. When she explained she cared nothing about what people thought, and under the influence of his passion, he accepted her offer. But then he was ostracized, was limited to his life with her, and that wasn't enough for him. I was born—against my mother's wish, according to what I've been able to understand. I was to be brought up by my mother as a child of nature, and to top that even learn everything a boy gets to learn so I'd be an example of how a woman is just as good as a man. I was dressed like a boy, I had to learn to look after horses but not to work in the barn; I had to curry and harness horses and go hunting; I even had to learn how to butcher. That was horrible! And on the estate the men were given the women's jobs and the women the men's—with the result that the property almost was ruined and we became the butt of ridicule in the whole neighborhood. Finally Father must have awakened from his enchantment, and he rebelled so that everything was changed according to his wishes. So they were married quietly. Mother got ill—what was wrong, I don't know—but she often had convulsions, hid in the

attic and in the orchard, and could stay out-of-doors all night.
Then came the big fire you've heard them talk about. The house,
the stables, and the barn burned up—under circumstances that
hinted at arson, for the misfortune happened the day after the
quarterly insurance expired, and the premium that had been
sent in by Father had been delayed through the carelessness of
the messenger so it didn't get there in time. (*She fills the glass
and drinks.*)

JEAN: Don't drink any more!

JULIE: Oh, what does that matter?—We were penniless and had to
sleep in the carriages. Father didn't know where he'd get the
money for rebuilding. He had neglected his old friends, so they
had forgotten him. Then Mother advised him to borrow from a
friend she'd had since she was young, a brick manufacturer in
the neighborhood. Father borrowed, but wasn't allowed to pay
any interest—that amazed him. So the buildings were restored!
—(*Drinks again*) Do you know who set the fire?

JEAN: The countess, your mother!

JULIE: Do you know who the brick manufacturer was?

JEAN: Your mother's lover?

JULIE: Do you know whose money it was?

JEAN: Just a minute—no, I don't!

JULIE: It was my mother's!

JEAN: Consequently the count's if there hadn't been any premarital
agreement?

JULIE: There wasn't any agreement!—Mother had a little fortune
she didn't want Father to manage so she invested it with—her
friend.

JEAN: Who stole it!

JULIE: Absolutely right! He kept it!—Father learned about all
this; he couldn't sue, couldn't pay his wife's lover; couldn't prove
it was his wife's money!—That was Mother's revenge for Father's taking over the power on the estate.—He almost committed
suicide that time!—There were rumors he had tried to shoot
himself but had failed! But he recovered, and Mother had to

pay for her acts! Those were five terrible years for me, you may believe! I loved Father, but I took Mother's part, because I didn't know the facts. She had taught me to suspect and hate men—because she hated men, as you've heard—and I swore to her I'd never be any man's slave.

JEAN: So you got engaged to the sheriff!

JULIE: For this reason—he'd become my slave.

JEAN: And he didn't want to?

JULIE: He wanted to, all right, but I didn't let him! I got tired of him!

JEAN: I saw what happened—in the stable yard.

JULIE: What did you see?

JEAN: What I saw—how he broke the engagement.

JULIE: That's a lie! I was the one who broke it! Has he said he did, the scoundrel?

JEAN: He wasn't a scoundrel, I suspect! You hate men, my lady?

JULIE: Yes!—Usually! But sometimes—when my weakness comes over me, when nature makes me wild with desire—Oh, the shame of it—that the fire never dies!

JEAN: So you hate me, too?

JULIE: Absolutely! I'd like to have you killed like an animal . . .

JEAN: The criminal's to be sentenced to two years at hard labor, and the animal killed! Isn't that it?*

JULIE: Exactly!

JEAN: But there isn't any prosecutor now—and no animal! What are we going to do?

JULIE: Leave!

JEAN: To torture each other to death?

JULIE: No—to enjoy life, two days, eight days, as long as one can enjoy it and then—die . . .

JEAN: Die! That's stupid! Starting a hotel would be a lot better!

JULIE (*without listening to* JEAN): . . . on Lake Como, where the

---

*Tidelag: an unnatural act; sexual intercourse between a human being and a lower animal. From an aristocratic point of view: Julie and Jean.

sun always shines, where the laurels are green at Christmastime and the oranges glow.

JEAN: Lake Como's a rainy hole, and the only oranges I saw there were in the stores; but it's a good place for foreigners—there are a lot of houses that can be rented to couples in love, and that's a business that really pays off.—Do you know why—? Well, they sign a contract for six months—and they leave after three weeks!

JULIE (*naïvely*): Why after three weeks?

JEAN: They quarrel, of course! But the rent has to be paid all the same! And then the house is rented again. And so it goes on and on, for there's plenty of love—though it doesn't last very long!

JULIE: You don't want to die with me?

JEAN: I don't want to die at all! Both because I like living and because I think suicide's a sin against Providence, which has given us life.

JULIE: *You* believe in God?

JEAN: Of course I do! And I go to church every other Sunday.— Frankly, I'm tired of all this—I'm going to bed.

JULIE: So! You think I'll be satisfied with that? Do you know what a man owes a woman he's ruined?

JEAN (*takes his purse and throws a silver coin on the table*): There you are! I don't want to be in debt!

JULIE (*pretending not to notice the insult*): Do you know what the law provides . . .

JEAN: Unfortunately the law doesn't provide any punishment for a woman who seduces a man!

JULIE: Do you see any way out of this other than leaving, getting married, and getting divorced?

JEAN: And if I refuse to enter the misalliance?

JULIE: Misalliance . . .

JEAN: Yes, for me! You see I have finer ancestors than you, for I haven't any arsonist in my family!

JULIE: Can you know that?

JEAN: You can't know I do, for we don't have any family records

—except with the police! But I've read about your family tree in a book on the drawing-room table. Do you know who the founder of your family was? A miller who let the king sleep with his wife one night during the Danish war. I don't have ancestors like that! I don't have any ancestors at all, but I can become an ancestor!

JULIE: That's what I get for confiding in someone unworthy, because I've given my family's honor . . .

JEAN: Dishonor!—Well, you see, I told you! One shouldn't drink, for then one starts talking! And one should *not* talk!

JULIE: Oh, how I regret all this! How I regret all this!—If you at least loved me!

JEAN: For the last time: What do you mean? Shall I weep, shall I jump over your whip, shall I kiss you, shall I fool you into going to Lake Como for three weeks, and . . . What shall I do? What do you want? This is getting painful! But that's how it is when one sticks his nose in women's business! Lady Julie, I see you're unhappy, I know you're suffering, but I can't understand you. We commoners don't have notions like that; we don't hate each other! Love is a game for us when work gives us time to play at it, but we don't have time all day and all night as you do! I think you're sick, and your mother must have been crazy; why, whole parishes have gone crazy through reading the Bible, and that nonsense about women that's raging now *is* a sort of religion.

JULIE: Be good to me—now you're talking as if you were a human being.

JEAN: Yes, but be human yourself! You spit on me, and you don't let me wipe it off—on you!

JULIE: Help me, help me! Just tell me what I should do—where I should go?

JEAN: Good God, if I only knew!

JULIE: I have been beside myself, I have been mad, but isn't there any way out?

JEAN: Stay here—take it calmly! No one knows anything.

JULIE: Impossible! The people know—Kristin knows!

JEAN: They don't know, and they could never believe anything like that!

JULIE (*slowly*): But—it could happen again!

JEAN: That's true!

JULIE: And the consequences?

JEAN (*frightened*): The consequences!—Why hadn't I thought of them? Well, then there's only one thing—to leave! Right away! I won't go along; then everything would be lost, but you have to go alone—away—anywhere at all!

JULIE: Alone? Where?—I can't!

JEAN: You have to! And before the count comes back! If you stay, you know what will happen. If you've made a mistake once, you want to go on since the damage has already been done . . . Then you get more and more daring and—at last you're found out. So: leave! Then write to the count later on, confessing everything except that it was I. And he can't guess that. I don't think he'd ever be anxious to find out.

JULIE: I'll go if you come along!

JEAN: Are you crazy, woman? Lady Julie eloping with her servant! It'd be in the papers the day after tomorrow, and the count would never live through it!

JULIE: I can't go! I can't stay! Help me! I'm so tired, so thoroughly tired.—Command me! Set me going, for I can't think any more; I can't act any more . . . !

JEAN: You see? What miserable creatures you are! Why do you draw yourselves up, stick your noses in the air as if you were the lords of creation? Well, I'll command you! Go up—get dressed; get money for traveling and then come down!

JULIE (*softly*): Come with me!

JEAN: To your room?—Now you're crazy again! (*Hesitates for a moment*) No! Go—right now! (*Takes her hand and conducts her out*)

JULIE (*while she's going*): Speak gently to me, Jean!

JEAN: An order always sounds harsh! Learn that right now! (*He returns alone; draws a sigh of relief; sits down at the table; takes*

up a notebook and pen; counts out loud now and then; silent play
of features until KRISTIN enters, dressed for church, with a false
shirt front and a white tie in her hand.)

KRISTIN: Good Lord, what a mess! What have you been up to in
here?

JEAN: Oh, it was Lady Julie who dragged in the people. Did you
sleep so hard you didn't hear anything?

KRISTIN: I've slept like a log!

JEAN: And already dressed for church?

KRISTIN: Yes! You promised to go with me to communion today!

JEAN: Yes, I did, didn't I? And there you have the shroud! Well,
come on then! (*Sits down.* KRISTIN *begins to put on him the
shirt front and the white tie. Pause*)

JEAN (*sleepily*): What's the text today?

KRISTIN: It's about the beheading of John the Baptist, I imagine.

JEAN: Then it'll be terribly long!—Ouch, you're choking me!—Oh,
how sleepy I am!

KRISTIN: Well, what have you been doing staying up all night?
Why, you're green in your face.

JEAN: I've been sitting here talking with Lady Julie.

KRISTIN: That woman certainly doesn't know what's proper!
(*Pause*)

JEAN: Listen, Kristin!

KRISTIN: Yes-s?

JEAN: It's strange all the same when one thinks it over.—She!

KRISTIN: What's so strange?

JEAN: Everything! (*Pause*)

KRISTIN (*looks at the half-empty glasses on the table*): Have you
been drinking together, too?

JEAN: Yes!

KRISTIN: For shame!—Look me in the eyes!

JEAN: Yes!

KRISTIN: Is it possible? *Is* it possible?

JEAN (*after considering*): Yes! It is!

KRISTIN: *Usch!* I never could have believed *that!* No, no. *Usch!*

JEAN: You're not jealous of her, I hope?

KRISTIN: No, not of her! If it had been Clara or Sofi, I'd have scratched your eyes out!—Well, that's how it is; why I don't know.—No, that was nasty!

JEAN: Are you angry with her, then?

KRISTIN: No, but with you! That was badly done, very badly! Poor girl!—No, you know what? I don't want to be in this house any longer—when you can't respect the family any more.

JEAN: Why should we respect them?

KRISTIN: Well, you tell me—you're so clever! But you surely don't want to work for people who behave indecently? Huh? One gets disgraced oneself by doing that, I think.

JEAN: Yes, but it's a comfort for us that the rest aren't a bit better than we!

KRISTIN: No, I don't feel like that—if they aren't better, there's nothing to strive for.—And think of the count! Think of him who's had so much grief in his days! No, I don't want to stay in this house any longer!—And with somebody like you! If it had been the sheriff; if it had been a better man . . .

JEAN: What's that?

KRISTIN: Yes, yes! You're no doubt fine in yourself, but there's a difference between people all the same.—No, I'll never be able to forget this.—Lady Julie, who's been so proud, so arrogant about men so one would never have believed she'd give herself— and to someone like you! She who was about to have poor Diana shot because she was running after the gatekeeper's mutt!—Yes, I do declare!—But I don't want to stay on here any longer, and on October 24 I'll move.

JEAN: And afterward?

KRISTIN: Well, since we're talking about that, it's about time you looked for something, since we're going to get married.

JEAN: Well, what would I look for? If I'm married, I can't get a place like this.

KRISTIN: No, that's clear! You can take a job as porter, I suppose, or try to get a place as caretaker in some government office or

other. Government wages are low, but you'd have security, and
then the wife and children get a pension . . .

JEAN (*grimacing*): All that's fine, but it's not my style to begin
thinking of dying for wife and children. I'll have to admit I really
had a somewhat higher ambition.

KRISTIN: Your ambition, yes! You have obligations, too! Think of
those!

JEAN: Don't irritate me by talking about obligations; I know what
I have to do! (*Listening*) We've plenty of time to think this over.
Go in and get ready, and we'll go to church.

KRISTIN: Who's wandering about up there?

JEAN: I don't know . . . maybe it's Clara.

KRISTIN (*going*): It surely can't be the count, come home without
anyone's hearing him.

JEAN (*frightened*): The count? No, it can't be—he would most
likely have rung.

KRISTIN (*goes*): Well, God help us! I've never been in on anything
like this.

(*The sun has risen and is shining on the treetops in the park;
the glow moves slowly until it falls in through the windows.* JEAN
goes to the door and signals. LADY JULIE *enters, dressed for traveling and carrying a little bird cage covered by a handkerchief.
She puts the cage on a chair.*)

JULIE: I'm ready!

JEAN: Sh-h! Kristin is awake!

JULIE (*extremely nervous in the following*): Did she suspect anything?

JEAN: She doesn't know anything about it! But, good God, what
you look like!

JULIE: What? What's wrong?

JEAN: You're as pale as a ghost and—excuse me—your face is
dirty.

JULIE: Let me wash up, then!—There! (*She goes to the hand basin;
washes her face and hands.*) Give me a towel!—Oh—it's the sun
rising!

JEAN: And then the troll bursts!

JULIE: Yes, it's the trolls that have been out tonight!—But, Jean, listen! Come along—I have the money now!

JEAN (*hesitantly*): Enough?

JULIE: Enough to start with! Come along, for I can't travel alone today. Imagine: Midsummer Day, on a stuffy train, packed in with crowds of people, who'll stare at me; standing still at stations when one would like to fly! No, I can't, I can't! And then come my memories: childhood memories of midsummer days with the church decorated with birch leaves and lilacs; dinner with the table beautifully set, relatives, friends; the afternoon in the park, dancing, music, flowers, and games! Oh, one runs away, but one's memories will follow in the baggage car . . . and remorse and pangs of conscience!

JEAN: I'll go along—but right now before it's too late. This minute!

JULIE: Get dressed, then! (*Takes the bird cage*)

JEAN: But no baggage! Then we'll be found out!

JULIE: No, nothing! Only what we can have in the compartment!

JEAN (*has taken his hat*): What do you have there? What is it?

JULIE: It's only my finch. I don't want to leave her!

JEAN: There we are! Are we going to have a bird cage along? Why, you're crazy! Let go the cage!

JULIE: The only thing I'm taking along from my home; the only living being who likes me, since Diana was faithless to me. Don't be cruel! Let me take it along!

JEAN: Put the cage down, I say—and don't talk so loudly—Kristin'll hear us!

JULIE: No, I won't leave her in strangers' hands! Kill it rather than that!

JEAN: Give me the creature then, and I'll twist its neck!

JULIE: Yes, but don't hurt her! Don't . . . No, I can't!

JEAN: Give it to me; I can!

JULIE (*takes the bird out of the cage and kisses it*): Dear little Serena, are you going to die and leave your mistress?

JEAN: Please don't make a scene! This is a matter of your life, your welfare! There, quickly! (*Grabs the bird, carries it to the chopping block, and picks up the kitchen axe.* LADY JULIE *turns away.*) You should have learned to butcher chickens instead of shooting revolvers—(*chops off the bird's head with one blow*) —and you wouldn't have fainted at the sight of a drop of blood!

JULIE (*screams*): Kill me, too! Kill me! You who can kill an innocent animal without trembling. Oh, I hate and despise you— there's blood between us! I curse the moment I saw you; I curse the moment I came alive in my mother's womb!

JEAN: Well, what good does your cursing do? Go!

JULIE (*approaches the chopping block, as if drawn to it in spite of herself*): No, I don't want to go yet; I can't . . . I have to see . . . sh-h, there's a carriage out there—(*Listens, while she keeps her eyes fixed on the block and the axe*). Don't you think that I can bear the sight of blood? Do you think I'm that weak . . . Oh—I'd like to see your blood, your brain on a block—I'd like to see everything that makes you a man swimming in a lake like that . . . I think I could drink out of your skull, I'd like to bathe my feet in your chest, and I could eat your roasted heart!—You think I'm weak; you think I love you because the fruit of my womb desired your seed; you think I want to carry your offspring under my heart and nourish it with my blood—bear your child and take your name! Listen, you, what is your name? I've never heard your family name—I suppose you don't have any. I'd become Mrs. Gatehouse—or Mrs. Garbagepile—you dog—you carry my collar, you servant—you carry my coat of arms on your buttons—I share you with my cook! be my maid's rival! Oh!— you think I'm weak and want to run away! No, now I'm staying —and let the thunder roll! Father will come home . . . find his writing desk broken open . . . his money gone! Then he'll ring— on that bell—twice for his valet— and then he'll send for the police—then I'll tell everything! Everything! Oh, it will be wonderful to have it over with—just so it is over! Then he'll get a stroke and die! . . Then we'll all be gone—and there'll be calm . . . peace! . . . eternal rest! And his escutcheon will be crushed on his coffin—the count's family will have died out—and the valet's family goes on in an orphanage . . . wins its laurels in the gutters and ends up in prison!

JEAN: That's the royal blood speaking! Fine, Lady Julie! Just stuff the miller into the sack now.

(KRISTIN *comes in, fully dressed for church and carrying a psalmbook in her hand.*)

JULIE (*hurries up to her and falls into her arms as if seeking protection*): Help me, Kristin! Help me against this man!

KRISTIN (*immovable and cold*): What sort of nonsense is this on Sunday morning? (*Looks at the chopping block*) And what a mess you've made here!—What's the meaning of all this? And all your screaming and noise?

JULIE: Kristin, you're a woman, and you're my friend! Watch out for this wretch!

JEAN (*a little shy and embarrassed*): While you ladies are talking things over, I'll go in and shave! (*Steals out to the right*)

JULIE: You must understand me, and you must listen to me!

KRISTIN: No, I don't really understand sluttish behavior like this! Where are you going—dressed for traveling—and he had his hat on—eh?—eh?

JULIE: Listen to me, Kristin; listen to me and I'll tell you everything—

KRISTIN: I don't want to know anything . . .

JULIE: You must listen to me . . .

KRISTIN: What's it about? Is it about that foolishness with Jean? Well, see, I don't care about that at all, for I won't interfere about that. But if you try to fool him into skipping out, I'll put a stop to that!

JULIE (*extremely nervous*): Try to be calm, Kristin, and listen to me! I can't stay here, and Jean can't stay here—so we have to leave . . .

KRISTIN: Hm, hm!

JULIE (*brightening*): But, you know, I just got an idea—what if we should go abroad, all three of us—to Switzerland and set up a hotel together.—I have money, you see—and Jean and I would be in charge of the whole project—and you, I thought, would take the kitchen . . . Wouldn't that be fine!—Say yes! And come with us; then everything will be arranged!—Say yes! Do! (*Embraces Kristin and pats her*)

KRISTIN (*cold; speculating*): Hm, hm!

JULIE (*presto tempo*): You have never traveled, Kristin—you must get out and look about in the world. You can't imagine how much fun it is to travel on a train—new people all the time— new countries—and we'll get to Hamburg and take a look at the zoological gardens in passing—you'd like that—and we'll go to the theater and the opera—and when we get to Munich, we'll have the museums, and there are Rubens and Raphael, the great painters as you know—Why, you've heard about Munich where King Ludwig lived—the king who became insane.—And we'll see his castles—he still has castles that are furnished just as in fairy tales—and it's not far from there to Switzerland—with the Alps—imagine the Alps with snow in the middle of summer— and there grow oranges and laurels, which stay green all year round—

(JEAN *can be seen in the right wing, sharpening his razor on a strop which he holds with his teeth and his left hand; listens with satisfaction to the conversation and nods in agreement now and then.*)

JULIE (*tempo prestissimo*):—And there we'll run a hotel—and I'll sit at the cash register, while Jean receives the guests . . . goes out shopping . . . writes letters—It will be a life, you may be sure—The train whistle will blow, then the bus will come, and the telephone will ring in the apartment, and then in the restaurant—and I'll make out the bills—and I *can* salt them . . . you can't believe how shy travelers are when they're going to pay the bill!—And you—you'll be the lady of the kitchen.—Of course, you won't be working at the stove yourself.—And you'll have to be nicely and neatly dressed when you're to see people—and with your looks—I'm not flattering you—you'll be able to catch

a man one fine day! A rich Englishman, you see—that kind of
person it's so easy to . . . (*slows down*)—catch—and then we'll
get rich—and build a villa on Lake Como—Oh, it rains there
now and then—but—(*subsiding*)—and the sun must shine
sometimes—though it looks so dark—and if not we can go home
—and come back—(*pause*)—here—or somewhere else—

KRISTIN: Listen! Do you believe all that yourself, Lady Julie?

JULIE (*crushed*): Do I believe it myself?

KRISTIN: Yes!

JULIE (*wearily*): I don't know; I don't believe in anything any
more. (*She collapses on the bench; puts her head between her
arms on the table.*) Nothing! Nothing at all!

KRISTIN (*turns to the right where* JEAN *is standing*): So you were
going to run away?

JEAN (*crestfallen, puts his razor on the table*): Run away? That's
not quite right! You heard Lady Julie's project, and though she's
tired after being up all night, the project can very well be carried
out!

KRISTIN: Listen to him! Did you intend I should be the cook for
that creature . . .

JEAN (*sharply*): Please use decent language when you talk to your
mistress! You understand?

KRISTIN: Mistress!

JEAN: Yes!

KRISTIN: Listen! Listen to him!

JEAN: Yes, you listen, you need to, and talk a little less! Lady Julie
is your mistress, and for the same reason you despise her, you
ought to despise yourself!

KRISTIN: I've always had so much respect for myself—

JEAN: —that you could be disrespectful of others!—

KRISTIN: —so I've never lowered myself below my class. You
can't say the count's cook has had anything to do with the stableman or the swineherd! Can you?

JEAN: Yes, you've had to do with a fine man; that's lucky for you!

KRISTIN: Yes, it's a fine man who sells the count's oats from the stable—

JEAN: You're the one to talk—you get your cut from storekeepers and take bribes from the butcher!

KRISTIN: What's that?

JEAN: And you can't respect your employers any more! *You!*

KRISTIN: Are you coming along to church? You could use a good sermon after what you've done!

JEAN: No, I'm not going to church today! You'll have to go alone to confess what you have been up to!

KRISTIN: Yes, I'll do that, and I'll come home with enough forgiveness to do for you, too! The Saviour suffered and died on the cross for all our sins, and, if we come to Him with faith and a penitent spirit, He will take all our sins upon Himself.

JEAN: Your grocery sins, too?

JULIE: Do you believe that, Kristin?

KRISTIN: It's my living faith, as surely as I'm standing here, and it's my childhood faith that I've always kept, Lady Julie. And where sin overflows, grace overflows!

JULIE: If I only had your faith! If I only . . .

KRISTIN: Yes, but you see, you can't get that without God's special grace, and it's not given to all to get that—

JULIE: Who gets it, then?

KRISTIN: That is the great secret of grace, Lady Julie, and God has no consideration for the person, but there the last shall be the first . . .

JULIE: Yes, doesn't He have consideration for the last, then?

KRISTIN (*continues*): . . . and it is easier for a camel to go through a needle's eye than for a rich man to enter into Heaven! You see, that's how it is, Lady Julie. Now I'm going—alone, and when I go by, I'll tell the stableman not to let anyone take any horses if anyone should want to leave before the count gets home!— Good-bye! (*Goes*)

JEAN: What a devil!—And all this because of a finch!—

JULIE (*dully*): Let the finch be!—Do you see any way out, out of this, some end to this?

JEAN (*thinking*): No!

JULIE: What would you do if you were in my place?

JEAN: In yours? Wait a minute!—As a noblewoman, as a woman, as—a fallen woman. I don't know—yes, now I know!

JULIE (*takes a razor and makes a gesture*): Like this?

JEAN: Yes!—But I wouldn't do it—note that: for there's a difference between us!

JULIE: Because you're a man and I'm a woman? What sort of difference is that?

JEAN: The same difference—as—between a man and a woman!

JULIE (*with the razor in her hand*): I want to! But I can't!—My father couldn't either, the time he should have done it.

JEAN: No, he shouldn't have! He had to get his revenge first!

JULIE: And now Mother's getting her revenge again, through me.

JEAN: Haven't you loved your father, Lady Julie?

JULIE: Yes, very, very much, but I must have hated him, too! I must have without being aware of it! But he's the one who brought me up to despise my own sex, who made me a half-woman and a half-man! Whose was the blame for what has happened? My father's, my mother's, my own? My own? Why, I haven't anything that's my own! I haven't a thought I haven't got from my father, not a passion I haven't got from my mother, and the last—that notion all people are alike—I got that from my fiancé—whom I therefore call a scoundrel! How can it be my own fault? Push the guilt on Jesus as Kristin did—no, I'm too proud and too sensible—thanks be to my father's teaching—And that a rich man can't get into Heaven, that's a lie, and at least Kristin, who has money in the bank, won't get in! Whose is the fault?—What does it matter to us whose fault it is! It's still I who'll have to bear the guilt, bear the consequences . . .

JEAN: Yes, but—

(*The bell rings sharply twice.* LADY JULIE *leaps up;* JEAN *changes his coat.*)

JEAN: The count is home! Imagine if Kristin—(*Goes to the speaking tube; knocks; and listens*)

JULIE: Now he has been at his desk?

JEAN: This is Jean, sir! (*Listens. The audience cannot hear the count.*) Yes, sir! (*Listens*) Yes, sir! (*Listens*) Yes, right away. In half an hour.

JULIE (*extremely anxious*): What did he say? Good Lord, what did he say?

JEAN: He wanted his boots and his coffee in half an hour.

JULIE: So, in half an hour! Oh, I'm tired; I'm not up to anything, not up to regretting what I've done, not run away, not stay, not live—not die! Help me now. Command me, and I'll obey like a dog! Do me this last service, save my honor, save his name! You know what I *should* want to do, but don't want to . . . You *will* it, and order me to carry it out!

JEAN: I don't know—but now I can't, either—I don't understand —It's as if this coat made it so—I can't order you—and now since the count talked to me—then—I can't explain it properly —but—it's that damn servant in me!—I think if the count came down now—and told me to cut my throat, I'd do it on the spot.

JULIE: Pretend you're he, and I'm you!—You were such a good actor a while ago when you were on your knees—then you were the aristocrat—or—haven't you ever been at the theater and watched the hypnotist? (JEAN *nods "yes."*) He says to his subject "Take the broom"; he takes it; he says, "Sweep"; and he sweeps—

JEAN: Then the other one has to be asleep!

JULIE (*ecstatically*): I'm already asleep—the whole room is like smoke to me . . . and you look like an iron stove . . . which resembles a man dressed in black and wearing a high hat—and your eyes are glowing like coals when the fire is going out—and your face is a white spot like white ashes—(*The sunlight has now reached the floor and is shining on* JEAN.) It's so warm and comfortable—(*she rubs her hands together as if she were warming them before a fire*)—and so light—and so calm!

JEAN (*takes the razor and puts it into her hand*): Here's the broom!
Go while it's light—out to the barn—and . . . (*Whispers in her
ear*)

JULIE (*awake*): Thank you! Now I'm going to my rest! But just
say—that the first can also get the gift of grace! Say it, even if
you don't believe it.

JEAN: The first? No, I can't—But wait—Lady Julie—now I know!
Why, you're no longer among the first—you're among the—last!

JULIE: That's true—I'm among the very last; I am the very last! Oh!—
But now I can't go—Tell me once more that I must go!

JEAN: No, now I can't either! I can't!

JULIE: And the first shall be the last!

JEAN: Don't think, don't think! Why, you're taking all my strength,
too, so I get weak—What! I thought the bell moved!—No! Shall
we stuff paper in it!—To be that afraid of a bell!—Yes, but it's
not only a bell—there's someone in back of it—a hand sets it
going—and something else sets the hand going—but cover your
ears—cover your ears! Well, then he'll ring still louder! will just
ring until someone answers—and then it's too late!—and then
come the police—and then—(*Two strong rings*)

JEAN (*almost collapsing; then pulling himself together*): It's terrible!
But there isn't any other answer!—Go!

   (JULIE *goes determinedly out through the door.*)

                         CURTAIN

Introduction to 'Creditors'

LITTLE EXCEPT A smattering of details can conceivably be added to the analysis of the autobiographical basis of *Creditors (Fordringsägare,* 1888) presented by the late Martin Lamm in his *Strindbergs dramer* (Stockholm: Bonnier, 1924), I, 330-48. But that analysis is frankly and almost completely an examination of the play as a reflection of Strindberg's personal idiosyncrasies, his reading, his troubles with his wife as recorded in *En dåres försvarstal (A Madman's Defense,* 1887) and elsewhere, and possible influences in his immediate environment. Illuminating as all these matters are, they can hardly fail to color any reader's interpretation of a play that must and can stand on its own merits as literature and theater for non-Swedish readers and theatergoers, who neither have access to the wealth of biographical and period background nor care particularly about the author's personal frustrations and dilemmas.

For the Strindberg scholar, it is certainly important to know that Strindberg exploited more or less accurately facts from his first marriage as he saw them and as he recorded them in highly artistic form in the novel *A Madman's Defense;* that he like many of his contemporaries was interested in hypnosis and psychiatry and their possible value for his own writing; and that he, in general, probably more than any other major writer, used himself and his environment as sources for what he wrote. For people who are particularly interested in the details of other people's lives, the autobiographical elements will remain fascinating in much the same way as the gossip columns of our newspapers.

The play itself will, however, be the concern of most theatergoers and certainly of most readers. In this introduction I shall examine the play without regard to autobiographical or other background in an attempt to discover why Herbert Grevenius' comment in the Blanche Theater program of February 2, 1938, *"Det är en bra otäck pjäs, men den är otäckt bra"* (freely translated, "It is a pretty terrible play, but it is terribly good") is particularly apt either when the play is read or when it is seen on the stage.

Creditors is a thorough application of the principles of characterization, economy of staging, compactness of structure, and naturalness of dialogue that Strindberg had advocated in the preface to *Lady Julie,* 1888. The play consists of one tightly packed act; the three major characters are complex and dynamic; the dialogue is reminiscent of that of real life, but intensified in Strindbergian fashion to fit his characters; and the staging is simplified to a minimum. Equally important is the fact that his broad theme—the relationship between man and woman within marriage—is universal and timeless.

The play emphasizes the give and take within the first and second marriages of one specific woman. It is a play deliberately conceived and composed within the framework of accounts; consequently, such terms as *creditors* (and *debtor,* by implication), *bills, payment, first mortgage, accounts, settling, tearing up bills,* and *dun* are basic. The use of terms borrowed from everyday financial transactions, startling as they may be at first glance when applied to an institution as human and complex as marriage, is a device that Strindberg exploits with harrowing effectiveness.

The three characters—a brilliant teacher of Greek and Latin (Strindberg says "dead languages"), a highly gifted and extremely sensitive artist, and a beautiful woman with some claims to achievement as a creative writer—are the very sort of people whom the world in general would find interesting and even charming. But what Strindberg does is to present them not primarily at their social best, but as they are either when all pretense and camouflage are stripped away or when pretense and camouflage are used for the attainment of deliberate ends. It becomes almost immediately clear that the play deals with the dissection of souls, as we see Gustav, the first husband, going to work on Adolf, the second husband, who does not know that his new friend is his predecessor; then Adolf attempting to make clear his condition and his Gustav-inspired analysis of his [Adolf's] marriage to Tekla; finally, Gustav going to work on Tekla.

Gustav is ideally suited to serve as the person who forces both Adolf and Tekla to examine themselves and their marriage, for Gustav—as Strindberg tells us by supplying the crucial bits of information piecemeal, when they are needed, as in life itself—is the intellectual, trained and disciplined, usually coldly rational, given to analysis and intellectual dissection of both ideas and people, and arrogantly aware of his intellectual superiority. He is self-confident about his ability to analyze others and their problems and to prescribe for them; he can "translate" what others say and has little or no doubt about the accuracy of his own analyses and the rightness of his therapy. He knows how to question, how to lead discussion, how to grope his way toward the truth; he knows how to deal with individuals.

Gustav is the consummate teacher-actor who can use both voice and manner to instill confidence and even gratitude in his subject. He gauges his approach carefully to the individual. What he has wanted to do from the beginning of his eight-day-old acquaintance with the sensitive and sick artist who has succeeded him as Tekla's husband is clear; he even defines what he will do to Adolf's wife: "But don't get frightened later when you see me cut open a human

soul and place its contents here on the table. It's terrible for beginners, but once you've seen it, you won't regret it!" Once having
instilled faith and gratitude, Gustav uses the direct approach through
skillful probing, suggestion, and even brutal frankness. He succeeds
in directing Adolf's thoughts about his art, his wife, their marriage,
and his ideals. Gustav also succeeds in taking away Adolf's illusions
about his physical state.

Gustav is, of course, no unimpeachable counselor who has merely
his subject's welfare in mind. Instead, Gustav is personally involved
(his secret wounds stemming from hurt pride and humiliation, his
loss of honor, his insatiable desire to analyze and probe, and his
human desire for revenge). To be sure, he is an effective teacher.
He does make Adolf think and come to the conclusions Gustav has
wanted. He does prescribe (sculpture instead of painting, self-
respect, contempt for his wife, examination of the facts, understanding), but in the process reduces everything Adolf has valued to
ashes and, because of his analysis of Adolf has not been perfect or
his motives pure, fails to sow successfully in the ashes. For Gustav
makes the mistake of assuming that Adolf will react as he himself
had done years before. His expression of regret over helping to
destroy Adolf is neither profound nor convincingly sincere; Strindberg obviously did not intend it to be.

Gustav's dealing with Tekla is nicely adjusted to his concept of
her. By means of flattery, a sympathetic manner, physical approach (pinching her ear while helping her adjust her earring),
deliberate belittling of himself, nicely timed frankness, a dash of
vulgarity, and lies (his planning to remarry), he quickly establishes
rapport with her, emphasized in the proposed and accepted celebration of reconciliation. But Tekla, too, has been an apt pupil; he
had, as she says, taught her to think. She proceeds to do so on the
basis of what Adolf and he have said. The result is the impressive
exposé of Tekla and both her marriages. Throughout both portions
of the play in which he appears, Gustav is revealed with ever-
increasing clarity as the creditor who is a cold-blooded and arrogant intellectual with human flaws. He has had his saving forms

of self-expression in his work and his intellectual activity; he has come close to mastering the art of self-control; he has almost succeeded in freeing himself of feelings: "That's why I can *think,* which you've rarely done, and *act,* as you've just found out." But even the self-confident Gustav is not always sure which way his subject will leap.

While Gustav has been vulnerable physically and is vulnerable in his pride, his successor is vulnerable physically, emotionally, mentally, and professionally. An abnormally sensitive artist who, although he is highly intelligent, is primarily a man of feelings and emotions, Adolf is an idealist about himself, his art, his marriage, and life. He is in a very real sense a moral man with high standards of conduct; it is he who is conscience-stricken about having "stolen" another man's wife, who believes that marriage should be a union of two people genuinely concerned about each other's welfare who do what they can to promote and protect each other. As the play amply demonstrates, he is the one who has tried to live up to his standards and in the process has been reduced to a state of physical, emotional, and mental exhaustion in which he is no longer able to function efficiently either as an artist or as a human being.

These, then, are the two men who are on stage when the play opens, but in the third speech it is clear that both are as intensely aware of Tekla as of themselves or each other. While she does not appear until one third of the play is over, she is certainly present in the thoughts and memories of both husbands; she is the one who, directly or indirectly, motivates every word and every act on the part of the two men. She is obviously the central character, a being with such great attraction and significance that they are unable to free themselves easily and permanently through, on the one hand, divorce and, on the other, therapeutic confession and counseling. Nor did the divorce result from the first husband's initiative, and the second husband does not express any determination to free himself from her but merely to change things in his marriage ("Things are going to be different").

It is with a great deal of curiosity that one looks forward to the physical appearance of a character about whom one has learned so much to her disadvantage; one wonders why the intellectual has not been able to forget her in spite of his low estimate of her and why the artist can not get along without her. To be sure, Gustav has labeled her a "cannibal," a "serpent," and a "phonograph," and Adolf has, under the guidance and encouragement of Gustav, indulged in an analysis of his marriage.

That analysis has revealed that Adolf has not previously thought much about either his wife or his marriage: "A man lives with a woman for years—he doesn't think much about her, or about their relationship—then . . . he begins to wonder—and he's in for trouble." It also reveals that he married her because he loved her; that he wanted her to be his better half; that he has helped her in many ways; that he has been tormented by thoughts of her first husband; and that he has become so obsessed with her that he depends on her, longs for her as soon as she is out of his presence, and is afraid he will lose her. It is only under Gustav's clever guidance and suggestions that he converts fairly vague feelings of uneasiness into convictions that she may be the cause of his physical, mental, and emotional exhaustion by depriving him of men friends, refusing to accept anything (particulary ideas) directly from him, pretending she has helped him, upsetting his peace of mind, forcing him to conform to her notions, and asserting her independent nature and her sexual role.

The woman who comes on stage when Gustav has set his trap (Gustav is in the adjoining room) is decidedly attractive. She is no simple character, however, but one who has mastered the social arts in their superficial forms, who carries herself well, and has the nuances of speech and manner that would stamp her for most Western people a delightfully interesting and charming woman.

She is certainly in control of the situation. Even though she and Adolf have parted in anger over a week earlier—he had called her a coquette, too old to get a lover—she indulges in behavior that for the most part can hardly be considered abnormal: she is affectionate, friendly, frank, cheerful, seductive, facetious, and playful. In other words, she behaves as many a woman does with a man whom she loves and who loves her. There is no lack of the obvious manifestations of affection, but with diabolical effectiveness Strindberg demonstrates that Kitten's ("Kurre's") display of affection has the effect on Adolf that he has already mentioned to Gustav: "Strange! I long for her, but I'm afraid of her! She caresses me, and she is tender, but there's something suffocating in her kisses, something that drains me and puts me to sleep,"

But parallel to her displays of affection is her suspicion that he has had company while she has been gone—a man who may steal him from her; her awareness that he is looking at her in a new way; and her interest in arousing his jealousy of "chaste young men," and in threatening him with unfaithfulness that will make him ridiculous. It is a scene that might come out of any marriage in which, as Strindberg says, "quarreling alternates with kissing." It is behavior that might well come out of a modern comedy of manners as Strindberg's fairly sparse stage directions suggest—*(comes in; goes directly to him and kisses him; she is friendly, open, cheerful and seductive; looks about the room as if she were looking for someone or were sniffing for something; observes him; draws him to her; he sinks down with his head in her lap; sniffing and observing; baby-talks, kisses his forehead; blithely; hits him playfully on the cheek; searchingly; goes towards him threateningly; without losing her self-control; facetiously baby-talks; puts her hands on his head and kisses him; grimaces; smiles; playfully; stretches out her arms toward him).*

Not only is she in control of the situation, but she upsets Adolf by what she says and by what she does. Not for a moment does she consider that he is obviously sick. She tortures him by her tactlessness, her admitted selfishness and egotism, her admission that she plays up to other men (her heart, she says, is so big it can hold more than one man), her suspiciousness, her abnormal demands for attention, her tendency to contradict, her threats; above all, she abuses him with the fact that he cannot talk *with* her. She has the knack of interpreting everything he says personally, of twisting whatever he says to something he never intended; it is impossible for him to hold a reasonably rational conversation with her. The scene makes clear why Adolf is emotionally, mentally, and physically exhausted and why he is professionally at loose ends.

In this highly moving and distressing scene, Strindberg pinpoints with precision why Adolf's marriage has been a failure for him—it has not been a creative union of two well-mated human beings: "But I have to admit that I, too, find it difficult to understand her. The cogs in our brains don't quite mesh. Something goes to pieces in my head when I try to understand her!" For him it has been a marriage based on idealism looking to emotional, intellectual, and physical compatibility, originating in notions that have blinded him to facts, and ending in what might be called obsession that at its very core is sexual.

But the Tekla who emerges from a close reading of this scene is no diabolic vampire who deserves the labels of "cannibal" and "serpent" that Gustav has applied to her. To be sure, she has received much from Adolf, but it has usually been voluntarily and gladly given. It is only when, as Strindberg says, he borrows someone else's eyes to see her as she is, that he can consciously draw up a bill ranging from his teaching her to swim to helping her with her writing and providing her with place and status. In fact, Tekla's vampirism consists largely of her depriving him of his men friends and taking them for herself, her indirect borrowing of his ideas, and her depriving him of his child. It is not clear that she has deliberately hurt him physically, emotionally, mentally, or professionally; that is, there is no evidence that she has ever consciously set out to injure him in any way. It is clear, however, that his potential weaknesses—ironically enough what most people, including Strindberg, would consider admirable qualities in a civilized community —have led to his unfortunate state.

For the Tekla we meet is a common enough human phenomenon. Strindberg himself has classified the type beautifully in *A Dance of Death,* II:

ALICE: Is he a man?
KURT: When you asked me that the first time I said no! Now I

think he's the most common type of human being among those who possess the earth.... Perhaps we're a little like that, too? Use people and favorable opportunities!

Tekla *has* failed as Adolf's wife because of her selfishness, her tactlessness, and her thoughtlessness; she *has* certainly helped reduce him to a state of general collapse.

As she frankly admits—Adolf, ironically enough, has taught her to be honest—she is a terrible egoist who, while she *knows* nothing about herself, *thinks* only about herself. While she does admit that she likes men and insists that there is room for many of them in her heart, there is no evidence in the play that she has been unfaithful to Adolf in act, though she has disturbed him greatly by flirting with other men. She insists that she wants to be liked by all men; she neither likes other women nor cares whether she is liked by them or not. She is frankly very much interested in sex; she resents very much the possibility that they may have to refrain from sex for six months because of Adolf's health. In fact, her measure of personal happiness in her second marriage apparently rests on the facts that Adolf has been a satisfactory sexual companion; that he has allowed her to do pretty much as she has wanted to; that he has been attentive, kind, and not very analytical about her or their relationship; and that he has provided her with an adequate number of opportunities by means of which she has been able to get satisfaction—her "creative" writing, social position, a sense of superiority, and a flattering image of herself as a woman and a writer.

In spite of all this, Tekla is not inwardly fully secure. She is afraid that she may lose Adolf; she suspects other people's motives in prescribing for Adolf or in discussing ideas with him. She resents any allusion to the fact that she is getting older. The second scene becomes a ghastly illustration of what such an attractive but essentially nonintellectual, amoral human being not only can do but will do to protect her own ego and her own world—consciously as when she occasionally threatens to make him ridiculous, but unconsciously or at least instinctively when she interprets what he says illogically, when she does everything to increase his tension without giving any indication that she understands except in an extremely superficial sense what condition he is in.

What Tekla is becomes even clearer in the third scene. Faced with her former husband without any forewarning, she quickly gains self-control, adjusts herself instinctively to his approach, but is immediately trapped by his proposal that they celebrate their reconciliation. She improvises with skill, quickly takes advantage of the opportunities his statements provide, and deliberately sets out to be charming and agreeable. But she is unpleasantly touched when he refers to her creative work (her first book had been an account of their marriage); she is embarrassed when the talk veers to her creative writing or her inner self; she is uneasy yet excited about the "farewell" party. Significantly, she admits she likes to talk with Gustav because he is broad-minded, is free from moral scruples and moralizing, and demands little of people.

But Tekla has been Gustav's pupil! On occasion she, too, can analyze. Adolf's unusual analytical scrutiny of their marriage, his echoing of some of Gustav's old ideas about art, and Gustav's sudden appearance make her conclude that Gustav has deliberately gone to work to destroy her second marriage. Her reactions are quick and instinctive. She moves to protect her ego (she is not going to be trapped); when Gustav has coldly and bluntly presented his bill and outlined her guilt in injuring both himself and Adolf, she seeks to defend herself as innocent, for, as Gustav had taught her and as she thinks Christianity teaches, she believes that all human beings are innocent because nature and circumstances drive the individual to act as he does.

Like Adolf's bill, Gustav's is two fold. Having married her deliberately in order to make her the sort of mate he wanted, Gustav had freely and willingly given her many things—ultimately for his own sake:

> Reconciliation! You use so many words that have lost their meanings. Reconciliation indeed! Should we three live together? You're the one who should atone by making up for all this, but you can't.

What you have taken, you've absorbed so thoroughly you can't return it.—Will you be satisfied if I say: Forgive me because you clawed my heart to pieces; forgive me because you dishonored me; forgive me because for seven years you made me the butt of my pupils' ridicule; forgive me for freeing you from parental discipline, for releasing you from the tyranny of ignorance and superstition, for putting you in charge of my home, and giving you prestige and friends, for making a woman of you? Now I'm tearing up my bill! Go settle your account with your husband.

But the Gustav who had once been reduced to the same predicament Adolf is now in, is dunning her not for what he has given, but for what she has stolen: "You had stolen my honor, and I could recover that only by taking yours." Strindberg makes clear, of course, what Gustav means by his loss of honor: his loss of self-respect because of her behavior and his humiliation because of her conduct as his wife, her desertion, and her first book.

The woman who senses that there may be something to Gustav's assertion that there is a margin of responsibility toward oneself and one's fellowmen labels herself "wicked Tekla" as she caresses the dead body of her second husband. She is not consciously a vampire, but she serves as an illustration of Strindberg's own definition of the type in *The Dance of Death;*

> KURT: . . . for just now when he felt his life slipping away, he clung to mine, began to settle my affairs as if he wanted to creep into me and live my life.
> ALICE: That's his vampire nature exactly . . . to seize hold of other people's lives, to suck interest out of other people's lives, to arrange and direct for others, when his own life has become absolutely without interest for him. And remember. Kurt, don't ever let him get hold of your family affairs, don't ever let him meet your friends, for he'll take them away from you and make them his own. . . . He's a magician at doing that. . . . If he meets your children, you'd soon see them on intimate terms with him, he'd advise them and bring them up according to his own whims, and above all against your wishes.

To be sure, Tekla has done many of these things, but she has done them instinctively, without forethought, for her own egotistic ends; she has taken what has been given; she has, in Strindbergian terms, used "people and favorable opportunities." The only evidence that she has been aware of having stolen anything from her husbands has to do with her first book, the book based on her first marriage—humiliating to the husband she has labeled "idiot" because he did not "understand" her, and composed in part with the help of the critical supervision of her second husband. She shies away from close scrutiny only of her creative writing. Her role in the murder that is committed is essentially unintentional; Tekla does not deliberately set out to destroy her husband. She is instead a highly complex human animal with physical charm, the camouflage of useful but superficial intellectual behavior, and social graces. An amoral creature, she is not handicapped by ego-restraining concern for others. Fascinating and repulsive to the men who label her "cannibal," "serpent," "phonograph," "thief," "little devil," and "monster," she is, as she herself says, "a terrible egotist," an egotist quite capable of suffocating and smothering the "lamb," the idealistic and sensitive artist, and of upsetting the "wolf," the self-centered intellectual not too much inclined to emphasize the moral discipline of a young girl whom he believed he could mold to suit himself. The effect on the lamb is, however, even greater than on Kurt in *The Dance of Death,* for not only has Alice alerted Kurt to the dangers very early, but Kurt has learned from life that there are fellow human beings who intentionally or unconsciously destroy others.

Neither the careful reader nor the theatergoer need depend on any knowledge of either Strindberg's personal problems or the 1880's in order to understand or appreciate *Creditors.* Since it was first performed in 1889, it has stood the test of effective and gripping theater. Herbert Grevenius' comment, "It is a pretty terrible play, but it is terribly good," will remain a most valid comment on a drama-packed one-act exposé of three highly individualized and fascinating Strindbergian characterless characters caught in timeless and universal dilemmas.*

*An earlier version of this Introduction appeared as an article in *Modern Drama,* V (1962), 281-90.

Creditors · A Tragicomedy

Eva Dahlbeck and Olof Widgren in *Creditors* (The Royal Dramatic Theater, Stockholm)

Characters

TEKLA
ADOLF, *her husband, a painter*
GUSTAV, *her former husband, a teacher who is traveling under an assumed name*

SETTING

A sitting room at a bathing resort. A door to the veranda at the back with a view of the landscape. A table with papers on it somewhat to the right; a chair to the left, a couch to the right of the table. A door to a room on the right side.

Adolf and Gustav are at the table to the right.

ADOLF (*modeling a wax figure on a miniature modeling stand; his two crutches are placed beside him*): . . . and I have you to thank for all this!

GUSTAV (*smoking his cigar*): Nonsense!

ADOLF: Absolutely! The first days my wife was away, I lay on the sofa exhausted, just longing for her! It was as if she'd taken my crutches so I couldn't move from this spot. After I had slept for a few days, I came to; I began to pull myself together; my brain, which had been working feverishly, gradually became calm; ideas that I used to have came back; the desire to work and the urge to create came back—and my eyes could see accurately and daringly again—and then you came!

GUSTAV: Yes, you were pretty far down when I met you, and you were walking on crutches, but that's not saying that my being here has caused your recovery. You needed rest, and you need masculine companionship.

ADOLF: Yes, that's true, no doubt—like everything else you say. I used to have men friends, but after I got married I felt I didn't need them—I was satisfied with the one I had chosen. I got into new circles; I made many acquaintances; but my wife became jealous of them—she wanted me to herself—what was worse, she wanted my friends to herself as well—so I was alone with my jealousy.

GUSTAV: Yes, you do have a talent for jealousy.

ADOLF: I was afraid of losing her—I tried to prevent it. Was that strange? But I was never afraid she would be untrue to me . . .

GUSTAV: No, a husband never is!

ADOLF: No, isn't it strange? What I really feared was that friends would influence her and get me into their power indirectly—and that I couldn't bear.

GUSTAV: So the two of you didn't agree on everything!

ADOLF: Now that you've heard so much, you may as well hear everything. My wife has an independent nature.—What are you smiling at?

GUSTAV: Go on! . . . She has an independent nature . . .

ADOLF: . . . which doesn't want to accept anything from me . . .

GUSTAV: . . . but from everyone else!

ADOLF (*after a pause*): Yes! She seems to hate my ideas just because they're mine—not because they are absurd. Quite often she has expressed ideas I used to have as her own; yes, sometimes one of my friends will pass on my ideas to her and then they please her. Everything pleases her except what comes from me.

GUSTAV: You're saying you're not really happy?

ADOLF: Yes, I am happy! I got the one I wanted, and I've never wanted anyone else.

GUSTAV: You've never wanted to be free?

ADOLF: No, I can't say that! Well, sometimes I've imagined that

I'd have peace if I were free—but she has only to leave me and I've longed for her, longed for her as I might long for my own arms or legs! It's strange, but sometimes it seems to me as if she weren't anything in herself but a part of me; an intestine that carried away my will, my desire to live—as if I had deposited my urge to live with her!

GUSTAV: Perhaps that's how it is—when you get down to it.!

ADOLF: What would that be? Why, she's an independent being with a great many ideas of her own—when I met her, I was nothing—as an artist I was a child, whom she brought up!

GUSTAV: But afterward you did develop her ideas and bring her up, didn't you?

ADOLF: No! She stopped developing, and I kept on!

GUSTAV: Well, it's strange that her writing declined after her first book—at least she didn't write anything else! She did have an excellent subject that time—she used her husband as a model, didn't she? You've never met him? He must have been an idiot!

ADOLF: I never met him. He had been gone for six months, but he must have been a genuine idiot, to judge by her account! (*Pause*) And you may be sure that her account was accurate!

GUSTAV: I am! But why did she marry him?

ADOLF: Because she didn't know him—people aren't likely to get to know each other until afterward!

GUSTAV: That's why they shouldn't get married until—afterward! —Well, I suppose he was a tyrant!

ADOLF: Suppose?

GUSTAV: Why, all married men are—(*groping his way*)—and you not least!

ADOLF: I! Who let my wife come and go as she pleases . . .

GUSTAV: Yes, that's the least you can do! Maybe you ought to keep her locked up! But do you like her being away at night?

ADOLF: No, of course I don't!

GUSTAV: You see! (*Changing his tone*) Frankly—that makes you ridiculous!

ADOLF: Ridiculous? Is a man ridiculous because he trusts his wife?

GUSTAV: He certainly can be, and you are already! Thoroughly!

ADOLF (*convulsively*): I! That's the last thing I'd want to be. There's going to be a change here!

GUSTAV: Don't get excited! You'll have another attack!

ADOLF: But why isn't she ridiculous if I'm out nights?

GUSTAV: Why? That doesn't concern you, but it's so, and while you're speculating about it, the misfortune will have happened!

ADOLF: What misfortune?

GUSTAV: So her husband was a tyrant, and she had married him to get her freedom. A girl gets that only by securing a front—the so-called husband.

ADOLF: Naturally!

GUSTAV: Now you're the front.

ADOLF: I?

GUSTAV: You're her husband! (*Adolf is bewildered.*) Am I right?

ADOLF (*uneasily*): I don't know!—A man lives with a woman for years—he never thinks about her, or about their relationship—then . . . he begins to wonder—then it's started. Gustav, you're my friend! You're the only man I have for a friend! You've given me the courage to live again during the past eight days; it's as if you've given me life; you've been a watchmaker who has repaired the mechanism of my brain and set it going again. Don't you hear that I'm thinking more clearly, speaking more coherently, and, it seems to me at least, that my voice has regained its old vigor!

GUSTAV: I think so, too! How can that have happened?

ADOLF: Perhaps it becomes a habit to speak softly to women; at least Tekla has always complained that I shout!

GUSTAV: So you lowered your voice and put your neck in the yoke.

ADOLF: Don't say that! (*Reflectively*) I think it's worse than that! But let's not talk about that now!—Where was I?—Yes, you came, and you opened my eyes to the secrets of my art. I had known for a long time, of course, that I was gradually losing my interest in painting because it didn't offer me a suitable medium for expressing what I wanted to say. When you explained why and pointed out that painting cannot be the contemporary form for artistic expression, I suddenly understood, and I knew it would be impossible for me to produce anything else in painting.

GUSTAV: Are you absolutely sure you can't paint any more, that you won't go back to it?

ADOLF: Absolutely!—I've tried! The evening after we had talked and I had gone to bed, I examined your argument point by point, and I knew you were right. But after I had slept soundly all night and my brain had cleared, it struck me that you could be wrong; I jumped up, took my brushes and colors, but I couldn't paint! I didn't have any creative imagination; I was only daubing colors, and I was amazed that I could have believed and made others believe that a painted canvas was anything but a painted canvas. The veil had dropped from my eyes, and painting was just as impossible as becoming a child again!

GUSTAV: So you understood that the realistic struggles of our time —its insistence on reality, on tangibility—can find their form only in sculpture, which has body, extends into three dimensions . . .

ADOLF (faltering): Three dimensions . . . yes, in a word, body!

GUSTAV: So you became a sculptor; that's to say, you were, but you had gone astray; all you needed was to be shown the right way . . . Does your work give you great pleasure?

ADOLF: Now I am alive!

GUSTAV: May I see what you're doing?

ADOLF: The figure of a woman.

GUSTAV: Without a model? And so alive!

ADOLF (dully): Yes, but it looks like someone! It's strange this woman is in my body, just as I am in hers!

GUSTAV: The latter isn't strange! . . . Do you know what transfusion is?

ADOLF: Blood transfusion? Yes!

GUSTAV: Apparently you've emptied your veins too much. When I see this figure, I understand a number of things I only suspected before. You have loved her too much!

ADOLF: Yes, so that I can't say if she is I or I am she. When she smiles, I smile. When she weeps, I weep; and when she—can you imagine this—gave birth to our child—I felt the pains of labor myself!

GUSTAV: It hurts me to say this, my friend, but you already have the first symptoms of epilepsy.!

ADOLF (*shaken*): I! How can you say that?

GUSTAV: I saw the symptoms in a younger brother of mine who had overindulged—sexually!

ADOLF: What were they?

(GUSTAV *expressively demonstrating*. ADOLF *listens most attentively and unconsciously imitates* GUSTAV's *gestures*.)

GUSTAV: It was horrible to watch. If you're feeling weak, I don't want to torture you with a description.

ADOLF (*in agony*): Go on! Go on!

GUSTAV: Well! The fellow happened to marry an innocent little girl with curls, the eyes of a dove, the face of a child, and the pure soul of an angel. Nevertheless she managed to take over the masculine prerogative . . .

ADOLF: What's that?

GUSTAV: The initiative, of course! With the result that the angel almost took him to heaven. First, of course, he had to bear the cross and feel the nails in his flesh. It was horrible!

ADOLF (*breathless*): Well, what happened?

GUSTAV (*slowly*): We'd sit talking, he and I—and when I had talked for a while, his face would become white as chalk; his arms and legs would stiffen and his thumbs would turn in—like this! (*Gesture; is imitated by* ADOLF) Then his eyes would grow blood-shot and he'd begin to chew—like this! (*Chews and is imitated by* ADOLF) The saliva would gurgle in his throat, his chest would contract as if in a vise; his pupils would flicker like a gas flame, he would froth at the mouth, and he would sink—down—slowly—backward—into his chair, as if he were drowning! Then . . .

ADOLF (*whispering*): Stop!

GUSTAV: Then . . . are you ill?

ADOLF: Yes!

GUSTAV (*getting a glass of water*): There, drink this. We'll talk about something else.

ADOLF (*feebly*): Thanks. Go on.

GUSTAV: Well! When he'd come to, he'd remember nothing of what had happened: he had simply been unconscious. Have you been like that?

ADOLF: Yes, I've sometimes had fainting spells, but the doctor says that I'm anemic.

GUSTAV: Yes, that's the start. But, believe me, it will become epilepsy if you don't take care of yourself!

ADOLF: What shall I do?

GUSTAV: You'll have to be absolutely continent to start with.

ADOLF: For how long?

GUSTAV: Half a year at the very least.

ADOLF: I can't! That would upset our married life!

GUSTAV: Then you're finished!

ADOLF (*lays the cloth over the wax figure*): I can't do it!

GUSTAV: Can't you save your own life? But tell me, since you've told me so much, isn't there any other wound, something secret that torments you? Because a person rarely has only one cause for disharmony since life is so complicated and full of causes of frustrations. Don't you have a skeleton in your closet that you're keeping to yourself? For example, you said a bit ago that you have a child you've sent away. Why isn't he living with you?

ADOLF: That was my wife's idea.

GUSTAV: Why? Tell me!

ADOLF: Well, when he was three years old, he began to resemble him—her former husband!

GUSTAV: Well-l! Have you seen her former husband?

ADOLF: No, never! I've only glanced at a poor portrait, but I couldn't see any likeness.

GUSTAV: Well, portraits are never lifelike, and he could have changed. Didn't it even make you at all suspicious?

ADOLF: Not at all! Our child was born a year after we got married, and her husband was away traveling when I met Tekla here—I did meet her here at this resort—In this very house in fact. That's why we come here every summer.

GUSTAV: So you couldn't be suspicious! You don't need to be, either, because a remarried widow's child quite often looks like her dead husband. That's annoying, of course, but that's why widows in India are burned alive! But tell me. Haven't you ever been jealous of him, of his memory? Wouldn't it turn your stomach to meet him out walking and have him say to you as he fixed his eyes on Tekla: *We* instead of I?—*We?*

ADOLF: Yes, that thought has haunted me.

GUSTAV: See! And you can never be free from it. There are complications in life that can never be resolved. So you'll have to stuff wax into your ears and work. Work, become old, and put quantities of new impressions in the hold below the deck; then the corpse will be quiet.

ADOLF: Excuse me for interrupting you! But—it's strange how you look like Tekla when you're talking. You have a way of squinting your right eye as if you were aiming, and your glances have the same power over me that hers sometimes do.

GUSTAV: No, really!

ADOLF: And now you said, "Really," in absolutely the same indifferent tone she does. She used to say, "Really," quite often.

GUSTAV: Perhaps we're distantly related—since all people are! It's strange in any case. It will be interesting to meet your wife just to see that.

ADOLF: Yes, but you can understand that she never picks up an expression from me; rather she avoids mine, and I've never seen her use a gesture of mine. Other married people usually become alike.

GUSTAV: Yes. But do you know what? That woman has never loved you.

ADOLF: What!

GUSTAV: There, there. I beg your pardon. But you see a woman's love is taking, receiving, and if she doesn't take anything from him, she doesn't love him. She has never loved you.

ADOLF: Do you believe that she can't love more than once?

GUSTAV: No, a person lets himself be fooled only once; then his eyes are open! You have never been fooled: that's why you have to watch out for those who have been. They're dangerous!

ADOLF: Your words are cutting me like knives; and I feel that something is being cut into pieces, but I can't prevent that; and the cutting does me good, for they're boils that are bursting and that could never come to a head!—She has never loved me!— Why did she take me, then?

GUSTAV: Tell me first how she happened to take you. Did you take her, or did she take you?

ADOLF: God knows if I can answer that.—How it happened!—It didn't happen in one day.

GUSTAV: Shall I try to guess how it happened?

ADOLF: You can't!

GUSTAV: Oh, with the information you've given me about yourself and your wife, I can reconstruct the course of events! Listen, and I'll tell you. (*Dispassionately, almost facetiously*) Her husband was away studying, and she was alone. At first she felt a pleasure in being free; then came emptiness, for I assume that she was rather empty when she had lived alone for fourteen days. Then you came along, and the emptiness gradually disappeared. By comparison her husband began to pale for the simple reason that he was far away; you know, the square of the distance.—But when they felt their passions were being aroused, they became uneasy about themselves, their conscience; and him. So they looked for protection and crept behind the fig leaves, played brother and sister, and the more physical their feelings became, the more spiritual they pretended their relationship was.

ADOLF: Brother and sister? How did you know?

GUSTAV: I guessed! Children play father and mother, but when they get older, they play brother and sister—to conceal what ought to be concealed!—And then they take the vow of chastity

—and play hide-and-seek—until they find each other in a dark corner where they are sure no one sees them! (*With pretended sternness*) But they sense that one person does see them in the dark—and they become afraid—and in their fear the figure of the husband begins to haunt them—takes on dimensions—changes, and becomes a nightmare. That disturbs them in their love-making, like a creditor who knocks on the door, and his shadow comes between them; when they make love, they hear his reproachful voice in the silence of the night which should be disturbed only by the beating of their pulses. He can't keep them apart, but he does disturb their happiness. And when they learn that he has the invisible power to disturb their happiness, they finally run away—but they run in vain from the memories that pursue them, from the debt they left behind, and from public opinion which frightens them, and they haven't the strength to bear their guilt, they have to have a scapegoat from the grave and murder him! They were freethinkers; but they didn't dare to go to him and say openly to him: We love each other!—Well, they were cowardly, and so the tyrant had to be murdered! Is that right?

ADOLF: Yes! But you forget that she taught me, gave me new ideas . . .

GUSTAV: I haven't forgotten that! But tell me, how did it happen that she couldn't train the other one, too, to be—a freethinker?

ADOLF: Why, he was an idiot!

GUSTAV: That's true, he was an idiot! But that's a very vague term, and in her novel his idiocy consists mainly of his not understanding her. Forgive me, but is your wife really very profound? I haven't found anything profound in what she has written!

ADOLF: Neither have I!—But I have to admit that I, too, find it a little hard to understand her. It's as if the cogs in our brains can't quite slip into each other, as if something goes to pieces in my head when I try to understand her!

GUSTAV: Maybe you're an idiot, too?

ADOLF: No, I don't *believe* that! And I almost always feel that she *is* wrong.—As an example, do you want to read this letter that I got from her today? (*Takes letter from his wallet*)

GUSTAV (*glances through it*): Well, I seem to know that handwriting!

ADOLF: Masculine—almost?

GUSTAV: Yes, I've known at least one man who has a hand like that! She addresses you as "brother." Are you still pretending to yourselves? The fig leaves are still there, though withered! Don't you call her by her first name?

ADOLF: No, I feel I'd lose my respect for her if I did!

GUSTAV: Ah, it's to make you respect her that she calls herself sister?

ADOLF: I want to respect her more than myself; I want her to be my better self.

GUSTAV: No, be your own better self; though perhaps that's more uncomfortable than to let someone else be it. Do you want to be inferior to your wife?

ADOLF: Yes, I do! I always enjoy being a little beneath her! For example, I've taught her to swim, and now I think it's fun to hear her brag about her being a better and more daring swimmer than I! At first, I pretended I was less competent and afraid in order to give her courage, but however it happened, one fine day I *was* the less competent and more afraid than she. It seemed to me as if she really had taken my courage away from me.

GUSTAV: Have you taught her anything else?

ADOLF: Yes—but don't tell anyone—I taught her how to spell. She couldn't! But I'll tell you. When she took over the household correspondence, I quit writing; and—can you imagine—for want of practice since then I've forgotten my grammar—the details of it. But do you think that she remembers it was I who taught her? No, now I'm the idiot, of course.

GUSTAV: So you're the idiot, already!

ADOLF: Jokingly, of course.

GUSTAV: Of course! But this is cannibalism! Do you know what it is? Savages eat their enemies in order to acquire their outstand-

ing qualities!—She has eaten your soul, this woman; your courage, your knowledge . . .

ADOLF: And my faith. I was the one who encouraged her to write
her first book . . .

GUSTAV: So-o-o!

ADOLF: I was the one who praised her even when I thought what
she wrote was pretty bad. I was the one who introduced her into
literary circles, where she could suck honey from precious
flowers; I was the one who personally kept the critics at a distance from her; I was the one who puffed up her self-confidence;
I puffed so long I lost my own breath; I gave and gave—until I
didn't have anything left myself! You know—I'm going to tell
you everything now—you know, it seems to me now—and the
spirit is very strange—when my success as an artist threatened to
overshadow her—and her name, too—I tried to inspire courage
in her by belittling myself and ranking my art below hers. I
talked so long about the insignificant role of painting as an art,
I talked so long and hit upon so many reasons, that one fine day
I had convinced myself that it was insignificant—so it was only
a house of cards you needed to knock down!

GUSTAV: Forgive me for reminding you that when we began talking you insisted that she never takes anything from you.

ADOLF: Yes, not nowadays. For there isn't anything more to take.

GUSTAV: The serpent has eaten her fill, and is vomiting now!

ADOLF: Perhaps she has taken more from me without my knowing
it.

GUSTAV: Yes, that you can depend on. She took without your
seeing it, and that's called stealing.

ADOLF: Perhaps she never has taught me anything.

GUSTAV: But you've taught her. Most likely! But it was her technique to make you believe the opposite! May I ask how she went
about teaching you?

ADOLF: Yes. First . . . hm!

GUSTAV: Well-l-l?

ADOLF: Well, I . . .

GUSTAV: No, she was the one!

ADOLF: Yes, but I can't be sure now!

GUSTAV: You see!

ADOLF: However . . . She had devoured my faith, too, and so I slipped farther and farther down until you came and gave me faith again!

GUSTAV (*smiles*): In sculpturing?

ADOLF (*doubtfully*): Yes!

GUSTAV: And you believe in that? In that abstract, worn-out art from the childhood of the race, you believe you can influence with pure forms—with three dimensions, eh?—the realistic point of view of our time—that you can create illusion without color—without color, do you hear? Do you believe that?

ADOLF (*crushed*): No.

GUSTAV: Well! Neither do I!

ADOLF: Why did you say so then?

GUSTAV: I pitied you.

ADOLF: Yes, I am to be pitied. For I am bankrupt now. Finished. And the worst is: I don't have her!

GUSTAV: What would you do with her?

ADOLF: Well, she'd be what God was before I became an atheist— the object of my reverence.

GUSTAV: Get rid of that . . . let something else take its place. A little sound contempt, for example!

ADOLF: I can't live without respecting . . .

GUSTAV: Slave!

ADOLF: And a woman to respect, to worship.

GUSTAV: Good Lord, rather take back God! Since you have to have someone to cross yourself in front of. What an atheist, who still has the superstition about women left! What a free-thinker, who can't think freely about women! Do you know what the intangible, the sphinxlike, the profound quality in your wife is? It's only stupidity! Look! Why, she can't distinguish between *dt* and *t*! And that, you see, is the flaw in the machine. The case is that of a clock, but the mechanism is only a watch.

It's only her skirts! That's all! Put trousers on her and draw mustaches with a bit of charcoal under her nose; then make yourself listen to her objectively, and you'll hear how differently she sounds. A phonograph, merely, which plays back your words—and other people's—a little bit thinned down! Have you ever seen a naked woman? Yes, of course! A youngster with developed breasts, an unfinished man, a child who has shot up and then stopped in its growth, a chronic anemic who loses blood regularly thirteen times every year? What can anyone like that amount to?

ADOLF: Even if everything you say is so, how can I feel that she and I are equals now?

GUSTAV: Hallucination, the ability to fascinate that skirts have! Or—because you have become equals. You've come down to her level: her capillary power has drawn you down to her level. Tell me one thing—(*Takes out his watch*) We've talked for six hours, and your wife ought to be here soon. Shall we stop so you can get some rest?

ADOLF: No, don't leave me. I don't dare to be alone!

GUSTAV: Oh, just for a little while—then your wife'll be coming.

ADOLF: Yes, she'll come. Strange! I long for her, but I'm afraid of her! She caresses me, she is tender, but there's something suffocating in her kisses, something that drains me and puts me to sleep. It's as if I were a child at the circus, whom the clown pinches backstage to make it look healthy to the audience when it comes on stage.

GUSTAV: I pity you! Though I'm not a doctor, I can tell you anyway that you're dying. All one has to do to understand that is to look at your latest paintings.

ADOLF: You say that? In what ways?

GUSTAV: Why, your color is watery blue, pale, thin, so that the canvas shines through yellow as a corpse; it is as if I saw your hollow, pasty-colored cheeks looking through . . .

ADOLF: Stop! Stop!

GUSTAV: Well, I'm not the only one who thinks so. Have you read today's paper?

ADOLF (*collapsing*): No.

GUSTAV: It's here on the table.

ADOLF (*reaching for the paper but not daring to take it*): Does it say that?

GUSTAV: Read it! Or shall I?

ADOLF: No!

GUSTAV: I'll leave if you'd like.

ADOLF: No! No! No! I don't know—I feel as if I were beginning to hate you, and still I can't let you go! You pull me out of the water in which I am lying, but when I'm up, you hit me on the head and force me under again! As long as I kept my secrets to myself, I still had guts, but now I'm empty. There's a painting by an Italian master that represents torture; they're winding out on a wheel the intestines of a saint; the martyr lies there seeing how he's becoming thinner and thinner and how the roll on the wheel becomes thicker and thicker!—It seems to me you've grown since you emptied me, and when you leave, you go away with everything from within me and leave only an empty shell!

GUSTAV: Now you're imagining! Why, so far as that goes, your wife is coming home with your heart, isn't she?

ADOLF: No, not any more—you've destroyed her for me. You've reduced everything to ashes behind you: my art, my love, my hope, my faith!

GUSTAV: Why, that had already been thoroughly done.

ADOLF: Yes, but I could have been saved! Now it's too late, you arsonist!

GUSTAV: We've just scorched you a little. Now we'll sow in the ashes!

ADOLF: I hate you! Damn you!

GUSTAV: Good signs! You still have strength! Now I'm going to pull you up again. Listen to me! Will you listen to me and will you obey me?

ADOLF: Do what you want to with me. I'll obey.

GUSTAV (*gets up*): Look at me!

ADOLF (*looks at Gustav*): Now you're looking at me with those other eyes that draw me to you!

GUSTAV: And, listen to me!

ADOLF: Yes, but talk about yourself. Don't talk about me any more; I'm like an open sore and can't bear being touched.

GUSTAV: No, there's nothing to say about me. I'm an instructor in dead languages, and I'm a widower! That's all.—Take my hand!

ADOLF: What terrible strength you must have. It's like touching a generator.

GUSTAV: Think of this: I have been just as feeble as you.—Get up!

ADOLF (*gets up; falls, throwing his arms about Gustav's shoulders*): I'm like a child without legs, and my brain's exposed.

GUSTAV: Walk across the floor!

ADOLF: I can't!

GUSTAV: Do it, or I'll hit you!

ADOLF (*straightens up*): What did you say?

GUSTAV: I said, I'll hit you!

ADOLF (*jumps back, furious*): You!

GUSTAV: There! The blood's back in your head, and your ego's awake! Now I'll give you strength!—Where is your wife?

ADOLF: Where . . . is . . . she?

GUSTAV: Yes!

ADOLF: She's . . . at . . . a meeting.

GUSTAV: Are you sure?

ADOLF: Absolutely!

GUSTAV: What kind of meeting?

ADOLF: A child welfare meeting.

GUSTAV: Were you on friendly terms when she left?

ADOLF (*hesitatingly*): No, not friendly.

GUSTAV: You were enemies, then! What did you say that irritated her?

ADOLF: You are terrible! I'm afraid of you! How could you know?

GUSTAV: I have three knowns, quite simply, and I discard the unknown. What did you say to her?

ADOLF: I said—only two words, ugly words, and I regret them.

GUSTAV: Don't! Tell me!

ADOLF: I said: Old coquette!

GUSTAV: And then?

ADOLF: I didn't say anything else.

GUSTAV: Yes, you did, but you've probably forgotten, because you don't dare to remember: you've stuffed it into a secret chamber, but go ahead, open it!

ADOLF: I don't remember!

GUSTAV: But I know! You said: You ought to be ashamed of being a coquette when you're so old you can't get a lover any more!

ADOLF: Did I say that? I must have. But how can you know?

GUSTAV: I heard her tell the story on the steamer I came on.

ADOLF: To whom?

GUSTAV: To four young fellows she had with her. She's already enthusiastic about chaste young fellows, just as . . .

ADOLF: That's perfectly innocent.

GUSTAV: As playing brother and sister when you're father and mother?

ADOLF: So you have seen her?

GUSTAV: Yes, I have! But you have never seen her, when *you* haven't seen her. I mean, when you're not present. And, you see, that's why a man never *can* know his wife. Do you have a picture of her?

(ADOLF *takes a picture from his wallet; looks at it curiously.*)

GUSTAV: You weren't there when that one was taken?

ADOLF: No.

GUSTAV: Look at it! Is it like the portrait you painted?—No! The features are the same, but the expression is different. But you can't see that, because you put your own image under it. Look at this one—as a painter—without thinking of the original— What does it portray? I can't see anything but an affected coquette making a play for someone. Observe that cynical expression about the mouth that you're never allowed to see? Observe that her eyes are seeking another man, not you. Look how her dress is cut low, her hair has been recombed, one sleeve is pushed up. Do you see?

ADOLF: Yes . . . I see it now.

GUSTAV: Watch out, man!

ADOLF: For what?

GUSTAV: Her revenge! Don't forget you hurt her at the very core of her being when you said that she couldn't attract a man! If you had said that what she wrote was rubbish, she could have laughed at your poor taste, but now—believe me, if she hasn't already got her revenge, it isn't her fault!

ADOLF: I have to know!

GUSTAV: Find out!

ADOLF: Find out?

GUSTAV: Look into it! I'll help you if you'd like.

ADOLF: Yes, since I'm going to die anyway—I'll do it; now is as good a time as any!—What's to be done?

GUSTAV: First, a bit of information. Hasn't your wife a single vulnerable point?

ADOLF: Hardly! I think she has nine lives—just like a cat.

GUSTAV: Well—there's the steamboat's whistle—she'll be here soon.

ADOLF: Then I'll have to go meet her.

GUSTAV: No! Stay here! Be impolite! If she has a clear conscience, you'll get a storm of reproach. If she's guilty, she'll come and caress you!

ADOLF: Are you sure?

GUSTAV: Not quite—a rabbit does double back to conceal its tracks sometimes and leaves gaps, but I'll find out about them. My room is next to yours. (*Points to the right-hand door behind the chair*) I'll station myself there while you're performing in here. When you're done, we'll trade roles: I'll come into the cage and work with the serpent while you listen at the keyhole. Then we'll meet in the park and compare notes. But be firm! And if you do get weak, I'll strike the floor twice with a chair!

ADOLF: Right!—But don't go away! I have to know that you're in the next room.

GUSTAV: You can depend on that! But don't get frightened later when you see how I cut open a human soul and place its contents here on the table. Most likely that's terrible for beginners, but if you see it once, you won't regret it!—Remember just one thing. Not a word about your meeting me or having made an acquaintance during her absence! Not one word! I'll discover her vulnerable point myself. Sh-h! She's already up in her room. She's singing to herself softly. Then she's furious!—There, control yourself now; sit on your chair there, so she'll have to sit down on mine, and then I can see you both at the same time.

ADOLF: There's an hour left until dinner—none of the other guests have come for no one has rung—we'll be alone then—unfortunately!

GUSTAV: Are you weak?

ADOLF: I am nothing!—Yes, I am afraid of what is coming! But I can't prevent its coming! The stone is rolling, but it wasn't the first drop of water—or the last—that set it going—it was all of them together!

GUSTAV: Let it roll, then—since there won't be peace until it has! I'll see you later. (*Goes*)

(ADOLF *nods farewell: has been holding the photograph, tears it to pieces, and throws the pieces under the table; then sits down on his chair, fingers his necktie nervously, brushes back his hair, fingers his lapels, etc.*)

TEKLA (*comes in; goes directly to him and kisses him; she is friendly, open, cheerful, and seductive*): Hello, little brother. How are you?

ADOLF (*half won over; resistingly, facetiously*): What have you been up to that you're kissing me?

TEKLA: Well, I'll tell you!—I've spent a lot of money!

ADOLF: Did you have fun?

TEKLA: A lot! But not at the meeting, though! That was rubbish! But what have you been doing while Kitten was away, little brother? (*Looks about the room as if she were looking for someone or were sniffing for something*)

ADOLF: I've had a dull time.

TEKLA: And no company?

ADOLF: Absolutely alone.

TEKLA (*observes him; sits down on the couch*): Who has been sitting here?

ADOLF: There? No one.

TEKLA: That's strange. The sofa's still warm, and here's the mark from an elbow. Has a woman been here?

ADOLF: To see me? You don't believe that?

TEKLA: But you're blushing! I think you're fooling me, little brother. Come and tell Kitten what is on your conscience. (*Draws him to her; he sinks down with his head in her lap*)

ADOLF (*smiling*): You are a little devil! Did you know?

TEKLA: No, I don't know anything about myself.

ADOLF: You never think about yourself!

TEKLA (*sniffing and observing*): I think only about myself—I am a terrible egotist! But, how philosophic you have become!

ADOLF: Put your hand on my forehead!

TEKLA (*baby-talks*): Do you have ants in your head again? Shall I chase them away? (*Kisses his forehead*) There! Is that better?

ADOLF: It is better!

(*Pause*)

TEKLA: Well, tell me what you've been doing? Have you done any painting?

ADOLF: No! I've quit painting!

TEKLA: What! You've quit painting!

ADOLF: Yes, but don't scold me. I can't help it that I can't paint any more.

TEKLA: What are you going to do?

ADOLF: I'm going to become a sculptor!

TEKLA: What a lot of new ideas again!

ADOLF: Yes, but just don't scold. Look at that figure!

TEKLA (*uncovers the wax figure*): Well, just look! Who is that supposed to be?

ADOLF: Guess!

TEKLA (*blithely*): Is it supposed to be Kitten? Aren't you ashamed?

ADOLF: Isn't it a real likeness?

TEKLA: How could I know when it doesn't have a face?

ADOLF: Yes, but it has many other things that are—beautiful!

TEKLA (*hits him playfully on the cheek*): If you don't stop talking like that, I'll kiss you again!

ADOLF (*defensively*): There, there. Someone might come!

TEKLA: What do I care about that? Mayn't I kiss my husband? Yes, that's my legal right.

ADOLF: Yes, but do you know what? Here at the hotel they believe we aren't married because we kiss each other so much! And our quarreling occasionally doesn't destroy their belief, for lovers do that, too!

TEKLA: Well, why should we quarrel? Can't you always be good like this? Tell me! Don't you want to? Don't you want us to be happy?

ADOLF: Yes, I do! But . . .

TEKLA: What is it now? Who has given you the idea that you're not going to paint any more?

ADOLF: Who? You always suspect someone's back of me and my thoughts! You are jealous!

TEKLA: Yes, I am! I'm afraid that someone will come along to take you away from me!

ADOLF: You're afraid of that! You who know that no other woman can force you out and that I can't live without you!

TEKLA: Well, it's not women I'm afraid of, but your friends who give you ideas.

ADOLF (*searchingly*): So you are afraid!—What are you afraid of?

TEKLA (*gets up*): Someone has been here! Who?

ADOLF: Can't you bear my looking at you?

TEKLA: Not in that way! You haven't looked at me like that before.

ADOLF: How am I looking?

TEKLA: You're looking under my eyelids . . .

ADOLF: Yes, under yours! I want to see what you look like back of them!

TEKLA: Go ahead! There's nothing I need to hide.—But—you—
—are talking differently—you're using expressions—(*searchingly*) you're philosophizing—eh? (*Goes toward him threateningly*) Who has been here?

ADOLF: No one but my doctor.

TEKLA: Your doctor! Who's he?

ADOLF: The doctor from Strömstad.

TEKLA: What's his name?

ADOLF: Sjöberg.

TEKLA: What did he say?

ADOLF: He said—well—among other things—that I'm on the verge of epilepsy—

TEKLA: Among other things? What else did he say?

ADOLF: Something very unpleasant.

TEKLA: Tell me!

ADOLF: He said we must not live as husband and wife for a while.

TEKLA: There! I can believe that! They want to separate us! I've been aware of that for a long time!

ADOLF: You can't have been aware of what has never happened!

TEKLA: Can't I?

ADOLF: How could you have seen what doesn't exist unless your fear has heightened your imagination to the point where you've seen what has never existed? What are you afraid of? That I have borrowed someone else's eyes to see you as you are, and not as you seem to me?

TEKLA: Control your imagination, Adolf! It's the animal in the human soul.

ADOLF: Where did you learn that? From the chaste young men on the boat? Eh?

TEKLA (*without losing her self-control*): Yes! One can learn something from the young, too!

ADOLF: I think you're already beginning to love the young!

TEKLA: I always have! And that's why I have loved you! Have you anything against that?

ADOLF: No, but I'd prefer to be the only one!

TEKLA (*facetiously baby-talks*): My heart is so big, little brother, that it has room for many others, too.

ADOLF: But little brother doesn't want several brothers!

TEKLA: Come to Kitten, and I'll pull your hair for being jealous —no, envious is the word!

(*Two knocks with the chair in Gustav's room can be heard.*)

ADOLF: No, I don't want to play! I want to talk seriously!

TEKLA (*baby-talking*): Good lord, do you want to talk seriously? How terribly serious you've become. (*Puts her hands on his head and kisses him*) Laugh a little. Yes, like that.

ADOLF((*smiles unwillingly*): Damn woman! I think you can bewitch a person.

TEKLA: Yes, you see. So don't quarrel—if you do, I'll make you disappear!

ADOLF (*gets up*): Tekla! Sit a moment in profile; then I'll give your figure a face.

TEKLA: Of course. (*Turns her profile toward him*)

ADOLF (*fixing his gaze on her; pretends to model*): Don't think about me. Think about someone else.

TEKLA: I'll think about my latest conquest!

ADOLF: The chaste young man?

TEKLA: Exactly! He had such a very small, sweet mustache—his cheeks looked like peaches—so soft and pink I wanted to take a bite!

ADOLF (*darkens*): Hold that expression by your mouth!

TEKLA: Which expression?

ADOLF: The cynicism and coarseness I've never seen there before!

TEKLA (*grimaces*): This one?

ADOLF: Exactly! (*Gets up*) Do you know how Bret Harte pictures the adulterous wife?

TEKLA (*smiles*): No. I've never read Bret what's his name.

ADOLF: Yes, as a pale woman who never blushes.

TEKLA: Never? But when she meets her lover, I should think she'd blush even if her husband or Mr. Bret never gets to see it!

ADOLF: Are you sure of that?

TEKLA (*as before*): Yes, since her husband can't make her blood rush to her head, I don't suppose he ever gets to see her blush!

ADOLF (*furious*): Tekla!

TEKLA: You little idiot!

ADOLF: Tekla!

TEKLA: Call me Kitten, and I'll blush beautifully for you! Shall I?

ADOLF (*defenselessly*): I'm so angry with you, you monster, that I could bite you—

TEKLA (*playfully*): Come and bite me! Come! (*Stretches out her arms toward him*)

ADOLF (*puts his hands behind her head and kisses her*): Yes, I am going to bite you so you die!

TEKLA (*facetiously*): Careful! Someone might come!

ADOLF: What do I care? I don't care for anything in the whole world if only I have you!

TEKLA: And when you don't have me any more?

ADOLF: Then I'll die!

TEKLA: Yes, but you're not afraid of that since I'm so old that no one else wants me!

ADOLF: Tekla, you haven't forgotten what I said! I take it back!

TEKLA: Can you explain why you're jealous and absolutely sure of me at the same time?

ADOLF: No, I can't explain anything! Perhaps the thought that you've belonged to someone else may be sprouting and growing. Sometimes it seems to me as if our love were a poem, a defense, a passion become a matter of honor, and I know of nothing that would torture me more than his knowing I'm unhappy. Ah! I've never seen him, but the very thought that there is a person who sits waiting for my unhappiness, one who calls down curses on me every day, and who will shout with laughter when I go under—the very idea rides me, drives me to you, fascinates me, and cripples me!

TEKLA: Do you think I'd let him have that pleasure? That I'd want to make his prophecy come true?

ADOLF: No, I shouldn't think so.

TEKLA: Can't you be calm, then?

ADOLF: No, you're forever making me uneasy by playing up to other men! Why do you play that game?

TEKLA: It isn't a game! I want to be liked—that's all.

ADOLF: Yes, but only by men!

TEKLA: Of course. Women never like each other.

ADOLF: Listen!—Have you heard anything about—him—lately?

TEKLA: Not for half a year.

ADOLF: Don't you ever think about him?

TEKLA: No!—Since our child died, we haven't any ties.

ADOLF: And you haven't seen him when you've been out?

TEKLA: No, most likely he's living on the west coast somewhere. But why are you worrying about that just now?

ADOLF: I don't know. But the last few days, when I've been alone, I've thought of how he must have felt when he was left alone— that time!

TEKLA: You're having pangs of conscience!

ADOLF: Yes!

TEKLA: You feel like a thief, don't you?

ADOLF: Almost!

TEKLA: That is nice! A man steals a woman as he'd steal children and chickens! So you consider me his property. Thank you.

ADOLF: Oh, no! I consider you his wife. And a wife is more than property. She can't be replaced.

TEKLA: Oh, yes! If you found out that he had married again, you'd get over these notions. You've made up for him—to me!

ADOLF: Have I?—Did you ever love him?

TEKLA: Of course I did!

ADOLF: And . . .

TEKLA: I got tired of him!

ADOLF: What if you get tired of me?

TEKLA: I won't!

ADOLF: If another man who had what you look for in a man should come along—just assume that! Then you'd desert me!

TEKLA: No!

ADOLF: If he fascinated you? So that you couldn't give him up—you'd give me up, of course!

TEKLA: That doesn't follow!

ADOLF: You certainly couldn't love two men at the same time?

TEKLA: Yes, Why not?

ADOLF: That I don't understand.

TEKLA: There can be such things even though you don't understand them. We're not all made alike.

ADOLF: I'm beginning to understand.

TEKLA: No, really!

ADOLF: No, really! (*Pause, during which Adolf seems to remember with difficulty something he cannot quite hit upon*) Tekla! Your frankness is becoming painful!

TEKLA: And yet that was the highest virtue you knew and that you taught me.

ADOLF: Yes, it seems to me you're hiding yourself behind your frankness.

TEKLA: That's the new technique, you see!

ADOLF: I don't know, but I feel it's getting unpleasant here. If you want to, we'll go home—tonight.

TEKLA: What an idea! I've just come and I don't want to leave!

ADOLF: Yes, but I want to!

TEKLA: What do I care about what you want?—You go!

ADOLF: I order you to come with me on the next boat!

TEKLA: Order? What kind of talk is that?

ADOLF: Are you aware you're my wife?

TEKLA: Are you aware you're my husband?

ADOLF: Yes, but there's a difference!

TEKLA: So! That's how you feel! You've never loved me!

ADOLF: No?

TEKLA: To love is to give!

ADOLF: To love as a man is to give; to love as a woman is to take! And I've given, given, given!

TEKLA: Huh! What have you given me?

ADOLF: Everything!

TEKLA: That is a lot! And, if it were so, I've accepted! Are you presenting me with a bill for your gifts? And, if I have taken, then I've shown you in that way that I've loved you. A woman accepts gifts only from her lover.

ADOLF: Lover, yes! There you told the truth! I've been your lover but never your husband!

TEKLA: So much the more pleasant, I should think, not to have to be my front! But if you're not satisfied you can go, because I don't want a husband!

ADOLF: So I've noticed! Lately, when I've seen you wanting to steal away from me like a thief and seek your own crowd where you could show off with my feathers, and parade my jewels, I've wanted to remind you of your debt. And then I was changed into an unpleasant creditor that you'd prefer to be rid of. Then you wanted to tear up the bill and quit taking anything from me but went to others. I became your husband without wanting to, and then you began to hate me! But now I am going to be your husband whether you like it or not, since I may not be your lover.

TEKLA (*playfully*): Don't talk nonsense, you idiot!

ADOLF: Listen, it's dangerous to go about believing that everyone else is an idiot.

TEKLA: Yes, but everybody does, I suspect!

ADOLF: And I'm beginning to suspect that he—your former husband—may not have been an idiot.

TEKLA: Good Lord, I believe you're beginning to sympathize with —him!

ADOLF: Yes, almost!

TEKLA: You see! You'd like to meet him, probably pour out your heart to him! What a pretty picture!—But even I am beginning to feel drawn to him since I've become tired of being a nurse to a child. At least he was a man, though he did have the fault of being *mine*!

ADOLF: You see! But don't talk so loudly—someone might hear us!

TEKLA: What difference would that make if they took us for married people?

ADOLF: So you're getting crazy about masculine men, too, and about chaste young men at the same time!

TEKLA: My admiration has no limits, as you see. My heart is open to everyone, to everything, for the great and the insignificant, for beauty and ugliness, for young and old—I love the whole world!

ADOLF: Do you know what that means?

TEKLA: No, I don't know anything! I just feel!

AOLD: That's a sure sign you're middle-aged.

TEKLA: Are you back to that? Watch out!

ADOLF: Watch out for yourself!

TEKLA: For what?

ADOLF: The knife!

TEKLA (*baby-talks*): Little brother mustn't play with such dangerous things!

ADOLF: I'm not playing any more!

TEKLA: So you're serious! Really serious! Then I'll show you— that you've made a mistake. That's to say—you'll never get to see it, to know it, but everyone will know it—but you! But you will suspect it, you'll sense it, and you aren't going to have a moment's peace again! You'll sense you're ridiculous, that you're deceived, but you're never going to get any proof—a husband never does! You're going to feel it!

ADOLF: You hate me?

TEKLA: No! I don't, and I don't think I'm going to, either. Probably because you're a child.

ADOLF: Now, yes! But do you remember when the storm hit us? Then you lay wailing like an infant; then you sat on my lap, and

I had to kiss your eyes to sleep. Then I was your nurse; I had to see to it that you combed your hair before you went out, I had to see to it that your shoes were sent to the shoemaker, see to it that we got food. I had to sit by your side and hold your hand for hours, because you were afraid, afraid of the whole world, because you didn't have a single friend and public opinion was crushing you. I had to give you courage by talking until my tongue was dry and my head ached. I had to sit there pretending to be strong, to force myself to believe in the future, and succeeded at last in getting life into you again, for you were as if dead. Then you admired me: then I was *the* man, not like that athlete you had left, but the strong man, the hypnotist who stroked his strength into your feeble muscles, filled your empty brain with new power. I revived you; supplied you with friends, provided you with a little court, which I tricked into admiring you, set you above me and my home. Then I painted you in my most beautiful pictures in rose and azure blue against a background of gold, and there wasn't an exhibit where you didn't have the best place. Sometimes you were St. Cecilia, sometimes you were Mary Stuart, Karin Månsdotter, Ebba Brahe,* and I centered the interest in you and forced the hooting crowd to see you with my eyes. I forced your personality on them, forced them to accept you, until you had won the sympathy of the public and you could go ahead by yourself!

When you were ready, my strength was gone, and I collapsed from overexertion—I had raised you and crippled myself. I became ill, and my illness embarrassed you now that life had begun to smile on you—and sometimes you were driven by a secret longing to dispose of the creditor and the witness! Your love became like a big sister's, and for want of anything better I had to get used to my new role of little brother. You're still affectionate, even more than ever, but it's tinged with a great

---

*Mary, Queen of Scots; Queen Karin of Sweden (see Strindberg's *Erik XIV*); Lady Ebba Brahe, the Swedish noblewoman loved by Gustav II Adolf (see Strindberg's *Gustav Adolf*).

sympathy, which includes quite a bit of condescension which is turning into contempt when my talent is setting and your sun is rising.

Be that as it may, your spring, too, seems to be drying up, since I can't replenish it, or, rather, when you want to show that you don't want to take anything from my spring. And then we'll both go under! And now you have to have someone to blame! A new one! Because you are weak, and you can never carry your guilt yourself, so I'm to be the scapegoat that's to be slaughtered alive! When you cut my tendons, you didn't take into account that you were crippling yourself, because the years have made us twins. You were an offshoot from my bush, but you wanted to free your shoot before it took root. That's why you couldn't grow by yourself; the bush couldn't do without its main stem—so both died!

TEKLA: All this, I take it, means that you have written my books!

ADOLF: No, that's what *you* want me to say—to make me a liar!— I didn't put it as crudely as you, and I've talked for five minutes to give all the nuances, all the halftones, all the transitions, but in your register there is only one tone!

TEKLA: Yes, yes! But the gist of all this is that you have written my books!

ADOLF: No, there isn't any gist! You can't resolve a chord into one tone; you can't translate a complex life into the number one. I haven't said anything so stupid as to say I've written your books.

TEKLA: But that is what you meant?

ADOLF (*furious*): I have not meant that!

TEKLA: But the total—

ADOLF (*wild*): There isn't any total when one doesn't add; it's a quotient, a long, endless decimal number as quotient when one divides, and the result isn't even. I haven't added!

TEKLA: Yes, but I can add!

ADOLF: I believe that, but I haven't added!

TEKLA: But you've wanted to!

ADOLF (*exhausted, closes his eyes*): No, no, no—don't talk to me any more! I'll have an attack! Quiet! Go away! You're destroying my brains with your pincers—you set the claws in my thoughts and tear them to pieces! (*Becomes unconscious; stares straight ahead, and rolls his thumbs*)

TEKLA (*tenderly*): What's wrong? Are you ill? Adolf! (ADOLF *wards her off.*) Adolf! (*He shakes his head.*) Adolf!

ADOLF: Yes.

TEKLA: Do you admit you were wrong just now?

ADOLF: Yes, yes, yes, I admit it!

TEKLA: And beg my forgiveness?

ADOLF: Yes, yes, yes, I beg your forgiveness! Just so you won't talk to me!

TEKLA: Kiss my hand, then.

ADOLF (*kisses her hand*): I kiss your hand. Just so you won't talk to me!

TEKLA: And now you're going out to get a bit of fresh air before dinner.

ADOLF: Yes, I need to! And then we'll pack and leave!

TEKLA: No!

ADOLF: Why? There must be a reason!

TEKLA: Because I've promised to take part in the entertainment tonight.

ADOLF: So that's what it was!

TEKLA: That's what it was! I've promised to be there—

ADOLF: Promised! You probably said you thought you'd come; that doesn't prevent your saying now that you won't come.

TEKLA: No, I'm not like you—I keep my word!

ADOLF: A person can keep his word, but he doesn't need to keep everything he says. Is there anyone who made you promise that you'd come?

TEKLA: Yes!

ADOLF: Then you can ask to be released from your promise because your husband is ill!

TEKLA: No, I don't want to, and you're not so sick that you can't come along!

ADOLF: Why do you always want me along? Does it make you feel less uneasy?

TEKLA: I don't understand what you mean.

ADOLF: That's what you always say when you know I mean something—that you don't like.

TEKLA: Oh-h! What don't I like now?

ADOLF: Stop; don't begin again!—Good-bye for now! And consider what you're doing!

(ADOLF *goes out through the door at the back and then goes to the right.* TEKLA *left alone;* GUSTAV *comes in immediately and goes to the table to get a newspaper, pretending not to see* TEKLA.)

TEKLA: (*starts; controls herself*): Oh, is it you?

GUSTAV: It's I!—Excuse me . . .

TEKLA: How did you get here?

GUSTAV: By the highway. But—I won't stay, since—

TEKLA: Stay by all means!—Well, it has been a long time!

GUSTAV: It has been a long time!

TEKLA: You've changed a lot!

GUSTAV: And you're as charming as ever! Almost more youthful! —Forgive me, though; but I shan't disturb your happiness by staying! If I had known that you were here, I would never . . .

TEKLA: If you don't find it embarrassing, I beg you to stay!

GUSTAV: As far as I'm concerned, there's nothing to hinder, but I'm thinking—well, whatever I do say will hurt you.

TEKLA: Sit down for a while. You're not hurting me—you have the rare gift—that you've always had—to be tactful and nice.

GUSTAV: You're too polite! But it's not certain that—your husband would be as forbearing about me as you are!

TEKLA: On the contrary, he was just now expressing a great deal of sympathy with you!

GUSTAV: Really!—Yes, everything disappears eventually—like carving one's names in a tree—not even ill will can last forever!

TEKLA: He has never had any ill will toward you, for he has never seen you.—So far as I'm concerned, I've always dreamt about—getting to see you two for a moment as friends—or that you'd at least meet each other in my presence—that you'd shake hands —and part!

GUSTAV: I've had a secret longing, too, to see the person whom I've loved more than life itself—in really good hands! And I've certainly heard a great deal of good about him, I know all that he has produced, but all the same—before I get old—I'd have liked to press his hand, look into his eyes, and beg him to protect this treasure that destiny has placed in his possession. That's how I wanted to destroy the involuntary hate I bear him, and I wanted peace and humility of mind so that I could live out my unhappy days.

TEKLA: You have expressed my thoughts, and you have understood me.—Thank you!

GUSTAV: Oh, I'm an insignificant person, and I was too insignificant to be able to overshadow you. My monotonous life, my dull work, my narrow circle weren't for your spirit, which longed for freedom. I admit it! But you understand—you've delved into the human soul—what it has cost me to admit this to myself!

TEKLA: It is noble, it is great to be able to admit one's weaknesses —it's not everyone who can! (*Sighs*) But you always were a sincere, faithful, dependable person—that I valued—but . . .

GUSTAV: I wasn't—I wasn't then, but suffering purifies us, sorrow ennobles us, and—I have suffered!

TEKLA: Poor Gustav!—Can you forgive me? Can you?

GUSTAV: Forgive? What? Why, I'm the one who should beg for forgiveness!

TEKLA (*changing her manner*): Why, I believe we're both weeping—old people that we are!

GUSTAV (*changing his manner*): Old! Yes, I am old! But you! You get younger and younger! (*Sits down without her noticing on the chair to the left, whereupon Tekla sits down on the couch*)

TEKLA: Do you think so?

GUSTAV: And you certainly know how to dress!

TEKLA: Why, you taught me that! Don't you remember your discovering what colors really become me?

GUSTAV: No.

TEKLA: Yes! You don't remember! Hm—I remember that you even became angry with me the days I wasn't wearing anything in flaming red!

GUSTAV: Surely I didn't get angry! I was never angry with you!

TEKLA Oh, yes, you were, when you were going to teach me to think! Do you remember that? Because I couldn't think!

GUSTAV: Of course you could think! Why, everyone can! And now you're really sharp-witted, at least when you write!

TEKLA (*unpleasantly touched, speeds up her dialogue*): Yes, darling, it's fun all the same to see you again, and under such quiet curcumstances.

GUSTAV: Well, I suppose I wasn't a really difficult person, and your life with me was rather quiet.

TEKLA: Yes, a little too quiet.

GUSTAV: Oh-h! But that's what I thought you wanted! At least that's what you said when we were engaged.

TEKLA: I didn't know what I wanted then. And Mother had told me that I had to pretend!

GUSTAV: Well, now everything's right for you. Why, the life of an artist is brilliant, and your husband doesn't seem to be any lazybones.

TEKLA: You can get too much of a good thing, too!

GUSTAV (*changing his manner*): What! You're still wearing my earrings!

TEKLA (*embarrassed*): Yes, why not?—We've never been enemies—and I thought I'd wear them as a symbol—and a reminder—that we aren't enemies—besides, you know, you can't buy any like these any more! (*Disengages one earring*)

GUSTAV: Yes, that's fine, but what does your husband say about it?

TEKLA: What do I care what he says!

GUSTAV: You don't care! But you can hurt him by wearing them! You can make him ridiculous!

TEKLA (*shortly, as if to herself*): He's that already!

GUSTAV (*who has seen that she is having a hard time fastening the earring, gets up*): May I help you?

TEKLA: Thank you!

GUSTAV (*pinches her ear*): Dear little ear! Just think if your husband saw us!

TEKLA: Then there'd be weeping!

GUSTAV: Is he jealous?

TEKLA: Is he jealous? Yes, I'll say he is!
  (*Sounds from the room to the right*)

GUSTAV: Whose room is that?

TEKLA: I don't know—Well, tell me about yourself and what you're doing.

GUSTAV: Tell me about yourself!
  (TEKLA *embarrassed; lifts the cloth from the figure.*)

GUSTAV: Ah! Who is it?—What!—It's you!

TEKLA: I don't think so!

GUSTAV: But it looks like you!

TEKLA (*cynically*): That's what you think!

GISTAV: It reminds me of the story: How could Her Majesty see that?

TEKLA (*laughs loudly*): You're too crazy!—Do you know any new stories?

GUSTAV: No, but you ought to.

TEKLA: I never hear any good ones any more.

GUSTAV: Is he bashful?

TEKLA: Oh—yes! When he's talking.

GUSTAV: Not otherwise?

TEKLA: He's very ill right now.

GUSTAV: Poor fellow! But why should little brother go sniffing at someone else's wasp's nest?

TEKLA (*laughs*): You're too crazy!

GUSTAV: Do you remember that once when we were newly mar-

ried—we lived in this room? Eh? The furniture was different
then. For example, there was a bureau by that pillar, and the
couch was there.

TEKLA: Sh-h!

GUSTAV: Look at me!

TEKLA: I certainly can!

(*They look at each other.*)

GUSTAV: Do you think a person can forget what has made a strong
impression on him?

TEKLA: No! And memories are powerful! Especially the memories
of youth.

GUSTAV: Do you remember when I first met you? You were a
little, lovable child, a slate on which your parents and your
governness had made a few scratches, which I had to erase.
And then I wrote new lessons in my own spirit until you felt you
were completely covered. That's why, you see, I wouldn't want
to be in your husband's place—well, that's his business!—But
that's why there's a certain pleasure in meeting you again. Our
thoughts are alike, and sitting here talking to you is like opening
an old bottle of wine of my own making. I get my own wine,
but it's mature! And now when I'm getting married again, I've
deliberately selected a young girl I can bring up to suit myself
for, you see, woman is man's child, and, if she doesn't become
his child, he becomes hers, and then the world's turned upside
down!

TEKLA: Are you going to get married again?

GUSTAV: Yes. I'm going to tempt fortune once more, but this time
I'm going to hitch up better, so there won't be any runaway.

TEKLA: Is she beautiful?

GUSTAV: Yes, to me. Maybe I am too old! It's strange—now that
chance has brought us together—I'm beginning to doubt that it's
possible to play that game again.

TEKLA: How so?

GUSTAV: My roots are still left, I feel, in you, and the old wounds
are reopening. You're a dangerous woman, Tekla!

TEKLA: Oh-h! My young husband says that I can't attract men any more!

GUSTAV: That's to say: he doesn't love you any more!

TEKLA: What he means by love I don't understand!

GUSTAV: You've played hide-and-seek so long you can't catch each other! That does happen. You've had to play innocent so that he doesn't dare. Yes, you see, changing has its inconveniences. It has its inconveniences.

TEKLA: You're reproaching . . .

GUSTAV: Not at all! What happens, happens—out of necessity, because if it doesn't happen, something else does. But what happened, happened.

TEKLA: You are broad-minded! And I've never met anyone else with whom I'd rather exchange ideas. You're so free from moral scruples and moralizing, demand so little from people, that I feel free in your presence. You know, I'm jealous of the girl you're going to marry!

GUSTAV: And I'm jealous of your husband.

TEKLA (*gets up*): And now we're going to part! Forever!

GUSTAV: Yes, we're going to part. But not without a real farewell! Isn't that right?

TEKLA (*uneasy*): No!

GUSTAV (*follows her*): Yes! We'll have a farewell party! We'll drown our memories in ecstasy which will be so heavy that, when we wake up, we'll have lost our memories—there is ecstasy like that, you know! (*Puts his arm around her waist*) You've been pulled down by a sickly spirit who's infecting you with his consumption! I'll puff new life into you, I'll get your talent to bloom in fall, as an everblooming rose, I'll . . .

(*Two women in traveling garb appear at the veranda door; they look, amazed, point at the two with their fingers, laugh, and go on their way.*)

TEKLA (*freeing herself*): Who were they?

GUSTAV (*indifferently*): Travelers.

TEKLA; Leave me! I'm afraid of you!

GUSTAV: Why?

TEKLA: You're taking my soul.

GUSTAV: And giving you mine in return! You haven't any soul, so far as that goes; that's only an illusion!

TEKLA: You have a way of saying impolite things so that I don't get angry with you.

GUSTAV: That's because you know I hold the first mortgage! Tell me. When—and—where?

TEKLA: No! I pity him! He still loves me, and I don't want to do him any more harm!

GUSTAV: He doesn't love you! Do you want proof?

TEKLA: How could you get any?

GUSTAV (*picks up the pieces of the photograph from the floor*): Here, see for yourself!

TEKLA: Oh! That's disgraceful!

GUSTAV: There you see for youself! So:—When? And where?

TEKLA: What a false scoundrel!

GUSTAV: When?

TEKLA: He's leaving on the eight o'clock boat tonight.

GUSTAV: So . . .

TEKLA: Nine o'clock! (*Commotion in the room to the right*) Who's staying in there and making all that noise?

GUSTAV (*goes over to the keyhole*): We'll see.—A table has been knocked over and a water pitcher broken. Nothing else. Maybe they've locked up a dog. Nine o'clock, then!

TEKLA: Right! Let him blame himself! Just think, such duplicity, and from him who has preached honesty and who has taught me to tell the truth!—But, just a minute . . . how was it!—He was almost unfriendly when I came in—didn't come down to the dock—and then—and then he said something about the young fellows on the steamer which I pretended I didn't understand— but how could he know that?—Just a minute—and then he philosophized about woman, and you were haunting him—and then he said he was going to be a sculptor because that's the art of today—exactly as you reasoned it out in the old days!

GUSTAV: No, really!

TEKLA: No, really!—Ah, now I understand! Now I'm beginning to understand what a terrible scoundrel you are! You've been here and torn him to pieces! You're the one who had been sitting on the couch; made him believe he had epilepsy; that he had to live in celibacy; that he should show he was a man and revolt against his wife! Yes, it was you!—How long have you been here?

GUSTAV: I've been here eight days!

TEKLA: So it was you I saw on the steamer!

GUSTAV: It was I!

TEKLA: And you thought you'd trap me!

GUSTAV: I already have!

TEKLA: Not yet!

GUSTAV: Oh, yes!

TEKLA: You stole up on my lamb like a wolf! You had a damnable plan to destroy my happiness—You set it going, but I opened my eyes and destroyed it!

GUSTAV: What you're saying isn't exactly right!—This is how it really was!—That things wouldn't turn out well for you two was my secret wish, naturally! But I was almost certain I wouldn't have to interfere! Besides, I've had so many other things to take care of, I didn't have any time left for scheming! But when I happened to be out strolling and saw you with the young fellows on the steamer, I felt the time for looking at you two was ripe.

I came here, and your lamb threw himself into the arms of the wolf immediately! I aroused his sympathy through some reflex that I don't want to be impolite enough to try to explain; I sympathized with him for he was in the same predicament I had once been in. But then he began poking at my old wound —the book, you know—and the idiot—then I wanted to pick him to pieces—and mix up the pieces so that he could never be put together again—and I succeeded, thanks to your conscientious preparatory work! Then I had you left! You were the spring in the instrument and had to be screwed apart. Then there was humming!

 When I came in, I really didn't know what I was going to say! Of course, like a chess player I had a lot of plans, but how I was going to play the game depended on your moves! One thing led to another, chance helped, and there I had you.—Now you're caught!

TEKLA: No!

GUSTAV: Yes, you are!—What you wanted least of all has happened! The public—represented by two women—whom I hadn't sent for—because I'm no schemer—the public has seen how you've become reconciled with your former husband and—repentant, crept back into his faithful embrace! Is that enough!

TEKLA: It should be enough for your revenge!—But tell me, you who are so broadminded and honest in your thinking, how does it happen that you who consider everything that happens, happens of necessity, and that none of our actions is free—

GUSTAV (*correcting her*): To a certain extent is not free.

TEKLA: That's the same thing!

GUSTAV: No!

TEKLA: —how can you who consider me innocent since my nature and circumstances drove me to act as I did, how could you think you had the right to get revenge?

GUSTAV: Well, on the same grounds, and on the grounds that my nature and circumstances drove me to get revenge! Isn't it a tie? But do you know why you two happened to draw the shorter straw in this struggle? (TEKLA *grimaces contemptuously.*) Why you let yourselves be fooled?—Well, because I was stronger than you and wiser! You were the idiot!—and he! You see, a person doesn't have to be an idiot just because he doesn't write novels or paint. Remember that!

TEKLA: You are absolutely without feelings, aren't you?

GUSTAV: Absolutely!—But, you see, that's why I can *think,* which you've rarely done, and *act,* as you've just found out!

TEKLA: All this just because I've hurt your self-respect!

GUSTAV: It's not only that! Quit hurting other people's self-respect! That's a person's most vulnerable point!

TEKLA: Vengeful wretch! Shame on you!

GUSTAV: Wanton wretch! Shame on you!

TEKLA: It's my nature eh?

GUSTAV: It's my nature, eh? You had better look into other people's natures, before you let your own express itself freely! Otherwise it can hurt itself, and then there's weeping and gnashing of teeth!

TEKLA: You can never forgive . . .

GUSTAV: Yes! I have forgiven you!

TEKLA: You?

GUSTAV: Of course! Have I lifted my hand against you all these years? No! And I came only to look at you, and you cracked! Have I reproached you? Have I moralized, preached? No! I've joked a little with your husband, and that was enough to make him burst.

But I'm standing here as the plaintiff defending himself! Tekla! Haven't you anything for which to reproach yourself?

TEKLA: Nothing at all!—Christians say that it's destiny that controls our actions; others call it fate. Aren't we innocent?

GUSTAV: Yes, to a certain extent. But there is a margin of responsibility all the same; and the creditors appear sooner or later! Innocent but responsible! Innocent before Him, who doesn't exist any more, responsible before oneself and before one's fellow men.

TEKLA: So you came to dun me, then?

GUSTAV: I came to take back what you had stolen, not what you had received as gifts! You had stolen my honor, and I could get that back only by taking yours! Wasn't I right?

TEKLA: Honor? Hm! And now you're satisfied!

GUSTAV: Now I'm satisfied! (*Rings for the* WAITER)

TEKLA: And now you're going to your fiancée!

GUSTAV: I haven't any!—And I'll never want any! I'm not going home because I don't have a home, and don't want any. (WAITER

enters.) Please get my bill; I'm leaving on the eight o'clock boat!
(*The* WAITER *bows and goes.*)

TEKLA: Without any reconciliation?

GUSTAV: Reconciliation! You use so many words that have lost
their meanings. Reconciliation! Should we live together all three?
You're the one who should atone by making up for all this, but
you can't! You've only taken, but what you have taken, you've
absorbed so that you can't return it!—Will you be satisfied if I
say: Forgive me for your having clawed my heart to pieces; forgive me because you dishonored me; forgive me because through
seven years you made me the butt of ridicule for my pupils;
forgive me because I released you from parental discipline, released you from the tyranny of ignorance and superstition, put
you in charge of my home, gave you position and friends, made
you a woman! Forgive me as I forgive you! Now I'm tearing up
the bill! Go and settle your account with your husband!

TEKLA: What have you done with him? I'm beginning to suspect—
something—dreadful!

GUSTAV: With him!—Do you still love him?

TEKLA: Yes!

GUSTAV: And me just now! Was that true?

TEKLA: That was true!

GUSTAV: Do you know what you are, then?

TEKLA: You despise me?

GUSTAV: I pity you! That's a quality—I don't say a flaw, but a
quality that is disadvantageous because of its consequences. Poor
Tekla!—I don't know—but I almost regret what I've done though
I'm innocent—as you! But perhaps it will do you good to feel
what I felt that time.—Do you know where your husband is?

TEKLA: I believe I know now! He is in your room—in the next
room! And he has heard everything! And seen everything! And
the one who has seen his own ghost dies!

(ADOLF *appears at the veranda door; pale as a corpse, and
with a bleeding scratch on one cheek; unmoving, expressionless
eyes, and white foam about his mouth.*)

GUSTAV: (*starts*): No, there he is!—Settle with him; you'll see if he'll be as generous as I!—Good bye!

(GUSTAV *goes to the left; stops.*)

TEKLA (*goes toward* ADOLF *with outstretched arms*): Adolf! (ADOLF *sinks down by the door.*)

TEKLA (*throws herself over* ADOLF'*s body and caresses him*): Adolf! My dear child! Are you alive? Tell me!—Forgive your wicked Tekla! Forgive! Forgive! Forgive! Answer me, little brother, do you hear? No! God, he doesn't hear. He's dead! Oh, God in heaven, oh, my God, help us! Help us!

GUSTAV: Really! She loves him, too! Poor woman!

CURTAIN

Introduction to
'The Stronger'

AWARE AS HE always was of developments in the Western theater, Strindberg did not miss the opportunity of demonstrating that
he could write a *quart d'heure* of the kind that had been put on at
the Théâtre Libre and in other continental theaters. Of the several
he wrote, the most popular, most frequently produced, and best is
The Stronger.

Behind the writing of this play were Strindberg's old dream of
having a theater of his own and the possibility of his getting an ex-
perimental one in Copenhagen in 1889; his wife Siri's persistent
ambition to be an actress; their open dissension (he wrote the play
for her at a time when they were hardly on speaking terms); attention, real or imagined, paid him by other women; and the fact that
he remained under the influence of naturalism.

The Stronger can be called a *quart d'heure,* a monodrama, a
dramatic monologue, a battle of brains, or a tour de force. However one classifies it, it must be admitted that it is good theater,
that it does have something to say, and that it presents an interesting gambit for argument and discussion. The proof of its effective-

ness on the stage lies both in the enthusiasm with which actresses have accepted either of the two roles and the interest shown it by innumerable audiences. It is, moreover, an ingenious demonstration of the naturalistic idea that life is a struggle for survival and, one might add, for the comforts of security represented by marriage, family, and home. The perennial question of who is the stronger presents possibilities for discussion between idealists and those who subscribe to a more or less naturalistic approach to the human condition.

In 1889 Strindberg apparently did not hesitate about answering the question. When he wrote a note to Siri, who was to create the role of Mrs. X, he said, among other things:

> Play it 1. as if you were an actress—that is, not as an ordinary housewife; 2. as the stronger, that is as the pliable person who bends—and rises again; 3. dressed in the best of taste. 4. Study the role extremely carefully, but play it simply. That's to say, not "simply." Put 50% charlatan into it . . . and hint at depths that do not exist.

The play becomes the sudden solution of a puzzle by the married woman when she confronts her silent but far from passive rival and puts the pieces together. Mrs. X's analysis of their relationship (her fear of Miss Y, her cultivation of her even to the point of inviting her to her home time and again, Amelia's engagement, the christening and the breaking of the engagement, and the fact that she never visits them afterward) plus the telling little details (tulips embroidered on her husband's slippers; his choice of colors and books for her, of dishes for their table, of the name of their son, and of the place to spend their vacations, and even of his expressions of passion for her to respond to) are revealing illustrations of Strindberg's diabolically keen insight into human nature and his gift for putting what he saw into dramatically effective form.

The Stronger   ·   One Scene

Märta Ekström and Eva Dahlbeck in *The Stronger* (The Royal Dramatic Theater, Stockholm)

Characters

MRS. X, *actress, married*
MISS Y, *actress, unmarried*

SETTING

A corner of a women's café; two small iron tables, a red worsted shag sofa, and some chairs.

MRS. X *enters wearing a winter coat and hat and carrying an elegant Japanese basket on her arm.*

MISS Y *is sitting at a table with a half-empty beer bottle on it; she is reading an illustrated paper, which she exchanges for others from time to time later on.*

MRS. X: Hello, Amelia darling! You look as lonely on Christmas eve as a poor bachelor.

MISS Y (*looks up from her paper, nods, and goes on reading*)

MRS. X: You know, I feel really sorry for you—alone in a café, and on Christmas eve at that. I feel just as sorry as when I saw a wedding party in a Paris restaurant and the bride was sitting reading a humor magazine while the bridegroom was playing billiards with the witnesses. Huh, I thought, with a start like that how would it go and how would it end! He played billiards on his wedding night!—And she read a humor magazine, you're thinking! Well, it's not quite the same!

WAITRESS (*enters; puts a cup of chocolate in front of* MRS. X, *and exits*)

MRS. X: You know what, Amelia! I think you would have been better off if you had kept him! Remember I was the first one who told you to forgive him! Remember?—You could be married and have a home. Do you remember the Christmas when you were out in the country with your fiancé's parents? How you raved about the joys of a home and really longed to get away from the theater!—Yes, Amelia darling, a home of one's own is certainly the best—second to the theater—and the children, of course.—But you don't understand that!

MISS Y (*gets a contemptuous look on her face*)

MRS. X (*drinks a few sips out of her cup; then opens her basket and shows* MISS Y *the Christmas gifts*): I'll show you what I've bought for my darlings. (*Takes out a doll*) Look at that! It's for Lisa. See, she can roll her eyes and turn her neck! See!—And here's Maja's cork pistol. (*Loads and shoots at* MISS Y)

MISS Y (*makes a gesture of horror*)

MRS. X: Did I frighten you? Did you think I wanted to shoot you? Eh?—My word, I think you did! I'd be less amazed if *you* wanted to shoot *me* since I've stood in your way—I know you can never forget that I did—though I was absolutely innocent. You still think my scheming got you out of the Great Theater, but I didn't scheme! I didn't, though you think I did!—Well, there's no point in my saying so, for you still think I was the one! (*Takes out a pair of embroidered slippers*) And my husband's to have these. With tulips on them—I've embroidered them myself—I despise tulips, of course, but he has to have tulips on everything!

MISS Y (*looks up from her paper—with irony and curiosity*)

MRS. X (*puts a hand in each slipper*): Do you see what small feet Bob has? See? And you should see how elegantly he walks! You've never seen him in slippers! (*Miss Y laughs aloud.*) Look, and you'll see! (*She pretends to walk with the slippers on the table*.)

MISS Y (*laughs so it can be heard*)

MRS. X: And then when he's angry he stamps his foot like this, you see: "Eh! The damned maids who never can learn to make coffee! Now those idiots haven't clipped the lamp wick properly!" And then there's a draft on the floor, and his feet get cold: "Ugh, how cold it is! Those damned idiots who can't keep the fire going!" (*She rubs the sole of one slipper against the top of the other*.)

MISS Y (*laughs uproariously*)

MRS. X: And then he comes home and looks for his slippers which Marie has put under the dresser . . . Oh, it's a shame to make fun of one's husband like this. He is really kind, and he's a fine little man—you should have had a man like that, Amelia!— What are you laughing at? Eh? Eh?—And then I know he's faithful to me, you see—yes, I do know! He told me so himself . . . What are you grinning about? . . . that when I was on that tour in Norway that nasty Frederique tried to seduce him—can you imagine? (*Pause*) But I'd have torn out her eyes if she had come around when I was at home! (*Pause*) It's a good thing Bob told me himself so I didn't have to hear it from others! (*Pause*) But Frederique wasn't the only one, you may believe! I don't know why, but women are absolutely crazy about *my* husband. They must think he has something to say about contracts at the theater, because he's in the office!—Maybe you have been after him, too!—I didn't quite believe you—but now I *know* that he didn't care about you and you seemed to have a grudge against him, I always thought! (*Pause; they look at each other with embarrassment*.)

MRS. X: Come over tonight, Amelia, and show us you're not angry with us, not with me at least! I don't know why, but I think it's so unpleasant to be on bad terms with *you* especially. Maybe it's because I did stand in your way that time—(*gradual decrease in tempo*)—or—I don't know at all—why really! (*Pause*)

MISS Y (*stares at* MRS. X *with curiosity*)

MRS. X (*thoughtful*): It was so strange about us—when I saw you the first time I was afraid of you, so afraid I didn't dare to let you out of my sight. Wherever I was, I was always near you—I didn't dare to be your enemy, so I became your friend. But there was always something wrong when you came to visit us, for I saw my husband couldn't stand you—and then I felt uncomfortable, as when clothes don't quite fit—and I did everything to make him friendly toward you, but I didn't succeed—before you got engaged! Then the two of you really got so friendly that it looked as if you dared to show your real feelings when you felt secure—and then—how was it after that?—I didn't get jealous —strange!—And I remember at the christening when you were godmother I made him kiss you—he did, but you got upset— that's to say: I didn't notice it then—didn't think about it afterward either—haven't really thought about it before—now! (*Gets up violently*) Why don't you say something? You haven't said a word all this time, but just let me keep on talking! You've sat there staring, twisting out of me all these thoughts, which have lain like raw silk in their cocoon—thoughts—suspicions maybe —let me see.—Why did you break your engagement? Why did you never come to our house after that? Why don't you want to come to us this evening?

MISS Y (*has an expression as if she wanted to speak*)

MRS. X: Quiet! You don't need to say anything—now I understand everything! That was why! That was why! Yes! Everything falls into place now! That's it!—Ugh, I don't want to sit at the same table! (*Moves her things to the other table*)

That's why I had to embroider tulips, which I hate, on his slippers—because you like tulips: that's why—(*throws the slippers to the floor*)—we had to live on Lake Mälare in the summer because you couldn't stand the sea; that's why my son was to be christened Eskil, because that was your father's name; that's why I had to wear your colors, read your authors; eat your favorite dishes, drink your drinks—your chocolate, for example; that's why—oh, my God—it's terrible when I think about it, it

is terrible!—Everything came to me from you, even your passions!—Your soul stole into mine like a worm into an apple, ate
and ate, dug and dug, until all that was left was the shell . . . and
a little dark dust! I wanted to escape from you, but I couldn't;
like a snake with your dark eyes you fascinated me—I felt how
my wings rose only to drag me down. I lay in the water with
bound feet, and the more I tried to swim with my hands, the
deeper I worked myself down until I sank to the bottom, where
you lay like a giant crab ready to seize me in your claws—that's
where I am now!

I hate you! Oh, how I hate you! But you—you just sit there
keeping still, calm, indifferent; indifferent about whether it's up
or down, Christmas or New Year's, if others are happy or unhappy, without the ability to hate or love; as still as a stork by a
rat hole—you couldn't catch your victim yourself, you couldn't
pursue her yourself, but you could lie in wait for her! Here you
sit in your corner—do you know they call it the rat trap—because of your reading the papers to see if anyone's having a bad
time, if anyone has been ruined, if anyone has been fired from
the theater. Here you sit waiting for your victims, figuring out
your chances like a pilot his shipwrecks, receiving your payoffs!

Poor Amelia! Do you know, I'm sorry for you all the same?
I know you're unhappy, unhappy like someone who has been
hurt, and nasty because you're hurt!—I can't be angry with you
though I'd like to be—you're the weakling—Oh, that with Bob,
I don't care about that!—That doesn't really hurt me!—And if
you have taught me to drink chocolate, or someone else has,
what difference does it make! (*Drinks a spoonful out of her cup.
With extreme common sense*) Besides, chocolate is good for me!
And if you have taught me how to dress—well, thanks very
much—that has made my husband closer to me than ever—you
lost when I won—yes, to judge by certain signs, I think you've
already lost him!—I suppose you expected me to go my own
way—as you did, and which you regret now—but you see I'm

not going to leave him!—We mustn't be petty, you see! And why should I take what no one else wants!

Maybe when all is said I'm really the stronger right now—you never got anything from me, you simply gave, and now I'm like a thief—so that when you awakened, I had what you had lost!

Otherwise how could everything be so worthless, so sterile in your hands? You couldn't keep any man's love with your tulips and your passions—as I could; you couldn't learn the art of living from your authors, as I did; you didn't have a little Eskil, though your father's name was Eskil! And why do you always keep still? Well, I thought that was strength, but it's probably only that you haven't anything to say! Because you couldn't think! (*Gets up and picks up the slippers*) Now I am going home—and taking my tulips with me—*your* tulips! You couldn't learn from others, you couldn't bend—so you broke like a dry reed—but I didn't! Thank you, Amelia, thank you for everything you taught me! Thank you for teaching my husband how to make love!—Now I'm going home to make love to him! (*Exits*)

Introduction to 'The Bond'

THE THEME OF the child as the bond between husband and wife is one of the most universal and timeless in Western literature. At the beginning of the 1890's it had particular significance for Strindberg, for those were the years when his marital difficulties led to separation and then divorce from Siri von Essen. Throughout those years he was highly disturbed, not only by his own emotional suffering and the embarrassing and humiliating torture of hearings and the trial itself, but by his very real concern for the futures of his two daughters and son. What would happen to them as a result of the divorce and the price that they would have to pay for it were matters that troubled him then and would continue to trouble him.

The most important literary result was the one-act serious drama *The Bond*. Structurally, this divorce play is midway between *The Father* and the two plays that followed it—*Lady Julie* and *Creditors*. The preliminary case (Alexandersson *vs* Alma) is similar to the opening scene in *The Father:* just as the examination of Nöjd by Captain Adolf and Pastor Jonas provides excellent preparation for the dramatic action that follows and introduces the theme that

serves as a catalyst, the Alexandersson-Alma scene not only pre-
pares us for the sort of action that will follow but introduces two
ideas—the inadequacy of the legal system and the concept of human nature basic to an understanding of the play. The rest of *The
Bond* approaches *Lady Julie* and *Creditors* in tightness of structure with, however, necessary divisions into "scenes" because of
the actual setting and the far greater number of characters.

The legal system to which his divorce has exposed him has perhaps puzzled some Americans. The pastor and the church council
do participate in the preliminary investigation, the hearing, and the
trial itself. The judge and the elected jury have powers appreciably
different from those in the American system, which excludes church
officials, gives far greater authority to the judge, restricts participa-
tion by the selected jury, and has different courtroom procedures.

These differences are, however, minor in significance as far as
the play itself goes. What is universal and timeless is the stress on
the inadequacy of any human legal system in getting at the truth
and meting out justice. The unreliability of human testimony, the
limitations nature itself has imposed on human beings in terms of
their powers of observation, the human tendency to rationalize and
adjust what is observed to one's own interests, and the arbitrary
provisions of human laws themselves are facts in both Swedish and
non-Swedish courtrooms. Western literature has exploited these
facts; Strindberg's play ranks among the most effective presentation
of them in dramatic form.

Closely related to the inadequacy of human laws and justice is
the concept of human nature essential to an understanding of what
Strindberg has to say. While Strindberg had dealt with this concept
time and again in practically all of his works written before *The
Bond,* and would continue to deal with it in the works that followed,
he probably never expressed it more effectively than he did in the
pastor's speech:

JUDGE: You are a terrible skeptic, Pastor!
PASTOR: One becomes that when one's sixty and has cared for
    human souls for forty years. Lying persists like original sin, and

I think all people lie; we lie out of fear as children; out of self-interest, necessity, for self-preservation when we get older. I know people who lie out of pure human kindness. In this case, as far as these two are concerned, I think you'll have a hard time figuring out who comes closest to speaking the truth, and I only want to warn you not to let any prejudice unconsciously sway you. You haven't been married very long—you're still bewitched by your young wife's charm, so you'll easily be taken in by a charming young lady, who is also an unhappy wife and mother. On the other hand, you've just become a father, so you can't escape being moved by the father's impending separation from his only child. Watch out for feeling too much sympathy for either of them, because sympathy for the one is cruelty toward the other.

Implicit in this speech and throughout the play is a concept of human nature that is at once essentially naturalistic and Hebraic-Christian. The naturalistic concept of man as an animal struggling for survival and self-preservation is only in relatively minor details different from the pastor's concept of man as a highly limited egotistic creature with a dual capacity for good and evil. The emphasis in the play is on the Hebraic-Christian point of view because of the nature of the situation itself; only superficially obscured is Strindberg's continuing interest in the naturalistic view of man and his environment.

It is the pastor who is also assigned the speech that helps to clarify another exceedingly important idea:

> JUDGE: ... it's ghastly to see two human beings who have loved each other try to destroy each other like this! It's like watching animals butchered!
> PASTOR: That is love, Judge!
> JUDGE: What is hate, then?
> PASTOR: The lining of the garment!

The concept of love-hate appears again and again in Strindberg's works, but *The Bond* is among his best treatments of the extremely common fact about the most intimate of human relationships. The union of the two very human principals has universal applications

in marital problems stemming from such conflicting factors as
genuine liking and daily exposure to domestic friction, wanting a
home but resenting being tied down for life, physical attraction and
opposite reactions when satisfied—in other words, the ambivalence
between positive and negative impulses. As Strindberg saw it, marriage is likely to be in varying degrees a struggle that goes on and
on, leads to no decision, and wearies both the egotists involved.

The two agreements entered into by Axel and Hélène are certainly illustrative enough of the results of Strindberg's observation
of his own and others' marriages. The first one, designed to protect
the "emancipated" woman who was not at all sure marriage was
right for her (privacy, no claim of right to the other's person, and
financial equality); and the second one, designed for the protection
of the child (no accusations or counteraccusations in court, the
awarding of the child to the mother, the granting of visiting rights
to the father, his promise of financial support) are believable and
very human. The premarital agreement is broken when nature takes
its due course; the agreement not to wash dirty linen in public is
kept only until the baroness becomes irritated.

Surely it is above all else the display of dirty linen in the courtroom that has made both audiences and readers accept *The Bond*
as a highly valid and effective treatment of divorce. For anyone
who has been directly or indirectly exposed to a divorce court, the
charges and the countercharges, though they may differ from those
of other trials in detail, must be embarrassingly and recognizably
pertinent to the stripping of two people of all shreds of human
dignity. The charges against Baron Sprengel—denying his wife
sleep, food, and medical care; jealousy; refusal to let her bring up
their son according to her wishes; breaking promises; wasting her
dowry; and adultery—are as familiar to those who know anything
about divorce are as his charges against her—bad temper, masculine tendencies, lying, wastefulness, unwillingness to compromise,
and adultery.

In this presentation of a marriage in which the two principals
have failed largely because of inability to communicate with each

other and to cooperate with each other, it is the child who should have been a bond and whose interests they have agreed to protect, at least in the courtroom, who becomes the victim of their incompatibility. Emile does not appear. One wonders how much he is present in any serious sense in their thoughts; at any rate, he is the primary victim. As Strindberg tells the story, the child will pay the price of disgrace and humiliation, having to do without the advantages of a real home, and being given a twisted upbringing.

Both the baroness and the baron are characterized in keeping with what Strindberg said about characterless characters in the Preface to *Lady Julie*. They are, in other words, complex and dynamic human beings, who have been shaped by their heredity and environment, by time and chance. The other characters are like, for example, the doctor in *The Father;* they are characterized only as they are seen in their particular functions. As in *Creditors,* Strindberg here, too, stresses the margin of human responsibility.

The Bond is startlingly good drama and good theater, as its successful production on both the Swedish and non-Swedish stage amply testifies.

The Bond   ·   A Tragedy in One Act

Characters

THE JUDGE, *twenty-seven years old*
THE PASTOR, *sixty*
BARON AXEL SPRENGEL, *forty-two*
BARONESS HÉLÈNE SPRENGEL, *forty*
ALEXANDER EKLUND,
EMANUEL WICKBERG,
KARL JOHAN SJÖBERG,
ERIK OTTO BOMAN,
ERENFRID SÖDERBERG,
OLOF ANDERSSON OF VIK,
KARL PETER ANDERSSON OF BERGA,   [*Members of the jury*]
AXEL VALLIN,
ANDERS ERIK RUTH,
SVEN OSKAR ERLIN,
AUGUST ALEXANDER VASS,
LUDVIG ÖSTMAN
THE CLERK
SHERIFF VIBERG
CONSTABLE ÖMAN
THE LAWYER
ALEXANDERSSON, *a farmer*
ALMA JONSSON, *a servant*
THE MILKMAID
THE HIRED MAN
SPECTATORS

[Setting]

A courtroom. A door and windows at the back; through the windows can be seen the churchyard and the bell tower. A door to the right. To the left the judge's table on a platform; the judge's chair is decorated with gilded ornaments of the sword and the scale of justice. On both sides of the judge's table, chairs and tables for the jury. Facing the judge's table, benches for spectators. The walls consist of built-in cabinets, on the doors of which are lists of market prices and public notices.

SHERIFF: Have you ever seen so many people at the summer sessions before?

CONSTABLE: No, not since we had that big murder case fifteen years ago.

SHERIFF: What's coming up is quite a story, too. It's as good as murdering both one's parents. It's bad enough that the baron and baroness are going to be divorced, but when the families start squabbling about property and the estate, you can imagine

207

there'll be quite an explosion. If they were going to squabble about their only child, too, King Solomon himself couldn't pass judgment.

CONSTABLE: Well, what's the truth about this case? Some people say this, and some that. But surely someone's to blame?

SHERIFF: Not necessarily. Sometimes it's no one's fault when two people quarrel, and occasionally it's the fault of only one of them. Take my old battle axe at home: they say she goes around quarreling with herself when I'm not at home. Besides this case isn't a quarrel; it's an out and out criminal case. In most cases like that the one party is the plaintiff, that's to say, the injured party, and the other's the defendant or the one at fault. It's not so easy to tell who's to blame in this case—both parties are plaintiffs, and both are defendants!

CONSTABLE: So! But it's strange nowadays; it's as if women had gone crazy. My old woman has spells when she says I ought to bear children if there were any justice—as if Our Lord didn't know how He has created His children. And she goes on and on about her being a human being, too, just as if I didn't already know that or had said anything else. She says she doesn't want to be my maid, though I'm actually her hired man.

SHERIFF: Really! So you, too, have that disease in your home! My wife reads a paper she gets at the manor house, and then one day she tells me something extremely striking about a girl in Dalarna who has become a bricklayer, another time about an old woman who has attacked and beaten up her sick husband. I don't know what it's all about, but she seems to be angry with me because I'm a man!

CONSTABLE: Yes, isn't it absolutely amazing? (*Offers the* SHERIFF *snuff*) Fine weather we're having! The rye's like a fur rug, and we got by without frost damage.

SHERIFF: I don't raise any crops, so good years are bad ones for me: no seizures of property, no forced auctions. Do you know the new judge?

CONSTABLE: No, But they say he's a young fellow who has just taken his degree and is serving as judge for the first time . . .

SHERIFF: They say he's something of a pietist! Hm!

CONSTABLE: Well, well!—Then the sermon will be a long one today!

SHERIFF *(places a large Bible on the clerk's table, and twelve small ones on the jury tables)*: It ought to be over pretty soon—they'll soon have been at it for almost a whole hour!

CONSTABLE: The pastor's a whiz of a preacher once he gets going. *(Pause)* Will the baron and the baroness appear personally?

SHERIFF: Both of them, so there'll be quite a show . . . *(The bells in the belltower ring.)* There! Now's it's over! Dust the table a little; then we can begin, I think.

CONSTABLE: And there's ink in the inkwells?

(The BARON *and the* BARONESS *enter.)*

BARON *(softly to the* BARONESS*)*: So, before we're separated for a year, we're in complete agreement on all points! First: no accusations in court!

BARONESS: Do you think I'd want to stand here revealing all the details of our married life in front of a crowd of curious farmers?

BARON: Fine! Next: you're to have custody of Emile during the year on the conditions that he may visit me when I wish and that he's to be reared according to the principles I've set up and you have approved?

BARONESS: Absolutely!

BARON: That I'm to contribute from the income of the estate three thousand crowns for your and Emile's support during the year?

BARONESS: Agreed!

BARON: Then I haven't anything to add except to say good-bye to you. Only you and I know why we're being divorced; for our son's sake no one else should find out. But I ask for his sake: don't stir up any contest so that we'll be provoked into throwing dirt on his parents' good names. At best he'll probably have to pay a cruel penalty for our getting divorced.

BARONESS: I won't stir up anything as long as I can keep my child!

BARON: Let's concentrate simply on this then: our child's welfare, and forget what there has been between us! And think of this, too: if we start fighting about the child and deny each other's fitness to bring him up, the judge can take him away from both of us and place him with pietists to be brought up in hatred and contempt for his parents !

BARONESS: That isn't possible!

BARON: Yes, my friend, that's the law!

BARONESS: That's a stupid law!

BARON: Perhaps, but it's valid, and it applies even to you!

BARONESS: It's unnatural! I'd never submit to it!

BARON: You don't need to since we've decided not to challenge each other. We've never agreed before, but on this one point we do agree: we are going to part without ill feeling! *(To the* PROSECUTOR*)* May the baroness wait in that room?

PROSECUTOR: Yes, indeed. Go right in!

(The BARON *accompanies the* BARONESS *to the door at the right; then he goes out at the back.)*

(The LAWYER, *the* SERVANT GIRL, *the* MILKMAID, *and the* HIRED MAN *enter.)*

LAWYER *(to the* SERVANT GIRL*):* You see, my friend, I don't doubt for a minute that you did steal, but since your employer doesn't have any witnesses to your theft, you're innocent. But since he called you a thief in the presence of two witnesses, he's guilty of slander. You're the plaintiff, and he's the defendant. Just remember: a criminal's first duty is: to deny.

SERVANT: Yes, but the judge just said I wasn't any criminal, but my employer was.

LAWYER: You are a criminal since you did steal, but as you've asked for a lawyer, it's my unavoidable duty to wash you clean and get your employer pronounced guilty. So, for the last time: Deny everything! *(To the* WITNESSES*)* How are you going to testify? Listen: a good witness keeps to the point. So note carefully: it isn't a question of whether Alma has stolen or not; it's merely a question of whether Alexandersson has said she has stolen, because—note this carefully—Alexandersson does not have the right to prove his accusations, but we have. Why the devil knows! But that doesn't concern you. So: control your tongue and keep your fingers on the Bible!

MILKMAID: Goodness, I'm so scared—I don't know what I'm going to say.

HIRED MAN: Say what I say, then you won't be lying.

(*The* JUDGE *and the* PASTOR *enter.*)

JUDGE: Thank you for your sermon, Pastor!

PASTOR: Don't mention it, Judge.

JUDGE: As you know, I'm a judge for the first time. I've really feared this career that I've entered almost against my will. Partly because the laws are so imperfect, the system of trial so uncertain, and human nature so full of lies and pretense that I have often wondered how a judge can have the courage to express a definite opinion. And you have reawakened my fears today!

PASTOR: Being conscientious is one's duty, of course, but getting sentimental won't do. And when everything else on earth is imperfect, I suppose we musn't consider judges or judgments perfect.

JUDGE: That may be, but that doesn't keep me from feeling an unlimited responsibility when I hold the fate of human beings in my hands. And when what I say can have its effects for generations. I'm thinking particularly of this divorce case between the baron and his wife. You gave them the two warnings in the church council, so I must ask you what your opinion of their relationship and their relative guilt is.

PASTOR: That's to say you want to make me the judge or to base your judgment on my testimony. But I have to refer you to the minutes of the church council.

JUDGE: The minutes . . . yes! I've read them. But it's precisely what's not in the minutes I need to know.

PASTOR: What they accused each other of at their individual hearings is my secret. Besides, how can I know who spoke the truth

and who lied? I have to say to you what I said to them: I don't
need to believe the one more than the other.

JUDGE: But you certainly have formed an opinion during the
hearings?

PASTOR: I've had one opinion when I've listened to one of them,
and another when I've listened to the other. In other words: I
can't have any firm opinion about this case.

JUDGE: But I'm to express a definite opinion, I who don't know
anything at all about it.

PASTOR: That is a judge's heavy duty, a duty I could never bear.

JUDGE: But can't witnesses be produced? Evidence secured?

PASTOR: No, they're not accusing each other publicly. Besides,
two false witnesses provide full and valid evidence, and a per-
jurer is just as good. Do you think I'd base my judgment on
servants' gossip, envious neighbors' talk, or biased relatives'
revengefulness?

JUDGE: You are a terrible skeptic, Pastor!

PASTOR: One becomes that when one's sixty and has cared for
human souls for forty years. Lying persists like original sin, and
I think all people lie; we lie out of fear as children; out of self-
interest, necessity, for self-preservation when we get older. I
know people who lie out of pure human kindness. In this case,
so far as these two are concerned, I think you'll have a hard
time figuring out who comes closest to speaking the truth, and I
only want to warn you not to let any prejudice unconsciously
sway you. You haven't been married very long—you're still
bewitched by your young wife's charm, so you'll easily be taken
in by a charming young lady, who is also an unhappy wife and
a mother. On the other hand, you've just become a father, so
you can't escape being moved by the father's impending separation from his only child. Watch out for feeling too much sympathy for either of them, because sympathy for the one is cruelty
toward the other.

JUDGE: One thing will make my task easier—they are in essential
agreement.

to the SHERIFF): Call in the parties and the witnesses.
he parties, witnesses, and spectators enter.)
In the case between Alma Jonsson and Mr. Alexander
he is sentenced to pay a fine of a hundred crowns fo
ering her.

DERSSON: But I saw her steal!—That's what one gets fo
merciful!

(to ALMA): You see! If one only denies, all goes well
ndersson was stupid when he didn't deny. If I had bee
wyer, and he had denied the charge, I'd have challenge
witnesses and you'd have lost!—Now we'll go out an
up! *(Leaves with* ALMA *and the witnesses)*

ERSSON *(to the* SHERIFF): Now I suppose I'll have t
she has been honest and decent.
That's not my affair!

ERSSON *(to the* CONSTABLE): And for this I'm to lose my
Can you imagine justice is such that the thief gets the
and the victim gets punished! Good lord!—Come drink a
royal with me, Oman.

E: I'll come a bit later, but don't complain!

ERSSON: Yes, damn it, I'll complain even if it costs me
onths in jail!

E: Just don't complain! Don't complain!

SHERIFF): Call the divorce case between Baron Sprengel
wife, née Malmberg.
The divorce case between Baron Sprengel and his wife,
mberg. *(The* BARON *and the* BARONESS *enter.)*
the proceedings Baron Sprengel has brought against
, he states that he does not intend to continue his mar-
nd asks that, inasmuch as the warnings of the church
have proved fruitless, they be separated in bed and
r a year. Do you have any objection to this, Baroness?
I have nothing to object to about the divorce, providing
ep my child. That is my condition.

PASTOR: Don't rely on that, for everyone says that, and then, when they appear in court, the fire breaks out. All that's needed is a spark, and it's started! Here come the jurymen! I'll see you later. I'm staying though I'll keep out of sight.

(The twelve JURYMEN *enter. The* SHERIFF *rings a bell in the open door at the back. The* JUDGE, *the other officials, and the witnesses take their places; spectators stream in.)*

JUDGE: In keeping with the provisions of the penal code, chapter eleven, paragraphs five, six, and eight concerning order in the court, I hereby declare this session of court opened. *(Speaks softly to the* CLERK: *then says)* Will the newly elected jurymen take their oaths?

JURYMEN *(rise, place fingers on the Bible, then speak in unison except when their names are mentioned):*
I, Alexander Eklund,
I, Emanuel Wickberg,
I, Karl Johan Sjöberg,
I, Erik Otto Boman,
I, Erenfrid Söderberg,
I, Olof Andersson of Vik,
I, Karl Peter Andersson of Berga,
I, Axel Vallin,
I, Anders Erik Ruth,
I, Sven Oskar Erlin,
I, August Alexander Vass,
I, Ludvig Östman *(then all in unison, keeping time, in a low pitch, and low voices),* promise and vow in the name of God and His Holy Scriptures that I will, according to my best understanding and with a clear conscience, do what is right in all my judgments, no less for the poor than for the rich, and judge according to the laws of God and the statute laws of Sweden *(with higher pitch and raised voices)* never to distort the law or to promote injustice for the sake of kinship of any kind, friendship, envy, and ill will, or fear, nor for bribes or gifts, or any other cause, no matter what appearance it may have, and

not to declare him guilty who is guiltless, or him guiltless, who is guilty. *(The pitch is raised still more.)* I will never before the judgment is pronounced nor afterward reveal either to those who seek justice or to others those proceedings the court conducts behind closed doors. All this I will and shall faithfully keep as an honest and upright judge without malicious cunning and deception . . . *(Pause)*. As surely as God would help me in life and in soul! *(The members of the* JURY *sit down.)*

JUDGE *(to the* SHERIFF*)*: Call the case of Alma Jonsson versus Alexandersson.

    (The LAWYER, ALEXANDERSSON, ALMA JONSSON, *the* MILKMAID, *and the* HIRED MAN *enter.)*

SHERIFF *(calls out):* Alma Jonsson versus Alexandersson.

LAWYER: I hereby present my power of attorney for the plaintiff, Alma Jonsson.

JUDGE *(examines the document; then says):* Alma Jonsson is suing her former employer Alexandersson and charges him according to the eighth paragraph of the sixteenth chapter of the penal code with having called her a thief without having presented proof of or substantiating evidence for his accusation in legal action. The penalty is six months in prison or a fine. What do you have to say, Mr. Alexandersson?

ALEXANDERSSON: I called her a thief because I saw her steal.

JUDGE: Do you have witnesses who saw her steal, Mr. Alexandersson?

ALEXANDERSSON: No, I didn't happen to have any witnesses along —I usually am alone.

JUDGE: Why didn't you take legal action against the girl?

ALEXANDERSSON: I never sue anyone! Besides, we employers never complain about household thefts, partly because they're so common, partly because we don't want to ruin our servants' future.

JUDGE: What do you have to say to this, Alma Jonsson?

ALMA: Well-l-l . . .

LAWYER [*to Alma*]: Keep still! *(Then)* Since Alma Jonsson is the plaintiff, not the defendant, in this case, she asks that her wit-

nesses may be heard so that her ch: has slandered her may be proved!

JUDGE: Since he has admitted the sl nesses. On the other hand, I need steal, for if Mr. Alexandersson has that will affect the severity of the v

LAWYER: I object, your honor. Acc graph of the sixteenth chapter of 1 is charged with slander is not per statement.

JUDGE: The parties and the witness to leave the courtroom so that th case. *(All but the* JUDGE *and the* J

JUDGE: Is Alexandersson a reliable

JURYMEN: Yes, he is!

JUDGE: Is Alma Jonsson known as

ERIK OTTO BOMAN: I had to fire h stealing.

JUDGE: Just the same I will have can be done about that! Is he po

LUDVIG ÖSTMAN: He hasn't been crops failed last year. He can't l

JUDGE: And I can't find any leg; as the matter's clear and Ale dence. Does any one of you ha

ALEXANDER EKLUND: I'd like to like this where the innocent a the thief has his so-called hor consequences that people wi neighbors and that there will l

JUDGE: That's quite possible, b the minutes, and judgment h Alexandersson is to be cons teenth paragraph of the sixte

JURY: Yes!

JUDGE (
   (*T*
JUDGE:
  son:
  sland
ALEXANI
  being
LAWYER
  Alexa
  his la
  your
  settle
ALEXAND
  certify
SHERIFF:
ALEXAND
  farm!
  honor
  coffee
CONSTABI
ALEXANDI
  three n
CONSTABL
JUDGE (*to*
  and his
SHERIFF:
  née Ma
JUDGE: Ir
  his wife
  riage, a
  council
  board f
BARONESS:
  I may ke

JUDGE: The law does not recognize any conditions in this case, and it is the court which will decide about the child.

BARONESS: That's mighty strange!

JUDGE: And for that reason it is highly important for me as judge to find out who is responsible for the dissension on which the divorce is based. According to the attached minutes of the church council, you have apparently admitted, Baroness, that you sometimes have a difficult and quarrelsome temper; on the other hand, you, Baron, have not admitted to any guilt. So, Baroness, you seem to have admitted . . .

BARONESS: That's a lie!

JUDGE: I find it difficult to believe that the church council's minutes, witnessed by the pastor and eight other reliable men, can be inaccurate.

BARONESS: The minutes are false!

JUDGE: Such remarks cannot be uttered with impunity in court.

BARON: May I point out that I have voluntarily agreed to let the baroness have custody of the child—on certain conditions?

JUDGE: And I repeat what I said a moment ago: it is I as judge and not the parties to the case who decide the case. So: do you, Baroness, deny that you caused the dissension?

BARONESS: Yes, I do! And it isn't one person's fault that two people quarrel.

JUDGE: This is not a quarrel but a criminal case. Besides, you seem to be demonstrating that you have a quarrelsome temper and a reckless manner.

BARONESS: You don't know my husband.

JUDGE: Please explain—I can't pronounce judgment on the basis of insinuations.

BARON: In that event, I ask to have the case dismissed so I may seek a divorce in other ways!

JUDGE: The case has already come to trial and must be carried through!—So you insist, Baroness, that your husband is responsible. Can that be proved?

BARONESS: Yes, it can!

JUDGE: Please do so, but consider carefully that doing so will destroy your husband's claims to his child and his right to the property.

BARONESS: He has destroyed them many times, not least when he denied me sleep and food.

BARON: I'm forced to tell you I have never denied the baroness her sleep; I've simply asked her not to sleep till noon, because that meant the household wasn't properly supervised and our child was not looked after. As far as food goes, I have always let my wife decide about that, and I have simply refused to approve a couple of unnecessary parties when our mismanaged household did not permit such outlays.

BARONESS: And he has let me lie sick in bed without being willing to call in a doctor.

BARON: The baroness always got sick when she didn't get her way, but she soon got well again. After I had called in a medical professor from Stockholm once, and he had explained she was merely acting, I didn't call in a doctor the next time she got sick—because the new pierglass mirror was fifty crowns less expensive than she had estimated.

JUDGE: All this is not the sort of thing that can be considered in passing judgment on such a serious case. There must be more serious motives.

BARONESS: It ought to be a motive that a father doesn't permit a mother to bring up her child.

BARON: In the first place, the baroness has let a maid look after our child, and, whenever she herself has taken any part in his care, it has always been wrong; in the second place, she has wanted to bring up the boy to become a woman, not a man. She had him dressed as a girl until he was four years old; even today when he is eight his hair is as long as a girl's; he has to sew and crochet, and he plays with dolls. I think all this is dangerous for his normal development into a man. On the other hand, she had fun dressing up our employees' daughters as boys, cut their hair, and set them to doing work boys usually do. To cut it short: I took over my son's training when I noticed symptoms of mental disorder, the results of which I've seen lead to conflicts with the eighteenth chapter of the penal code.

BARONESS: And you still wanted to let me have custody over him?

BARON: Yes, because I've never had the cruel thought of separating mother and child, and because his mother has promised to improve. Besides, I promised only conditionally and with the assumption that the law did not concern itself with the matter. But I've changed my mind now that we've started in on accusations—especially since from having been the plaintiff I've become the defendant.

BARONESS: That's how that man always keeps his promises.

BARON: My promises like others' have always been conditional, and as long as the conditions have been fulfilled I've kept my promises.

BARONESS: And he promised me personal freedom in our marriage . . .

BARON: Naturally with the assumption that the laws of decency would not be violated, but when all limits were passed and freedom had become license, I considered my promise no longer binding.

BARONESS: So he tortured me with the most unreasonable jealousy, which is usually enough to make a marriage unbearable. He was even silly enough to be jealous of the doctor.

BARON: That jealousy amounted to my advising her not to be treated by a gossipy masseur with a bad reputation for an ailment usually treated by a woman . . . unless the baroness is referring to the time when I drove out the manager of our estate when he was smoking in my living room and treating the baroness to cigars.

BARONESS: Since we've passed the bounds of shamelessness, we might as well have the whole truth. The baron has commited adultery. Is that enough to make him unworthy of bringing up my child by himself?

JUDGE: Can you prove that, Baroness?

BARONESS: Yes, I can! Look at these letters!

JUDGE *(accepts the letters):* How long ago was it?

BARONESS: A year ago.

JUDGE: The time for instituting proceedings has elapsed, of course, but the fact itself weighs heavily against your husband and can lead to his loss of the child and partial loss of your common property. Do you admit that you commited adultery, Baron?

BARON: Yes, with shame and regret. But there were extenuating circumstances. I was forced to live in humiliating celibacy by the baroness' calculated coldness, in spite of the fact that I simply asked politely for a favor that the law considers a marital right. I got tired of buying her love when she introduced prostitution into my marriage and sold her favors, first for power, then for gifts and money. Finally, I saw myself forced to go to another woman—with the baroness' express permission.

JUDGE: Did you give your permission, Baroness?

BARONESS: That's not true! I demand proof!

BARON: It is true, but I can't prove it, since the only witness, my wife, denies it!

JUDGE: What is unproved need not be untrue. But an agreement like this in violation of the law constitutes moral turpitude and is void. You still have everything against you, Baron.

BARONESS: Since the baron had admitted the offense with regret and shame, I ask—now that I am plaintiff instead of defendant —that the court proceed to judgment since further details are unnecessary.

JUDGE: As chairman of the court, I'd like to hear what the baron can present by way of defense or at least excuse.

BARON: I have admitted adultery and presented as extenuating circumstances that, partly, it was done out of dire necessity when after having been married for ten years I found myself suddenly unmarried, partly, because I did so with the baroness' own approval. As I now have reason to believe that all this was a trap by means of which to establish my guilt, it is my duty to my son to go beyond this . . .

BARONESS *(cries out involuntarily):* Axel!

BARON: What made me commit adultery was the baroness' unfaithfulness.

JUDGE: Can you prove that the baroness has been faithless?

BARON: No! Because I wanted to protect the honor of the family,
I destroyed all the evidence I had, but I dare say the baroness
will confirm the confession she made to me!

JUDGE: Baroness, do you admit that you commited adultery first
and thereby probably brought on the baron's lapse?

BARONESS: No!

JUDGE: Will you swear to your innocence?

BARONESS: Yes!

BARON: Good lord, no! She mustn't! No perjury for my sake!

JUDGE: I ask you again, Baroness: Will you swear to this?

BARONESS: Yes!

BARON: I'll simply comment that for the monent the baroness is
the plaintiff and that as plaintiff she does not need to take an
oath.

JUDGE: Since you have accused her of an offense, she is the defendant. What do the members of the jury think about this?

EMANUEL WICKBERG: Since the baroness is a party in the case, it
seems to me she can hardly testify in her own defense.

ERLIN: It seems to me that when the baroness is going to testify
by oath, the baron, too, should be allowed to testify by oath in
the same case, but since oath may not be opposed to oath, the
whole thing remains in the dark.

VASS: We surely don't have a question of an oath by a witness but
of taking an oath of one's own innocence.

RUTH: Surely that's the question to be answered first.

VALLIN: But not in the presence of the parties, since the deliberations of the court are not public.

SJÖBERG: The jury's right to express its opinions is not restricted
by secrecy as a condition.

JUDGE: From so many differing opinions I cannot get any guidance. But since the baron's guilt can be proved, and the baroness'

guilt is still unproved, I have to demand that you swear to your innocence, Baroness.

BARONESS: I'm ready!

JUDGE: No, wait a moment!—If you had time, Baron, could you find proof of or witnesses for your accusation?

BARON: I neither can nor want to, because I'm not anxious to make any dishonor public.

JUDGE: Court is recessed while I talk to the chairman of the church council.

(Goes out to the right)

(The members of the JURY *talk the case over among themselves softly. The* BARON *and the* BARONESS *in the background. The spectators talk—in groups.)*

BARON *(to the* BARONESS*)*: You don't hesitate to commit perjury?

BARONESS: I hesitate at nothing when it concerns my child.

BARON: But if I have proof?

BARONESS: But you don't!

BARON: I burned the letters, but I have certified copies.

BARONESS: You're lying to frighten me!

BARON: To show you how much I love my child, and at least to rescue his mother when I'm lost, well—take the proof; but don't be ungrateful. *(Hands her a bundle of letters)*

BARONESS: That you were a liar I knew before, but that you were such a scoundrel that you had the letters copied, I didn't believe.

BARON: That's the gratitude! Now we're both lost.

BARONESS: Yes, may we both go under, so there'll be an end to this struggle.

BARON: Is it better to have Emile lose both parents and be alone in the world? . . .

BARONESS: That can never happen!

BARON: Your unreasoning conceit which makes you think you're beyond the law and above your fellow men has fooled you into starting this contest, in which the one certain loser will be our son! What were you thinking of when you began this attack, which could only make me defend myself? Certainly not about

tḥe child! Was it revenge? Revenge for what? Because I found
out about your guilt.

BARONESS: The child? Did you think about him when you stood
there covering me with filth in front of this mob?

BARON: Hélène!—We've torn each other bloody like wild animals;
we've revealed our shame in front of all these people who rejoice
over our going under. We haven't one friend in this courtroom.
From now on our child can never talk about respectable parents,
never go out into life with a good word from his father or his
mother; he'll see how our home is avoided, how his parents sit
alone, despised, and he'll reject and leave us!

BARONESS: What is it you want?

BARON: Let's go abroad when the estate is sold!

BARONESS: And begin quarreling again! I know how it goes: you'll
behave for eight days, and then you'll insult me.

BARON: Think of this: our fate is being decided in there! You can't
count on a good word from the pastor whom you called a liar a
little while ago; since they know I'm not a Christian, I can't
expect any mercy either. I wish I were lying under the roots of a
tree in the forest with my head under a stone—that's how
ashamed I am.

BARONESS: That's true: the pastor hates both of us, and it may go
as you say. Speak with him!

BARON: About what? Reconciliation?

BARONESS: About anything at all, just so it isn't too late. What
does that Alexandersson want? He's been stealing about near us
all the time! I'm afraid of that man!

BARON: Alexandersson is all right!

BARONESS: Toward you, yes, but not toward me.—I've seen him
look like that before!—Go to the pastor, but shake my hand first.
I'm so afraid!

BARON: Of what, my friend? Of what?

BARONESS: I don't know.—Everything, everybody!

BARON: Not of me, though?

BARONESS: Not any more! It's as if we've been drawn into the millrace and our clothes have been caught between the wheels! And all these evil people are standing looking on and laughing! What have we done? What have we done in our anger? Imagine how all of them are enjoying seeing the baron and the baroness stripped naked and beating each other.—I feel as if I were standing here naked. *(She buttons her coat tightly.)*

BARON: Calm yourself, my friend! This isn't the right place to say to you what I've said before. A human being has only one friend and one home, and we could start again!—God knows! No, we can't! It has gone too far. It's over! And may this be the last! And it had to follow what had gone before!—No, we're enemies for life! And if I let you go with the child now, you may get married again—I understand that now; and then my child will get a stepfather; and I'll see another man walking along with my wife and my child.—Or I'll be walking about with someone else's slut on my arm! No!—Either you or I! One of us must be struck down! You or I!

BARONESS: You! If I let you have Emile, you may remarry, and another woman will be my child's mother! That thought could make me a murderer! Stepmother of *my* child!

BARON: You might have thought of that before, but when you saw how I bit at the chain of my love that bound me to you, you thought I couldn't love anyone else.

BARONESS: Do you think I've ever loved you?

BARON: Yes, at least once! When I was unfaithful! Your love was really sublime then! And your pretended contempt made you irresistible. But you even respected me then! If it was the male or the sinner you most admired, I don't know, but I suspect it was both; it must have been both, for you're the most thoroughly female creature I've ever seen! And you're already jealous of what I haven't even thought of—my next wife! It's a shame you became my wife! As my mistress you'd have been an unqualified success, and your unfaithfulness would only have added a bouquet to my wine.

BARONESS: Yes, your love was always sensual!

BARON: Sensual as everything spiritual is; spiritual as everything sensual is! My weakness for you—the strength of my feeling— gave you the notion you were the stronger when you merely were meaner, coarser, more ruthless than I.

BARONESS: You, stronger? You who don't want the same thing for two minutes, who as far as that goes don't know what you want!

BARON: But I know what I want very well; I can both love and hate. I love you one minute and hate you the next! Just now I hate you!

BARONESS: Are you also thinking about the child?

BARON: Yes, now and always! Do you know why? Because he is the embodiment of our love. He's the memory of our beautiful moments, the bond that unites our souls, our meeting place where we always meet without wanting to. And that's why we never can separate even if we are divorced.—I wish I could hate you as I'd like to!

(*The* JUDGE *and the* PASTOR *come in conversing. They stop toward the front of the stage.*)

JUDGE: I see it's absolutely hopeless to try to be just and to find out the truth. And it seems to me as if our laws were a couple of centuries behind our concepts of justice. Didn't I have to sentence the innocent Alexandersson to pay a fine to restore the honor of a maid who is a thief? As far as this divorce case goes, I don't really know anything, and I haven't the conscience to hand down a judgment.

PASTOR: But a judgment *has* to be handed down!

JUDGE: Not by me!—I'll give up my position and go into another profession!

PASTOR: A scandal like that would only make you a laughing stock and close every other calling to you. Keep on a few years and hand down judgments—You'll see it goes quite easily then to crush human destinies like eggs. Besides, if you want to avoid responsibility in this case, let the jury outvote you, and they'll have to take the responsibility themselves.

JUDGE: That's one way of doing it, and I believe they'll be quite united against me. I do have an opinion about this case, though it's based on intuition and I don't dare rely on it.—Thank you for your advice!

SHERIFF *(who has been talking to* ALEXANDERSSON *comes up to the* JUDGE*):* As sheriff I wish to call Mr. Alexandersson as a witness against Baroness Sprengel.

JUDGE: Concerning her adultery?

SHERIFF: Yes!

JUDGE *(to the* PASTOR*):* This provides a new line for a solution!

PASTOR: There are most likely the ends of many lines if you could only get hold of them.

JUDGE: In any event, it's ghastly to see two human beings who have loved each other try to destroy each other like this! It's like watching animals butchered!

PASTOR: That is love, Judge!

JUDGE: What is hate, then?

PASTOR: The lining of the garment!

(The JUDGE *goes over to the* JURYMEN *and talks with them.)*

BARONESS *(comes up to the* PASTOR*):* Help us, Pastor! Help us!

PASTOR: I can't, and as a pastor I'm not permitted to! Besides, didn't I warn you not to play with such serious matters?—You felt it was so simple to get a divorce! Go ahead! The law isn't stopping you; so don't blame the law.

JUDGE [*having seated himself*]*:* Court is resumed!—According to the public prosecutor, Sheriff Viberg, a witness against the baroness has appeared to confirm the charge of adultery against her. Mr. Alexandersson!

ALEXANDERSSON: I'm here!

JUDGE: How can you prove your assertion, Mr. Alexandersson?

ALEXANDERSSON: I saw the crime commited!

BARONESS: He's lying! Have him prove it.

ALEXANDERSSON: Prove? Why, I'm testifying.

BARONESS: Your assertion isn't proof, even if you're called a witness for the moment.

ALEXANDERSSON: As a witness I should probably have two witnesses, and those witnesses new witnesses?

BARONESS: Yes, they might be needed when people don't know if they're all lying!

BARON: Alexandersson's testimony is superfluous. Your honor, may I present as evidence the whole correspondence which gives full proof of the baroness' guilt.—Here are the originals; the defendant has the copies.

(The BARONESS *cries out, but controls herself quickly.)*

JUDGE: Yet you were willing to take an oath a little while ago, Baroness?

BARONESS: But I didn't!—Besides, I think we're just about even now, the baron and I.

JUDGE: We don't cancel crime by crime! The account of each and every one is drawn up by itself.

BARONESS: Then may I at the same time officially present the baron with my claim for my dowry which he has wasted?

JUDGE: If you have wasted the baroness' dowry, Baron, now is the time to settle that matter.

BARON: The baroness had a dowry of six thousand crowns in bonds that could not be sold and became worthless. As she had a position as telegrapher when we got married, and declared she did not want to be supported by her husband, we had a marital agreement with the stipulation that each one was to support himself. But then she lost her position, and I have supported her ever since; I have had no objection to that, but, since she's presenting her bill, I request permission to present mine! It amounts to thirty thousand crowns, comprising a third of the household expenses during our marriage. I assume two thirds.

JUDGE: Do you have written proof of that agreement, Baron?

BARON: No, I don't!

JUDGE: Do you have proof for your charge about the dowry, Baroness?

BARONESS: I didn't believe at that time that I needed it in writing. I thought I was dealing with honorable people!

JUDGE: Then that matter can't be taken into consideration!—Will the members of the jury kindly go into the little juryroom to deliberate and come to a verdict?

(*The* JURYMEN *and the* JUDGE *go out to the right.*)

ALEXANDERSSON (*to the* SHERIFF): I'll never get the hang of justice!

SHERIFF: I think you had better go home, or it might go for you as it did with the farmer in Mariefred. Have you heard about him?

ALEXANDERSSON: No!

SHERIFF: Well! He was in court as a spectator, got involved in the case as a witness, became a party to it, and ended up with getting twenty lashes!

ALEXANDERSSON: Good lord! But I can believe that of them! I think they'd do anything! (*Leaves*)

(*The* BARON *goes up to the* BARONESS *toward the front of the stage.*)

BARONESS: You have a hard time staying away from me?

BARON: Hélène! I've struck you down, and I'm bleeding to death myself, for your blood is mine . . .

BARONESS: And how good you are at drawing up bills!

BARON: No, only counterclaims! Your courage is that of despair, that of someone condemned to death. When you get away from here, you'll collapse. Then you won't have me to blame, and your conscience will start giving you pangs. Do you know why I haven't killed myself?

BARONESS: You don't dare!

BARON: No! Not because of eternal agony—I don't believe in that —but because I've thought: if you get the child, you'll be gone in five years—the doctor said so; and then Emile will be without both father and mother! Imagine yourself alone in the world!

BARONESS: Five years!—That's a lie!

BARON: In five years! And then I'll have the child all the same, whether you approve or not.

BARONESS: Oh, no! Then my family will sue to get custody of Emile! I won't die when I die!

BARON: Evil never dies! That's true.—Can you tell me why you can't bear to let me have Emile, and Emile me, when he needs me? Is it pure meanness, the desire for revenge, which punishes the child? *(The* BARONESS *remains silent.)* You know I told the pastor I thought you weren't quite sure I am Emile's father, that that was why you didn't want me to have the child—my happiness would rest on a false basis. He answered, "No, I can't believe she has such a fine motive." I don't think you know yourself why you're so fanatical about it, but it's the struggle to survive that drives us into not wanting to give up our hold. Our son has your body, but my soul, and you can't root that out. You'll get me again in him when you least expect it; you'll get my thoughts, my inclinations, my passions in him, so you'll hate him some day as you hate me now! That's what I fear!

BARONESS: So you're still afraid I'll get him!

BARON: As a mother and a woman you have an advantage over me with both judge and jury, and justice plays dice with blindfolded eyes, but there's always a little lead in the bottom of the dice!

BARONESS: You can still say polite things at the moment of parting. Maybe you don't hate me so much as you say?

BARON: To tell the truth, I think it's my dishonor more than you that I hate, though I probably hate you, too! And why this ghastly hate? Maybe I have forgotten you're almost forty, and that you're getting masculine. Perhaps it's the masculine in you, in your kisses, in your embrace, that I can't bear!

BARONESS: Perhaps! As you know, what I've regretted more than anything else is that I wasn't born a man!

BARON: Probably that became the bane of my life! And you're getting revenge on nature by trying to bring up your son as a woman. Will you promise me one thing?

BARONESS: Will you promise me one thing?

BARON: What's the point? We never keep our promises anyway!

BARONESS: No, let's not promise anything any more!

BARON: Will you answer one question honestly?

BARONESS: Even if I did, you'd think I was lying.

BARON: Yes, I would.

BARONESS: Do you see it's over forever?

BARON: Forever! Just as we once swore to love each other!

BARONESS: Too bad we have to swear anything like that!

BARON: Why? It's always a bond—such as it is!

BARONESS: I can't bear any bonds.

BARON: Do you think it would have been better if there hadn't been any bonds?

BARONESS: Yes, for me!

BARON: I wonder! Then you would have had no hold on me.

BARONESS: Nor you on me.

BARON: Then it would have become just the same as—when you reduce fractions! So: it's not the fault of the law, not our fault, not other people's fault! And still we have to bear the guilt! *(The* SHERIFF *approaches.)* There! Now they have decided.— Good-bye, Hélène!

BARONESS: Good-bye!—Axel!

BARON: It's hard to part! And impossible to live together. But at any rate the struggle is over!

BARONESS: If it only were!—I'm afraid it's just beginning!

SHERIFF: You are both to step out while the court is deliberating.

BARONESS: Axel! One thing before it's too late! It's possible they'll take the child from both of us! Go home and bring the boy to your mother. Then we can flee far, far away afterward!

BARON: I think you're trying to fool me again!

BARONESS: No, I don't want to. I'm not thinking about you any more, not about myself or revenge. Just save the child! Please, please do!

BARON: I will. But if you have deceived me!—All the same: I will! *(Goes out hastily. The* BARONESS *goes out at the back.)*

(The members of the JURY *and the* JUDGE *enter and take their places.)*

JUDGE: Now that the deliberations are over, I'd like to have the members of the jury state their views before a verdict is handed down. As far as I am concerned, I can come only to the conclusion that the mother is to be given custody of the child. Both of them are equally responsible for the divorce, but the mother must be considered more suited to care for the child than the father. *(Silence)*

ALEXANDER EKLUND: According to the law, the wife assumes the station and circumstances of the husband, and not the opposite.

EMANUEL WICKBERG: And the husband is the wife's guardian!

KARL JOHAN SJÖBERG: In the marriage formula which gives marriage legal standing, the wife is made subordinate to the husband. According to that, it seems to me that the husband takes precedence over the wife.

ERIK OTTO BOMAN: And the children are to be brought up in the father's faith.

ERENFRID SÖDERBERG: According to that, the child follows the father and not the mother.

OLOF ANDERSSON OF VIK: But in the present case, when both husband and wife are equally guilty, and, according to everything that has come to light, are just as incompetent for bringing up a child, I believe the child should be taken away from both of them.

KARL PETER ANDERSSON OF BERGA: Agreeing with Olof Andersson, I point out that in that event the judge appoints two good men and true to care for the child and the property, and lets both husband and wife as well as the child receive their support through them.

AXEL VALLIN: In that event I propose as the good men and true Alexander Eklund and Erenfrid Söderberg since both of them are known as upright and Christian.

ANDERS ERIK RUTH: I agree with Olof Andersson of Vik about taking the child away from both father and mother, and with Axel Vallin about the good men and true, whose Christian spirit makes them particularly suitable for bringing up the child.

SVEN OSKAR ERLIN: I agree!

AUGUST ALEXANDER VASS: Agree!

LUDVIG ÖSTMAN: Agree!

JUDGE: Since the opinion of the majority of the members of the jury is obviously contrary to my own, I ask the jury to proceed to voting. I should probably put as the motion Olof Andersson's proposal that the child be taken away from both father and mother and that guardians be appointed. Is this the unanimous opinion of the jury?

JURY: Yes!

JUDGE: If anyone does not approve the proposal, let him raise his hand. *(Silence)* The jury's opinion has won over mine, and in the minutes I wish to have entered my reservations against what seems to me an unnecessarily cruel verdict.—Husband and wife are separated in bed and board for a year on threat of imprisonment if they seek each other out during that time. (*To the* SHERIFF) Call in the principals!

(The BARONESS *and spectators enter.)*

JUDGE: Isn't Baron Sprengel present?

BARONESS: The baron will be here immediately.

JUDGE: The one who neglects the time has himself to blame.— The verdict is this: Baron and Baroness Sprengel are sentenced to a year's separation in bed and board, their child is taken away from his parents and is to be given into the custody of two good men and true. The court has, moreover, appointed as guardians the jurymen Alexander Eklund and Erenfrid Söderberg.

(The BARONESS *cries out and collapses on the floor. The* SHERIFF *and the* CLERK *lift her up and put her on a chair. Some of the spectators leave.)*

BARON *(enters):* Your honor! After hearing the verdict out there, I ask permission to challenge the competence of the whole jury, all of whom are my personal enemies, as well as the guardians, Alexander Eklund and Erenfrid Söderberg, neither of whom has the economic security legally required of guardians; besides, I

am going to enter a suit against you, your honor, for not knowing the duties of your position, you could not understand that
the one who first was unfaithful in marriage is responsible for
the other one's unfaithfulness, and that therefore both are not
equally responsible.

JUDGE: If you are not satisfied with the verdict, you have the right
to appeal in a higher court during the designated period of
grace! Will the jury accompany me to the manse so that we
may inspect the manse in connection with the case against the
assessors in the district board? *(The* JUDGE *and the* JURY *go
out at the back.)*

   (The BARON *and the* BARONESS *are left alone as the spectators
leave.)*

BARONESS *(stands up):* Where is Emile?

BARON: He was gone!

BARONESS: You're lying!

BARON *(after a pause):* Yes!—I didn't take him to my mother—I
don't rely on her—but to the pastor's home.

BARONESS: To the pastor!

BARON: Your only reliable enemy! Yes! Whom else would I dare
rely on? And I did it because the way you looked made me
wonder if you might not kill both yourself and the child.

BARONESS: So you saw that!—How could I let myself be fooled
into believing you?

BARON: What do you say about the verdict?

BARONESS: I don't know, but I'm so tired I don't feel blows any
more. It seems a comfort to have been dealt the final blow.

BARON: You're not thinking of what's to come: how your son will
be brought up by two farmers whose crude and simple ways will
slowly torture the child to death; how he'll be pressed down into
their limited sphere; how his intelligence will be choked by
religious superstition; how he'll be taught to despise his father
and his mother . . .

BARONESS: Hush! Don't say any more, or I'll lose my mind. My
Emile living with farm women who can't keep clean, who have

vermin in their beds, and don't know if a comb is clean! My
Emile? No, it's not possible!

BARON: It's absolutely possible and real, and you have only yourself to blame!

BARONESS: Myself? Yes, but did I create myself? Give myself
evil inclinations, hatred, and wild passions? No! Who denied
me the strength and will to resist them?—When I look at myself
at this moment I feel I am to be pitied. Am I not pitiable?

BARON: Yes, you are! We're both to be pitied. We tried to avoid
the pitfalls of marriage and lived together without getting
married; but we had difficulties anyway, and we missed one of
the greatest pleasures in life—the respect of our fellow men, so
we got married. But we were going to trick the community with
its laws; our marriage wasn't to be consecrated by the church,
and we managed to get married in a civil ceremony. We weren't
going to depend on each other in any way . . . not have our
funds in common, not insist on any right to the other's person—
then it took the same old track; without the blessings of the
church and with a marital agreement: and the marriage went
to pieces! I forgave your unfaithfulness, and we lived separated
in the same house—for the sake of the child! But I got tired of
presenting my friend's mistress as my wife—so we had to part!
You know what? Do you know whom we have fought against?
You call him God, but I call him nature. And that force stirred
us up to hating each other just as he stirs people up to love!
And now we're doomed to hurt each other as long as there's a
spark of life in us. New suits in higher courts, presenting the evidence again and again, hearings before the church council, the
opinion of the cathedral chapter, the decision of the supreme
court! But then will come my complaint to the ombudsman,
my plea to be designated guardian, your challenges and counter-
suits: from guillotine to guillotine! Without finding one merciful
executioner!—Mishandling of the estate, financial ruin, neglect of
Emile's rearing! And why don't we end our miserable lives? Because the child holds us back!—You're weeping, but I can't! Not

even when I think about the coming night in our empty home! And you, poor Hélène, who are going home to your mother again! Your mother whom you left with joy to get your own home! Become her daughter again . . . that will perhaps be worse than being a wife!—A year! Two years! Several years! How many years of suffering do you think we can take?

BARONESS: I'll never go home to my mother! Never! I'll wander about on paths and in forests to hide myself and to cry out against God until I'm exhausted—the God who has let hellish love come into the world to torture human beings. And when it gets dark, I'll lie down in the pastor's barn so I can sleep near my child.

BARON: You think you'll sleep tonight?

[CURTAIN]

Bibliographic
and Other Notes

THE STANDARD but far from definitive Swedish edition of Strindberg's works is John Landquist's *Strindbergs samlade skrifter* (55 vols.; Stockholm: Bonnier, 1912-20). G. Carlheim-Gyllensköld supplemented the Landquist edition in *Samlade otryckta skrifter* (2 vols.; Stockholm: Bonnier, 1918-19).

The scholarly edition of three of the plays in this volume is, however, *August Strindbergs Dramer* (Utgivna med inledningar och kommentarer av Carl Reinhold Smedmark. III: *Herr Bengts hustru, Kamraterna, Fadren, Fröken Julie, Fordringsägare*. Stockholm: Bonnier, 1964). This edition of *The Father, Lady Julie,* and *Creditors* contains not only the texts based on the original manuscripts with detailed information about discrepancies between the manuscripts and the versions in the Landquist edition but also extended commentary on the plays both as literature and as theater.

For those who know Swedish the best bibliographies are available in E. N. Tigerstedt's *Svensk litteraturhistoria* (Stockholm: Bonnier, 1948), pp. 383-97—a new edition is about to appear—and in the journal *Samlaren,* which prints an annual bibliography.

For those who must rely on English sources, the basic bibliographies are Esther H. Rapp's bibliography of Strindberg in England and America (*Scandinavian Studies,* XXIII, 1-22, 49-59, 109-37); Alrik Gustafson's bibliography in his *A History of Swedish Literature* (Minneapolis: University of Minnesota Press, 1961), pp. 601-10; and the annual bibliographies in *Scandinavian Studies (SS)* and the *Publications of the Modern Language Association (PMLA).*

Harry G. Carlson's translation of Martin Lamm's *August Strindberg* (Bronx, N.Y.: Benjamin Blom, 1968), the most important biography of Strindberg, makes available at last to those who do not read Swedish the approach to Strindberg and his works which has until fairly recently almost completely dominated Strindberg scholarship and criticism in Sweden and even elsewhere in Scandinavia, not to mention the influence Lamm has had on many non-Scandinavian Strindberg scholars. Professor Carlson's notes will be very helpful to students of Strindberg.

Take *The Father* as an example of Lamm's approach, an approach which Strindberg himself for good reasons had foreseen.

Strindberg had every right to believe that his fellow Swedes would consider *The Father* an autobiographical document. From its appearance in print, Swedish critics and scholars have taken it for granted that the play is a revelation of Strindberg's emotional and mental condition, of his marital difficulties, and of his debt to other authors and to psychologists.

The most impressive and influential of all such scholarly treatments is Martin Lamm's in *Strindbergs Dramer* (Stockholm: Bonnier, 1924), I, 262-301. Basing his conclusions on Strindberg letters, *A Madman's Defense,* other people's testimony, and Strindberg's reading, Lamm insists that *The Father* was essentially shaped, in substance, by Strindberg's immediate environment, marital difficulties, mental and emotional illness, and current reading; and that it was shaped, in form, by such models as Aeschylus' *Agamemnon.* Fortunately, however, Lamm goes somewhat beyond all this to present the results of his own close reading of the play as well. While the latter is intensely interesting, it is the former— the emphasis on the biographical approach—that has largely determined Swedish scholars' treatment of the play, the nature of productions on the Swedish stage, and the Swedish public's view of the play.

Lamm's presentation is persuasive: the Strindbergs *were* living in Lindau, Bavaria, when the play was written; Strindberg *was* impressed by the masculinity of the German officers who had no doubt that the husband should dominate the home; Strindberg *did* try to be like them in manner; and Siri found that a little ridiculous. The Strindbergs *did* have marital difficulties; they *did* not see eye to eye on the matter of their son Hans's baptism; they *did* exchange angry words about the future callings of their very young daughters Karin and Greta; neither one of them ever learned that family matters are family matters not to be broadcast either by letter or word of mouth to a world inclined to delight in juicy tidbits. Strindberg was suspicious and had always felt persecuted; Siri was addicted to coquetry; and Strindberg tried to trap her into confessing she had been unfaithful. Strindberg was badly hit by the blasphemy trial in the 1880's and was afraid he might lose his mind.

It is on the basis of such facts that Lamm insists that *The Father* is a diagnosis of the author's mental state, an account of his own marriage, and a reflection of impulses from sources as varied as Shakespeare's *Othello,* and Paul Lafargue's essay on matriarchy and the battle of the sexes in *La nouvelle Revue* (1886). Relying almost completely on Karl Jaspers' *Strindberg and van Gogh* (1922), Lamm insists that *The Father* reflects Strindberg's schizophrenia of the paranoid type (jealousy, persecution feelings, fear of going insane). Lamm accepts without question the notions that Strindberg was a woman hater and that he admitted it in *The Father*.

But even Lamm apparently felt a little uncomfortable about stating as unqualified truths the results of his biographical approach. He admits, for example, that both *The Father* and *A Madman's Defense* are to a degree "*dikt,*" i.e., products of the creative imagination in the double sense that Strindberg's marital sufferings were creations of his imagination without actual basis and that Strindberg knew it. Lamm, moreover, strains himself to find models in earlier literature. He believed that *The Father* was deliberately written as a modern counterpart to *Agamemnon* (hence the simplicity of structure, the limitation of action to the catastrophe, and the tightened pathos); that Adolf is directly descended from such great Shakespearean tragic figures as Othello and Lear and therefore presented in *"kolossalformat"* as a giant engaged in struggle with small-minded pygmies; and that *"helve-teskvinnan"* (the woman devil) Laura was deliberately engaged in a struggle where she consciously employs the techniques of Iago.

The use of the questionable and dubious notion of "larger than life" format, the emphasis on Strindberg's inconsistency in, for example, portraying Laura as the perpetrator of an unconscious crime, the finding of the nature of Adolf's tragedy as merely inner factors which lead to his own destruction, and, above all, the overwhelmingly biographical approach and emphasis do not obscure completely Lamm's quite apparent conviction that *The Father* was indeed a very great play. The pity of it is that Lamm's brilliant essay has set the pattern for almost all Swedish and most foreign treatments of *The Father* ever since. For proof of such a statement, one need only glance at pictures of Swedish productions of the play or read what has been written about the play in Sweden.

Lamm's treatments of *The Father* in two later books—*August Strindberg* (1940-42; new edition, 1948, which Professor Carlson has translated and edited) and *Det moderna dramat* (1948; translated as *Modern Drama* by Karin Elliott, Philosophical Library, New York, 1953)—are essentially the same as that of 1924. Typical of all three are such statements in the last as, *"The Father* may be regarded as a study for *A Madman's Defense";* and, "That Laura is intended to be the incarnation of all feminine evil is not doubted by any one"; or, to take one from the middle book, *"The Father* is an excerpt from a hospital journal, but at the same time it is the first drama, in which Strindberg demonstrates the mastery of the style which would be characteristic of all his naturalistic [realistic] dramas, even those written after the Inferno crisis."

It is a pity that Lamm did not emphasize this last and non-biographical aspect of his criticism of *The Father*.

In the most recnt Swedish treatment of *The Father* in *August Strindbergs Dramer* III (Stockholm: Bonniers, 1964), Carl Reinhold Smedmark insists that the play is primarily autobiographical (p. 194, for example):

It is these intimate experiences [of Strindberg's] which form the core in *The Father*. . . . Strindberg's struggle for a philosophy of life and his personal crisis during the years 1884-1886, which forced him to make a final audit of his life, lives on with undiminished power in *The Father*. The play is the tragedy of the atheistic determinist, when he has lost faith in *his* god: woman, and *his* hope for eternal life: the children. Out of the woman question rises a powerful drama of fate with profoundly penetrating analysis of the husband's psyche. The social questions sink below the horizon. Up rise the confused and moving image of Strindberg's inner being, in which the struggle for the identity of his own ego and its preservation has reached a stage of despair.

Differing from Lamm mainly in emphasis and details, Dr. Smedmark presents an interesting case for considering *The Son of a Servant* rather than *A Madman's Defense* a major autobiographical source, sees Laura as less of an embodiment of feminine evil, and suspects that *The Father* may well have been written as a contrast and parallel to Ibsen's *Ghosts*. But Dr. Smedmark is well aware of the greatness of *The Father* as drama and theater in spite of his inclination to let his search for autobiographical sources overshadow his evaluation of the play itself.

What has been said about the Swedish emphasis on the autobiographical elements in *The Father* can be said about *Lady Julie, Creditors,* and *The Bond* as well. See Professor Carlson's translation of Lamm's *August Strindberg*. Aside from that, the major treatment of *Lady Julie* is Lennart Josephson's *Strindbergs drama Fröken Julie* (Stockholm: Almqvist & Wiksell, 1965), which, unfortunately, is not available in English translation. Dr. Josephson deals with almost every conceivable aspect of the play, but his emphasis is suggested in this quotation (p. 252):

> But [the probable models for Julie] we have found are sufficient for us to consider the role as an independent creation of Strindberg's poetic imagination. He has used his own experiences in life and in literature, which is also a part of life, but every writer does. And the figures of his imagination have developed from his experienced reality. Julie's role can be used as a warning against the tendency to see direct portraits in Strindberg's stage characters.

For those who would like to consider *Creditors* as an illustration of what Dr. Josephson says, the task is easy. All that needs to be done is to read what Lamm says in his biography and then compare the content of the play with the content of *The Confession of a Fool* (translated by Ellie Schleussner; Boston: Small, Maynard, 1913, and New York: Viking Press, 1925) as revised, edited, and supplied with notes by Evert Sprinchorn in *A Madman's Defense* (Garden City, N.Y.: Anchor Books A 492b, 1967). The defense or confession is appreciably an autobiographical document with the actual material transformed in the creative process. There are parallels between the novel and *Creditors,* however, but they should not be allowed to distract one's attention from the play as a play.

For the autobiographical background of *The Bond,* the Carlson translation of Lamm's biography is indispensable. For those who read Swedish, David Norrman's *Strindbergs skilsmässa från Siri von Essen* (Stockholm: Bonnier, 1953) is the fullest account of Strindberg's first divorce.

The question whether these pre-Inferno plays are naturalistic or not has interested scholars. Lamm, whose definition of naturalism is loosely that of extreme realism, treats the question in all the books already cited. Professor Børge Gedsø Madsen's *Strindberg's Naturalistic Theatre: Its Relation to French Naturalism* (Seattle: University of Washington Press, and Copenhagen: Munksgaard, 1962) clarifies Zola's formula for naturalistic literature, *"faire grand, faire vrai, et faire simple";* traces the influence on Strindberg of French naturalism and contemporary psychological theory; and demonstrates that, while Strindberg wrote great plays, he did not apply the Zola formula for a naturalistic drama fully in any one of them; "his ineradicable subjectivity" prevented him from doing so. "By exaggerating the *faire grand* part of the new formula, *The Father* . . . becomes deficient in the formula's requirement of *faire vrai,* as this term was defined by Zola."

But Professor C. W. E. L. Dahlström, author of the basic treatment of Strindberg's post-Inferno plays, *Strindberg's Dramatic Expressionism* (Ann Arbor: University of Michigan Press, 1930, and Bronx, N.Y.: Benjamin Blom, Inc., 1968) has also considered the pre-Inferno plays in a series of articles published in *Scandinavian Studies.* Three of them concern *The Father:* "Strindberg's *Fadren* as an Expressionistic Drama" (August, 1940), "Strindberg and the

Problems of Naturalism" (May, 1941), and "Strindberg's *The Father* as Tragedy" (May, 1955). The first, an examination of the play in terms of expressionistic norms, concludes that while it is not a full-fledged expressionistic play it has elements of expressionism, and serves as an effective reminder that Strindbergian naturalism is decidedly different from, say, Zola's. The second sets up a critical apparatus *through* the study of Zola *for* the study of the Strindberg plays that John Landquist included in the volume *Naturalistiska sorgespel.* The third article analyzes *The Father* in terms of Aristotle's *Poetics,* demonstrates that the play fulfills the requirements of classical tragedy and Shakespearean tragedy except for its ending, but concludes: "In its very exploitation of the denial of moral order and purpose in the lives of men, *The Father,* perhaps in spite of the author's conscious intent, affirms such order. In its direct form it does not, and cannot, establish emotional equilibrium." See the Rapp bibliography for other articles by Professor Dahlström.

For further information about material pertaining to the five plays in this volume, see the Rapp bibliography, Gustafson's *A History of Swedish Literature,* and the annual American Scandinavian bibliography which appears each May in *Scandinavian Studies.*